HEART OF DART-NESS

HEART OF DART-NESS

NED BOULTING

BLINK
bringing you closer

Published by Blink Publishing
3.08, The Plaza,
535 Kings Road,
Chelsea Harbour,
London, SW10 0SZ

www.blinkpublishing.co.uk

facebook.com/blinkpublishing
twitter.com/blinkpublishing

Hardback – 978-1-788700-47-4
Trade Paperback – 978-1-788701-50-1
Ebook – 978-1-788700-48-1

A CIP catalogue of this book is available from the British Library.

Designed by Envy Design Ltd

Printed and bound in Great Britain by Clays Ltd, Elcograf S.p.A

1 3 5 7 9 10 8 6 4 2

Blink Publishing is an imprint of Bonnier Books UK
www.bonnierbooks.co.uk

To Jamesy – The Welsh Wizard and Lord of Butlins.

Contents

Contents

Author's Note

This book was written over a three-year period and completed in the winter of 2017.

Shortly after I finished writing it, darts lost two of its most notable characters, both of whom feature on these pages.

Jim Bowen, the long-time host of *Bullseye*, died in March 2018 at the age of 80. He was widely, and rightly, credited with responsibility for the huge growth in popularity that darts enjoyed in the 1980s.

Three weeks later, Eric Bristow's death was also announced. He was just 60.

In the eyes of many, Bristow was the greatest player there had ever been.

Purfleet

The rest of the world was nowhere, as far as our eyes
and ears were concerned. Just nowhere. Gone, disappeared;
swept off without leaving a whisper or a shadow behind.

JOSEPH CONRAD – *HEART OF DARKNESS*

Purfleet is where Essex meets the Thames estuary. The English coast here is a broad, mud-brown and grey-grassed sweep of windy flatland, lapped unenthusiastically by the tidal reach of London's river. Here, breakers' yards, small paddocks, neglected industrial units, lorry stops and forlorn little towns vie for attention in a landscape that has given up on itself. Purfleet is not a place to linger.

And, at its heart, nestling between an Esso garage and a bleak electricity substation that hums with static power, the Circus Tavern sits, squat and unlovely. An arterial road roars by, ferrying articulated trucks onto the high span of the Dartford Crossing and away. Should you have taken a wrong turning somewhere in the maze of dual carriageways that intertwine like serpents on London's eastern fringes, then you might already have driven past this place en route to Suffolk or Kent without noticing it. It is an archetype of roadside anonymity, at once repelling interest and throwing down a silent challenge.

Think about it. Would you consider stopping here?

During the day, there are a handful of cars, Land Rovers, BMWs scattered sparsely across the expansive, weed-strewn forecourt. People come and go, rushing from doorway to vehicle, and are gone, with a growl of the engine. The odd delivery is made, with a clatter of metal cage. Then, at dusk, lights from within shine dimly against the night. Would you open its doors and walk in?

The back of the building is a brick-built, flat-roofed quadrant of indeterminate age. It is surrounded by a few acres of car parking. Perhaps once it had been used for office space, or an ill-sited community hall. Its original purpose is lost. Sometime in the mid-eighties, at best guess, the front end of the building, the façade that gazes blankly at the petrol station, was graced by the addition of a two-storey atrium finished in tinted glass. It is through this new entrance that the people come and go, getting in and out of minicabs and, occasionally, stretch limos in white or pink, on their way to and from the entertainment.

But inside is where the rare magic happens. Especially when night falls, and it is dark and cold outside on the A roads and the empty, fenced fields. Especially then, when the bright lights inside the building defy the isolation all around, when there is not a square foot of empty space, and everyone is pressed up close to watch them play.

It is around nine o'clock in the evening of New Year's Day, 2007.

It is here, beneath the low ceiling of the function room, that the Master of Ceremonies calls the seething crowd of people to order. He wears a light blue jacket, and he stands still and upright, facing the masses, all of whom are now standing, on chairs, or tables, leaning over the low balustrades of the raised areas to catch a glimpse of proceedings.

'Ladies and gentlemen!' he bellows. 'Welcome to the PDC: the Premiership of Darts!

'Introducing onstage the four-time World Darts Champion and reigning UK Open Champion, from the Netherlands, Raymond van Barneveld!'

Thump!

The first familiar, irresistible punch that marks the iconic opening to *Survivor*'s crowd-pleaser 'Eye of the Tiger'. Van Barneveld raises his head slowly towards a tightening camera shot, as instructed to by the television director. A touching attempt to look menacing by a faint narrowing of his eyes is undermined by almost everything else about him; from his fleshy, flushed cheeks and fulsome lips to his slightly rounded shoulders. The camera retreats at walking pace as everyone, not least the Dutchman, waits for the beat to kick in. Now, the shot is wide enough to show his whole shirt, a restrained navy blue polo with a clutch of clumsily applied stick-on sponsors' badges: Nifra.nl, building constructors based to the north of Amsterdam, AfAB, a Dutch loans company.

Rising up... Back on the street...

Awkwardly, but on the correct big beat, he breaks into a nervous stride, loping towards the stage in time with the music. He pushes good-naturedly through a forest of arms, reaching over the barriers, hands outstretched for a high-five, or clutching small posters with homespun messages. Barney Army! Hello Mum! Love The Darts! And, mysteriously, Swanage!

'Eye of the Tiger' is now belting out its irresistible call to arms as the big Dutchman lopes on. And now he spots his wife, Silvia. He stops briefly to embrace her. He kisses her on the cheek and stomps on. The din around him is outrageous. Lights swivel madly above him, suspended from the low ceiling of the Circus Tavern. One more embrace before mounting the steps and into the light. This time it's his agent, a tall, thin man with grey hair and a nervous shuffle. They hug awkwardly. Then van Barneveld takes to the stage.

He bows humbly to the crowd, then turns his back to them so that the Barney Rubble design on the back of his darts shirt is visible. He shakes the hands of the officials, kissing the walk-on girl in a black corset who has accompanied him onto the stage and then he flourishes a white hand towel. He'll need that, sooner rather than later, to mop his brow and dry his hands. It's like a tropical blaze on the stage under the lights.

In the hall, they clap thunderously, bellowing out the chorus.

He is about to rise up to the challenge of a rival.

But, for all the beery frenzy, it's not him they've come to see. Not really. The music fades. The MC lifts the microphone to his lips. The expectation levels in the room rise again.

'Now, ladies and gentlemen, the 13-time champion of the world.'

There is a rumble of thunder over the PA system. A few voices in the crowd, unable to control their excitement any longer, jump the gun and shout out his name slightly too soon. 'Phil!'

Then the MC: 'Philllll!'

A heavy crack of lightning.

'The Powerrrrrr!'

More lightning.

'Tay-looorrrrr!'

The place erupts.

At the back of the hall, where a minute before van Barneveld had stood, we catch our first glimpse of the great Phil Taylor. Wearing an orange shirt, the colour of which is quite deliberately chosen to needle his Dutch opponent, he grins impishly at the camera. He bobs about, and leans almost out of shot to snatch a casual word with someone in the wings, as if all this were the most natural thing in the world. Then he sets off while the voice of Penny Ford belts out her urgent war cry over that insistent beat.

I've got the power!

The Tavern bounces. By the time he has made it up onto the stage, there is no doubt who owns this occasion. Taylor stops to whisper in the ear of a powerful-looking man in a black suit who appears from nowhere. The two look like they are well connected, as if they are clinching a business deal, right there and then. They pull apart, exchanging an even closer look. Then some unseen flunky hands him his darts in a case. He has not had to carry them to the threshold of the stage; someone else has done that for him. Then Taylor pauses to allow his red-corseted walk-on girl up the steps first. The camera cuts to the waiting van Barneveld, smiling, but jigging nervously up and down to the music, an awkward uncle on the margins of a wedding disco.

Taylor makes his way over to the referee, and instead of shaking him by the hand, reaches his left hand behind his head and pulls him forward into a clutch. For what seems a long time, Taylor talks right into his ear, then pulls away, leaving the man smiling. Taylor starts to unpack his darts. It can begin.

I've got the power!

Outside, across the road, you might not hear it. But if you were filling up your car at the petrol forecourt to the side, and if the chill wind picked up in the right direction away from the Tavern, you might hear the thump of the bass fading out, and then the match referee issuing his final muffled instruction.

'Raymond to throw first!'

Resettling the nozzle in its cradle and heading into the petrol station to pay, you might not be aware you were a stone's throw from greatness. The greatest darts player that ever lived, and perhaps the greatest that there will ever be.

Beginnings

I don't want to bother you much with what happened to me personally, yet to understand the effect of it upon me, you ought to know how I got out there, what I saw, how I went up that river…

JOSEPH CONRAD – *HEART OF DARKNESS*

I am a freelance writer and broadcaster. I play darts against myself, on weekdays. One morning, as people with purposeful existences and real lives to be getting on with came and went along the damp London pavement outside my window, I struck a treble 20 with almost my first dart of the day.

Without hesitating, I drew back the arm and threw again. The next dart landed cheek by jowl with the first. I had thrown two consecutive trebles. I was on for a maximum.

I stared back at the board, pierced by two perfect darts. There they sat, goading me into imagining the final third dart arrowing into that holy remainder of space to their side, the application of absolution. I could almost see it: a 180, in my own front room.

I looked down at the remaining dart in my hand, with its classic Embassy flight, and drew breath.

Our neighbours had given me the dartboard when they'd moved house a few years ago. They had been clearing out the attic, and it was superfluous to their requirements, having been bought for their son and then neglected. Such is the fate of so many dartboards up and down the country.

It is a Winmau board, with folding cabinet doors on either side that act as chalkboards when opened, and neatly conceal the board when closed, hiding it from view as if it were somehow indecent, like a colour television in 1974; something to be mildly ashamed of.

When I excitedly mounted it on the wall, I only guessed at the correct height, although my options were limited. There is a wall-fitted light just above the dartboard that has lived a charmed life ever since. Darts have peppered its surrounds, without yet striking the glass lampshade. And I merely estimated the correct throwing distance too. My improvised 'oche' was a swirling knot in the pine floorboard. Beneath the board, fanning out like a rash around a central sore, the woodwork is pockmarked with holes from bounce-outs.

The darts themselves are special. The great Bobby George gave a set to me 15 years ago when I went to his house on a filming assignment for *Grandstand*. He lives in a mansion called George Hall, which he built himself. It has a pub in the living room.

George's signature is still visible, just, a swirl of blue biro over the front of the soft darts case above the dark red logo of Embassy cigarettes, itself a historical curiosity. These darts were a relic from the days when no one had spotted the contradiction between puffing away on fags and their association with sport. Embassy had become a byword for a bygone age of post-war carelessness and had little to do with health. The government went on to ban tobacco sponsorship in 2003, the summer when Bobby George had given me the darts.

The intervening years have not been kind to the Embassy flights that used to sit snugly in the shaft. Only one of them remains operable. The other two have snagged and become unthreadable after too many of my inept fumblings. So I now throw a shameful mismatch of flights; one Embassy, one Andy Fordham 'Viking' flight, and one generic shiny silver one from JD Sports. A darts purist would shudder at the horror of such a mixed set.

I can remember my first dartboard. Like almost every other British youth of a certain age, I was once the owner of a board that I was allowed to hang in the attic. It was one of those cheap ones from Woolworths, and was probably the result of some rather panicked last-minute Christmas present shopping from my parents.

It came with two sets of darts, one red and one green. I always played with the red ones. They were those nasty, stubby, integrated ones, where the shiny plastic flight was part of the stem, and the stem was welded onto the barrel, and they flew like faultily wired Scud missiles, missing their targets by unimaginable, dangerous margins. Needless to say, this board did not improve my game, nor really spark any lasting interest in developing it. A few years later, it was boxed up, along with a kettle and a squash racket, and they made their way in the back of a Datsun estate to my university hall of residence.

As a student, I rediscovered the game. We drank in an ordinary sort of pub called The Maypole that had a board in the back snug. The unimpressive group of darts-playing undergraduates to which I belonged was tolerated by the locals but positively encouraged by the rotund, jovial and balding Sicilian landlord Mario, who, altruistically, used to cash our cheques in exchange for lager. He kept the darts in a half-pint jug under the counter of the bar.

Unable to engage in the proper activity of '501', without the darts descending inevitably into a lame, inexorable grind towards trying, and failing, to check out double one, we stuck to 'Killer'. This game, or at least our strange hybrid version of it, necessitated nothing more unreasonable than the ability, every now and then, to hit a single specified number. Trebles and doubles were an exotic bonus.

My flatmate John, an engineering student from Retford, had a stabby little action and an ability to score sod all or plenty with no rhyme or reason attached. Giles, an Eton-educated student of Russian and Swedish languages with multiple earrings and an ethnic jerkin he'd acquired during a gap year in Thailand, was a steady kind of player, capable of occasional consistency, the one quality which is a prerequisite of darting progress. But mostly he was a bit rubbish. Then there was Sean, the Sorbonne-aspiring *flâneur* of the oche; a young man from Nottingham who thought he was D H Lawrence, but behaved more like a troubled Laurence Llewelyn-Bowen. As a darter, he was irrepressibly roguish, mostly imprecise, but occasionally inspirational when he threw; attributes he carried through into the rest of his life.

It was Sean who introduced me to literature. Passionate about the written word, he would wax lyrical about the lesser works of Samuel Beckett and expound with great poise and ease as to the merits or otherwise of Ezra Pound, Franz Kafka and Joseph Conrad. He was a lover of film, too. In his company I remember falling asleep to the languid art of Tarkovsky, but coming alive to the director's cut of *Apocalypse Now*, a film based on Conrad's *Heart of Darkness*. 'The horror', famously spoken by Marlon Brando, echoing the dying words of Conrad's anti-hero Kurtz, became a byword for our serial failure, not just in life, but also in darts.

'Seany requires a double one.'

Thud.

'The horror.'

Me? I was awkward. Struggling to find my place in the world, I sought solace in simple pleasures like beer and throwing pointed sticks at a cork board.

Our commitment to the game was fragile. We got embroiled in the drama of our matches, fabricating terminology (The Shuffle! The Tickler! The Nudge!), providing faux darts commentary ('And it's Giles to throw. Pressure darts for the privately schooled modern linguist!') and laughing uproariously at each other's failures. A win was a win. But a loss was as good as a win. It was fun.

Sometimes Mario the landlord would join in, near closing time when he'd had enough of serving drunken twerps frittering away their government grants and felt like punishing someone. None of us were ever able to match him at 'Killer'. If he needed sixteens, he got a double and two single sixteens. If he needed treble five, by and large he got treble five. He could take us all on and smash us all up. We were like a posse of children clambering all over a favourite uncle. He toyed with us, then put us firmly in our place.

From time to time the game threw us into close contact with a certain section of society the university did its best to keep us from: actual people. There was a central knot of regulars who drank in The Maypole whose money came not from a student grant or a parental allowance, but from the graft of a full-time job. Many of the locals were employed in the colleges as caterers, groundsmen, porters. And some of them, on a Saturday afternoon, would take delight in teaching us a lesson on the dartboard. But that did not matter. It was darts. It was funny.

Then darts packed away its tungsten shafts and left my life altogether. It was 1991 when I finished university and embarked on a decade-long attempt to grow up.

At the same time, darts, as if sensing that the fun was over, and having been at the heart of British television schedules for the best part of 20 years, had all but withered on the vine. Only the Embassy World Championships remained on the telly. As a spectacle, darts had flatlined. To me, the game seemed like a silly relic of a nicotine-stained era best forgotten. The childhood board that had accompanied me during those three, Marlboro-yellowed years of tertiary education had been thrown out somewhere along the line. God knows what happened to it. I gave it no more thought.

Darts passed out of my world as inconsequentially as it had entered it. In a puff of smoke.

Time passed. I drifted into adulthood. I got a job in telly, watched telly, cooked dinners, had children, read books. I didn't play darts.

But then the game returned in the most extraordinary of circumstances. I was sent to Wolverhampton by ITV in 2007. And that's how it all began again.

For ten days, the Wolverhampton Civic Centre played host to the Grand Slam of Darts. Phil Taylor, in his unbeatable pomp, was the hot favourite for tournament, despite having been deposed as world champion. It was the same year that he had lost that great encounter at the Circus Tavern in Purfleet. Those who were lucky enough to be there swear that it will probably never be beaten for drama. Both men matched each other shot for shot, but it was the Dutchman who edged the contest in the deciding set 7–6. Raymond van Barneveld won, by the width of a wire. If it had gone the other way, which it very nearly did, Phil Taylor would have won his fourteenth world title there and then. Of course, he went on to win two more. But this had been a glitch.

The Grand Slam was a stepping stone back to greatness for Taylor, and he almost inevitably won the first prize, walking away with £80,000 at the end. But the actual result was only half the story. For me, it wasn't the story at all: everything else was.

My first experience of a major darts tournament knocked the wind out of me, entirely. It was intense, bizarre, hilarious, raucous; a total assault on the senses. I had gone into it in a state of innocence, and I emerged out of the other end, blinking into the daylight, dimly aware that I had been confronted to something absolutely other, something I never knew existed.

The first man I met on day one of my exposure to professional darts was a black-clad, ex-SAS member of the extremely well-prepared Professional Darts Corporation security detail to whom I was simply an unfamiliar face without the correct accreditation. 'Excuse me. Where are you going?'

'I'm with ITV,' I had jabbered as he gazed suspiciously down on me from his six-foot-something advantage.

'What's your name, mate?'

'Ned,' I said, aware of how silly the one syllable sounded at the stage door of the Wolverhampton Civic.

It sounded even sillier when it was relayed through the lapel mic of his walkie-talkie to his superiors. 'We've got a Ned at the door.' He fixed me in his gaze as he spoke. 'With ITV, apparently.'

A few static crackles later, the Ned had been cross-referenced against the list, and I gained access to the darts. Crossing the Rubicon of the smokers' huddle outside the fire exit at the back of the venue, I caught a glimpse of a man who looked extremely like Eric Bristow. Only as I pushed through the doors did it occur to me that it was Eric Bristow. I had passed so close to him that my jacket must have brushed against his.

And then, suddenly, there I was.

I had entered the Civic just as Peter Manley, an extremely large Cumbrian who went by the name of 'One Dart' and always wore a huge bright pink shirt, was stamping his size 13 feet in time to the music as Tony Christie demanded whether anyone knew the way to Amarillo. The crowd was in a state of good-natured semi-riot, and the sound system rocked the place on its foundations, from the balcony to the floor. The air was alive with sickly alcohol fumes and chip fat, burger air and bodies marinating inside an array of nylon costumes that reflected the pillars of popular entertainment, from Bart Simpson to Super Mario, Snow White to the Grim Reaper. There were banks of disco lights, swivelling gloriously, hidden cameras, moving cameras, cameras with massive close-up lenses, cameras on cranes swooping low over the seething mass of darts fans, a human explosion of primary colours like a gigantic pack of fleshy fruit Polos split open across the fetid space of the Civic. This was a Tuesday lunchtime.

They started to play. I took a seat at the side and watched.

Then came the next surprise: the game itself. The bouncing joy of the win, and the explosions of fury in defeat! The roar of a winning dart, and jab of frustration at one that misses! The bear-like embraces of respect and relief when all was settled!

Darts was played out on the sharpest edge of precision, replete with heart-stopping tension, the double hitting home like a knife to the soul, or slipping the wire and sinking the ship. Darts was a constantly reloaded torpedo, crashing into the bull at the heart of the board in the centre of the stage amid the chaos of Wolverhampton Civic Centre in the middle of England one week in November. It was uproarious: a twenty-first-century reinvigoration of an outmoded game. Darts was an affront to taste, an abandoning of restraint and a giant two-fingered salute to anyone wanting a quiet life. It was a fantastical experience. The low-key, charming game of my childhood resembled this champagne supernova as a sparrow resembles an eagle.

Like most people who grew up on these shores, darts had been for most of my life a peripheral concern; something to be taken lightly and occasionally, a bit of a joke. I was no good at the game, and it just didn't seem important or relevant to my upbringing. I was a provincial middle-class child, the son of two teachers. I played the clarinet badly, and once, aged 15, sprayed quotes from the Romanian absurdist Eugène Ionesco on my bedroom wall. I was that kind of kid.

Yes, I watched *Bullseye* on Sunday afternoons, but so too did the entire nation. And, until the sport grabbed my attention, I didn't pay it much thought. I might have known who Eric Bristow was, but not much beyond that. Now darts had come and walloped me in the solar plexus of my senses. And in doing so, it shook up my comfortable preconceptions, showing me a little bit of Britain I scarcely knew, but one that pumped real blood and lived and breathed like no other.

Call it what you will: a sport, a game, a nonsense. But darts, self-evidently, was the noisy neighbour who demanded attention

by sparking up an impromptu barbecue in the garden next door, cranking up the volume and packing the lawn with hollering, gyrating revellers. 'Come on over!' it seemed to insist, stretching out a can of warm lager in welcome. It was too good an offer to miss, so I hopped over the fence.

And that's when my journey began, I suppose. With each passing year, I drilled just a little bit deeper into the core of this particular activity. My familiarity with the game and the vivid players who circulated in its fish-tank environment grew, and before too long I had grown fond and fascinated. Darts seemed endlessly funny, and yet deadly serious. I loved it.

I collected stories, overheard from my privileged seat at the breakfast table alongside the greats of the sport, and began hoarding them in my memory like match-day programmes; occasionally dusting them down and flipping back through them. From time to time, I'd give the tales an airing at middle-class dinner parties, 'dispatches from the world of darts' for an uncomprehending audience. They were greeted with benevolent amusement, but no great interest, no surge of understanding. I discovered that I could not adequately express my admiration and affection for this world, and that my experiences merited greater attention. One day, I realised that the stories had gained a critical mass, and a book started to emerge; this book, in fact.

It was a slow gestation. Midway through writing, I still had no idea what the book should be called. Then, out of the blue, came a moment of inspiration.

Heart of Dart-ness.

The working title for this book had been suggested to me. Even though it was not my idea, I liked it. For a start, it was a neat pun, and the darts world is touchingly fond of puns.

I thought straight away of Ted 'The Count' Hankey, the former two-time British Darts Organisation world champion and the single most lugubrious presence ever to have graced the oches of this great darting nation. Hankey, with his handsomely proportioned head, bedecked with thinning, oily black hair, rejoices in the look of an undertaker with an intimate rash. Some time ago he had already annexed for himself the nickname 'The Prince of Dartness'.

But *Heart of Dart-ness* drew neatly on the literary baggage of Joseph Conrad's seminal tale, *Heart of Darkness*, the very book that had spawned my earliest efforts at commentating like Sid Waddell, forcing a literary allusion into a darts match: 'The horror!'

Waddell was, until his untimely death in 2012, the undisputed Voice of Darts and one of the modern game's founding fathers, in whose honour the World Championship trophy itself is named. And it was Sid Waddell who produced the most memorable, the funniest, and the most pretentious line of commentary in the history of televised sport. When commentating on Eric Bristow's first-ever World Championship, he opined enthusiastically that: 'When Alexander of Macedonia was 33, he cried salt tears because there were no more worlds to conquer. Bristow's only 27!'

It was, of course, tremendously silly to compare a book about darts to one of the greatest novels in the history of the English language. And to compare nineteenth-century Belgium's colonisation of the Congo to the growth of the Professional Darts Corporation might perhaps induce the reader to snort derisively into their lager. But this was darts! Different rules applied. And besides, as I constantly reminded myself, it was a pun.

Heart of Darkness tells the story of one man's ghastly journey in a steamboat up the Congo, into a wild, unfamiliar landscape in search of a mysterious and fascinatingly dark character called Kurtz. For me, it seemed the perfect metaphor for my mission: the Congo became the darts world, and the mysterious brooding presence of Kurtz was a distant figure in the gloom, three darts clasped in the palm of his hand, his identity as yet unexplored.

Conrad's tale begins with a description of a French gunship, moored off the coast of an impenetrable landscape, firing unimpressively into the unending jungle. The similarities were not lost on me: 'In the immensity of earth, sky and water, there she was, incomprehensible, firing into a continent. Pop, would go one of the six-inch guns; a small flame would dart...' (*And see! Conrad actually uses the word 'dart'!*) '...and vanish, a little white smoke would disappear, a tiny projectile would give a feeble screech – and nothing happened. Nothing could happen.'

This felt like an apt metaphor: darts seemed to me to be the unimaginable continent. I was bewildered by the sheer volume of games, and scores, and players; the twisted contusions, almost lost in history, of at best ill-remembered, half-forgotten, semi-recorded tournaments, from the *News of the World* to the Poker Stars Isle of Man International Festival of Darts or the Dry Blackthorn Cider Masters and the MFI World Pairs. Where to begin with it all?

Back at my dartboard, there I stood, on the brink of greatness.

Outside, a cloud scudded across the winter sun, turning the world dark. The pressure grew, unbearably.

The third and final dart lay in my curled palm, its potential unspoilt by the prospect of failure, gleaming with the promise of a 180 maximum. I shook out my throwing arm, took a deep breath, squinted at the board with its two perfect darts sitting side by side in the treble 20, then I threw.

I hit a single 14.

I put the darts back in their case and left them gently on the mantelpiece.

And in that vast jungle, another shell landed impotently, exploding to no effect.

The Power

'Tell me, pray,' said I, 'who is this Mr Kurtz?'

JOSEPH CONRAD – *HEART OF DARKNESS*

'**Y**ou all right, bud?'

That, accompanied by a pleasant enough smile, was the extent of our communication for many years as Phil Taylor strode into yet another venue through the back entrance, his black anorak pulled over his rounded shoulders. He was a cheerful presence backstage at the darts, somebody who should be wearing a peaked cap; a bus conductor, perhaps, or a parkie.

'Hi Phil.' I'd walk past him in the corridor, thinking nothing more of the encounter. Greeting this exceptional man was as normal as eating a steak and mushroom pie.

My working area for ITV was the players' bar, a place of unreconstructed verbal jousting, where political correctness sat shyly in the corner with a Diet Coke. It was here that I interviewed players (for television) before and after their matches.

I watched the players go about their pre and post match rituals, in their acres of fantastically embroidered nylon shirts. They were variously bearded, tattooed, pierced, gelled, primed, oiled and larger than life, glad-handing their way through the hordes to get onto the stage. I warmed to them and their constant merriment, though I felt excluded by their familiarity with each other and what I perceived as a wariness towards me, the intruding stranger.

At first it was hard to speak the language, in terms of both vocabulary and accent. I opted for a softening of my vowels into an approximation of Estuary English, dropping the tell-tale consonants that betrayed my background. I was anxious I might be unmasked as the darts newbie I was. I trod as carefully as I could around the darts vernacular, choosing my moments to drop in my hastily learnt key phrases such as 'out shot', 'holding the throw' and 'ton plus'.

And yet, at the end of every evening, close to midnight, I'd often see some bedraggled loser wearily chucking on their jacket, patting the pockets to check for fags and darts, then mumbling a few farewells and taking his leave of the players' bar. Alone, and possibly in search of a kebab, the legends of the oche would slope off into the night, just men with a craving for grilled meat and chilli sauce. And there's no more ordinary sight than that.

Taylor was no different. He was, in Joseph Conrad's words, 'a very remarkable person'. Although you wouldn't always know, from a cursory encounter with The Power, that you were in the presence of a near-perfect practitioner.

The dissonance between man and myth was at its greatest where Phil 'The Power' Taylor was concerned. Such was the low-key presence of a middle-aged man who used to manufacture porcelain toilet handles and now threw darts for a living, and the cacophonous, almost idolatrous reception he elicited with each of his many public appearances.

And yet, without question, Phil Taylor was the motor that drove it all and the fuel that fed it. He redefined what was possible with three darts in your hand and a board to aim at, taking a game of skill and chance into the realms of the calculable, the mathematical, the astronomical. He spanned eras, eclipsed others. If Taylor had been a tennis player, he'd have started as Borg and finished as Djokovic. If he'd gone into politics, he'd have been Churchill, Kennedy and Putin, with more than a hint of Trump. He enjoyed a singular status that, for a while at least, outstripped the game itself. At times his legend, made flesh by his presence on the dartboards of Blackpool and Bolton, Glasgow and Antwerp, seemed to outweigh the worth of the sport that had given him the stage on which to shine.

And yet, when I knew him, you'd most likely find the greatest player the game has ever produced sitting down with a cup of tea discussing, for example, the latest lease terms for his car, and would often seem to be full of admiration for the wisdom of his choice, the sharpness of the deal he struck, the sheer command he exerted over the whole enterprise. Never lacking in self-belief, Phil Taylor, or 'Philip Douglas Taylor' as commentators liked to intone portentously when the gravity of his brilliance weighed heavily in the air, was by common consent the Greatest. Indeed, on the eve of his retirement, Sky Sports (whose fate was interwoven to some extent with Taylor's ascendancy over two decades or more) aired a biopic documentary film titled: *Phil Taylor: The Greatest*.

Nonetheless, backstage, in that hidden off-camera realm that is the reserve of players, their guests and the functionaries of the tournament, Taylor sometimes cut an isolated figure; not lonely, but exuding an apartness of spirit. From time to time he would joust with opponents, but often he'd be silently warming up, always alert to the comings and goings of the practice boards. Even towards the end, greying, thinning and gaunter than he once was, Taylor still had his feet planted firmly on the ground. A more rooted, self-assured, balanced

figure I had not seen among the preening peacocks of the darts world. Taylor simply was.

For a long time, all players were equal except for Taylor, who was, by the solid five per cent with which his average scores exceeded those of his nearest rivals, more equal than others. Other players' games were known to have been paused in the middle of a set on the orders of Sky TV directors, so that they could film Taylor's arrival at the venue. And I saw at first hand how the officials rallied around and pandered to his demands, pulling him back to earth minute by minute. It could be a delicate operation, but necessary. He had to be protected.

'What do I know? I'm just a humble bloke from Stoke...' I once heard him say in front of a television camera. 'A humble bloke from Stoke... who just happens to be a major shareholder in the PDC.'

And with that, he turned and swaggered out of the interview area, bobbing from side to side in the manner of a boxer entering a ring.

'A major shareholder in the PDC' was a particularly well-turned phrase, both a stinging rebuke to a darting world that was beginning to count him as simply a good player among a clutch of peers, and an acknowledgement that his brilliance had built the whole sandcastle and could just as easily be wiped out with one swing of his black-trainered foot.

The last time I had spoken to him at length, in 2015, he was aware that things were changing, and he was trying to find a way to adapt. He cut a weary figure, sitting in the foyer of a Milton Keynes hotel without removing his black anorak. Some weeks previously, Taylor had been narrowly beaten in the final of the World Championships by the popular Scotsman Gary Anderson. It had been a tense encounter. He had been criticised in some quarters for seeming to turn his back on his opponent when the winning double went in. It was not the first time that Taylor had been accused of bad losing, but this was perhaps of greater significance, coming as it did on the biggest stage of all: Alexandra Palace in the World Championship Final.

His career was being spoken of more and more often in the past tense. He didn't like that. He was downcast, terse.

Because there was an awkward silence, I made an outrageous suggestion. 'Have you ever thought about changing your image, giving it a complete makeover?' I thought maybe he might be tired of having to be The Power every single day of his working life.

'I can't,' he replied instantaneously, as if that was precisely what he was thinking too. 'Sky won't let me change my nickname.'

'I like the idea of you changing it.' I was seized by sudden enthusiasm for the idea. 'I think it'd be great for you, moving on.'

'I do, too. I'm all for change, me. But it wouldn't happen. It just won't.'

'It's a big year for you, this, isn't it?'

'It is.' I thought I could see self-doubt momentarily cloud his placid expression. 'It's like starting out all over again.'

For so long, Taylor had been unbeatable. Over a period of 23 years, he amassed an astonishing 16 World Championships, starting out with the Embassy title with the British Darts Organisation in 1990 and 1992 before switching, along with 15 others, to the newly formed Professional Darts Corporation and then beginning a prolonged era of complete domination.

Great players came close, and occasionally got the better of him, even, sometimes, when it really mattered, in the final of the World Championships: Dennis Priestley (1994), John Part (2003) and Raymond van Barneveld (2007). Gary Anderson was the last man to beat him in the final, in 2015, before his last-ever match and defeat to Rob Cross, in 2018.

But more often than not, Taylor prevailed. At his peak, between 1995 and 2002, he won eight consecutive titles, like a one-man darting version of Glasgow Rangers in their mid-nineties unassailability. As a champion he was simply a different breed from any of the greats who had gone before.

He was Phil Taylor, the Power; his frailties were scarcely visible with little of the maverick genius that accompanied the feats of Leighton Rees, Eric Bristow or Jocky Wilson. His winning was remorseless. By sheer weight of his achievement, his inclusion in any tournament added the necessary lustre required to sell subscriptions and keep the eyeballs glued to the darts in ever-larger numbers. Sky Sports, after taking a significant risk by investing in a sport that seemed to be on the way out, built their broadcasting narrative around Taylor's continuing domination and the game moved from cheap and cheerful sideshow to a staple of the satellite constellation. Such were the benefits of backing a winner.

Taylor's soft features and playful grin featured again and again on their high-definition screens as he lined up against an endless string of soon-to-be plucky losers, his inked arms folded to reveal his Power tattoo, or as he stood back to back with his latest rival against a green screen background exploding into fireballs to the accompaniment of something classical and full of portent. The unlikely face of the sport, as homespun and down to earth as any of them, but supernaturally talented. They were on to a good thing with Taylor, and they knew it.

With Sky's darts coverage, this had given rise to a proliferation of televised events summoned up from thin air: the World Matchplay, the World Grand Prix, the UK Open and the Desert Classic. Taylor won them all, over and over again, year after relentless year.

His walk-ons were the stuff of high drama, ritualistically devoured by the hordes of his supporters who clambered over each other to extend an outstretched palm in the direction of the great man as he weaved and bobbed his way onstage. The thunderclaps before the intoning of the final 'Taylooorrrr!' and the crashing beats of his signature tune kicked in were timed to perfection, a routine celebrated and understood by hundreds of thousands, if not millions of darts fans in the increasingly overstuffed arenas of the PDC over two ambitious decades of growth.

And how the crowds loved to love him! His presence introduced a new and urgent frenzy into a boisterous crowd. They would stand on chairs, on tables, arms outspread in religious ecstasy, chanting with endless looped passion that there was 'only one Phil Taylor, one Phil Taylor!' and that they were all, collectively, 'walking along, singing a song, walking in a Taylor wonderland!'

People loved the cheek of him too, the wrinkled nose of his smile, the loping gait and the 'grandad in the playground' fist bumps with opponents. They revelled in the self-pumping snarls of vindication to camera after another brilliant checkout, the way he'd remove the board after every match, sign it and hand it to someone in the front row, annexing the largesse of a champion and putting that gesture out of reach for every other player, for ever more.

They laughed along with, as well as applauded, the slight little barbs with which he peppered his spiky post-match interviews, damning opponents with faint praise, indulging in a kind of head-patting, hair-ruffling condescension that was his by right, but rubbed people up the wrong way, or the right way, if you were Phil Taylor.

He adored winning. He also adored what came with winning: the money. I remember leaving the Circus Tavern in Purfleet sometime after midnight in the dead of winter in 2009. Taylor had just soundly beaten Robert Thornton by 16 legs to 9 to win the inaugural Players Championship. Unbeknown to everyone inside the cushioned red interior of the Tavern, a blizzard had been howling for several hours around the venue. A thick carpet of snow lay outside, and as we spilled out into the night to hail taxis or retrieve parked cars, there was a delightful sense of childish playfulness about the scene, grown men sliding, or hurling snowballs at each other.

Suddenly, I was grabbed from behind in a bear hug. A voice bellowed into my ear: 'Fucking yes!'

'Well played, Phil.' I spun around to see Taylor, eyes ablaze with excitement, wearing his ordinary-looking black coat over his darts shirt. He was clutching a trophy.

'Fifty fucking grand,' Taylor hollered. 'You beauty.' And with that extremely honest, if somewhat prosaic assessment of his weekend's work, he slid off into the Essex night. I watched the greatest player in the world attempting to hold his balance, and a trophy, in a snowy car park; an image of pride and pleasure that will live me for a long time.

It was mesmerising to watch him play. I'd often sneak away from the interview area and find a spot high up in the audience to watch him walk onstage and start to throw. Even to the untutored eye, there was something very special about the way Taylor threw a dart. His gaze was unlike any other in its breathless immobility: rock steady, unflinching, impossibly relaxed even in the moments of greatest tension, under the most intense pressure. The only indication you were ever likely to get that, underneath that expansive nylon shirt, there was a heart beating 20 to the dozen, was the occasional reddening of his cheeks. But even that was very rare. In his words: 'That's the paradox of top darts: you must be tense enough to compete, but relaxed enough to play your normal game.'

After a brief stuttering ghost throw, tiny in its suggestion of what's to come, his right hand draws back, slowly, smoothly, an action repeated to the millimetre with each successive dart. Then comes a momentary dead spot in the arc of his throwing arm, poised between both eyes, almost at the bridge of his nose, before the pendulum swings back in the opposite direction, now gaining sudden speed until the release, and an accompanying feathering out of his fingers, as the dart gets airborne. At this precise moment, Taylor's eyes widen a fraction, his eyebrows rise as if in comic surprise and he minutely straightens his back, making him seem a centimetre taller. His tattooed right arm continues to fall through the movement it started, his hand already seeking out the next dart from his left hand, limp at his side.

What follows, as the dart moves through the air, is nothing short of aerodynamic alchemy. Chaos is followed by calm certainty. Studied in slow motion, Taylor's darts are wild with irregular motion, known in the made-up darting lexicon of Sid Waddell as the 'wibble'. As they pass through the split-second dead zone between release and landing, it's as if they're buffeted by crosswinds, like a light aircraft pulling off a tricky approach in a gale. They lurch to one side, over-correct their line by flicking wildly back in the other direction, and they bob up and

down before the tip of the dart rears up like the nose of an aeroplane about to stall. This is known, for some reason, as the 'weep'. Now the flight, hanging back, drags through the air, applying a virtual handbrake to the movement. And then all the wild oscillating vanishes and the dart simply hits home, miraculously straight, and angled about ten degrees off 90 to the board. And they land on target.

His darts look unnaturally, incontrovertibly right. Taylor's darts make everyone else's, however brilliant the player, look like an act of faith rather than method.

Like so many other players, Taylor hails from Stoke-on-Trent. His was a tough childhood. What we read and hear in his words is a sanitised version of a reality that might have been harder still to have lived through. He was raised in the hard-pressed conglomeration of red-brick terraces and sixties brutalist towers that make up the unpretentious Staffordshire city built from the merging urban sprawl of seven towns. Collectively, they lack a centre, lack a major industry and lack much sense of purpose.

Forty years ago, coal pits and the steel industry, as well as the famous potteries, provided Stoke with an economic beating heart. But it's failing now.

It is, in the modern political landscape, exactly the kind of long-standing, white, working-class community that has been neglected by successive governments with their ineffectual tinkering and lack of serious investment. There are high rates of unemployment, immigration and exceptional levels of deprivation. Its careworn status is borne out by the battered look to its shopping precincts, and though there are well-kept and attractive gardens and public spaces, by and large it is the antithesis to the notion of the London 'elite'.

Stoke is Brexit in bricks and mortar. That impression was borne out by the European Referendum result, in which Stoke-on-Trent produced a higher percentage of Leave voters than anywhere else in the country. Recent activists have railed against this labelling of their city: too glib, too patronising, too easy to dispense. In 2017, the *Guardian* commissioned a series of documentaries that aspired to emphasise the positive nature of the city's culture. Not one of them included a reference to darts.

Yet here in the Potteries, while the industry that gave it its identity has been ripped out, there's always been football – and darts. The sport may have been drying up into residual pockets in the Greater London area, but boards still hang in pubs and clubs throughout this city. As Taylor puts it, with his own bullet-proof self-esteem, 'I may be one of the only thriving business concerns still going in the Potteries.' That's the second sentence in his autobiography. The first starts with the words, 'I am very proud of this little patch of England…'

A tiny dilapidated house on Boothfield Street in Tunstall, just around the corner from the comically aptly named Dart Avenue, constituted that 'little patch'. The ceilings were caving in, the windows glass-free and boarded up. There was no running water and no electricity. It was, in Taylor's words, 'a world of poverty and hardship'. His mother Liz and father Doug both ran the gamut of hard, poorly paid jobs. Doug's were back-breaking; Liz's were demoralising. Together with their infant son, they used to scour the scrapyards for discarded copper to sell, as well as scavenge the colliery waste yards for coal and rip out fencing from allotments to burn in an effort to keep the house warm.

The Stoke-on-Trent of Taylor's childhood is still generating the same opening lines to countless biographies that will, unlike Taylor's, never be written. As recently as 2014 there were frequent reports of bands of kids seen scavenging for food in dustbins in the district of Fenton. This doesn't make Stoke unique, of course, as urban poverty is endemic in much of the UK. Nonetheless, according to the Hardship Commission of Stoke-on-Trent City Council, almost 30 per cent of children live in poverty with an estimated 60,000 adults surviving on less than the 'minimum required to access basic goods and services'. The problems, it seems, are deeply engrained. And they are precisely the conditions in which Phil Taylor grew up.

His father died in 1997 from stomach cancer and his relationship with his mother remained very tight until her death in January 2015. In her last few days, and often by her bedside, Taylor would find himself steeped in nostalgia for their shared past, his childhood; 'episodes like hiding in the pantry, with Mum holding her hand over my mouth so I wouldn't call out when the landlord came to collect the rent and we pretended no one was home'.

Taylor was rocked badly by losing his mother. He was, at the bottom of it all, quite an emotional man, occasionally impulsive, private, proud, sentimental. Yet the day after burying her, he was in action in Bournemouth, playing in the Premier League. And a week or so after that, he was on the road again, this time heading to Milton Keynes to try and win the Masters

Championship. The darts world treated him with considerable sensitivity, having been made acutely aware over many years of the special bond there had been between mother and son. And Taylor now sought refuge in the familiarity of competition; all he'd ever known for most of his adult life.

'I'm sorry to hear your news, Phil,' I remember saying to him just before we filmed an interview. He thanked me, and then told me how much it hurt him to have lost her. I was struck, as I often was, by how blunt and open he would be, revealing, quite unprompted, his personal life. It was a not uncomplicated existence and he often sought to protect it, yet at the same time, quite spontaneously, he exposed surprising extents of it to the public gaze. Then we started the recorded interview, which dealt simply with his ambitions for the weekend's darts. It ended when I wished him good luck in the tournament.

'Thanks,' he said, grinning. 'I need the money. I've got a funeral to pay for.' Then he walked off.

At the time, none of us knew quite how to react. We edited his final line out of the broadcast to save the viewers from the same slight discomfort that I'd felt when he said it.

There has always, I suspect, been something of the square peg in a round hole about Taylor, despite him having acquired the self-confidence and swagger that befitted a man of his standing. Nonetheless, not far beneath the surface, lurked the shadow of a lonely kid: the only child who nearly drowned in a lake and then walked home in sodden clothes, who saw ghosts in his bedroom, and, later on, used to converse openly with a ghost called Charlie. As a child, he shunned the showers at school because of his chubbiness and spent hours with his best mate Fitzroy Ellis ('the only black kid in my school') cutting coal out of a hillside with an axe.

In childhood, Taylor developed coping mechanisms that he took with him into professional darts. Friends might have come and gone, but mother and father remained, home was home, darts were darts and money was most certainly worth having. When you'd had none, money was worth more: 'I thought school was a complete waste of time and I couldn't wait to get out when I was 15 and earn some money.'

As a young man, he drifted through a series of jobs in which, by his own admission, he scammed and skived his way to greater reward than was strictly legal, playing the system and beating it. But he found pleasure, attention and fulfilment at the Riley Arms, standing seven feet, nine and three-quarter inches from a dartboard. Taylor spent hours flinging darts at the back of the bedroom door where he now lived with his wife Yvonne and their growing young family. As his commitment to the game grew, he started to take a greater interest in what the future might offer.

When Eric Bristow, somewhat sensationally, moved to Stoke-on-Trent in 1985 ('it was like Jesus Christ moving from the Holy Land to Milton Keynes', according to Bristow), and opened a darting pub, the Crafty Cockney with his wife, and fellow dart player Maureen Flowers, it was only a matter of time before Taylor and Bristow's paths crossed.

Bristow knew a player when he saw one and in the end, Bristow offered him a way out of playing 'merely' for Staffordshire 'A'. He gave Taylor an opportunity to turn professional by sponsoring him to the tune of thousands of pounds. Taylor didn't think twice.

'"Pay me back if you win anything," was all he said.' He paid Bristow's investment back, over and over again.

It was an intervention that changed the course of Taylor's life and altered the history of the sport, as well as ultimately undermining Bristow's claim to have been the greatest player in the world. Little did any of them know what they had started.

And the rest, if you like, is a simple enough trajectory. Success piling upon success. He played his pivotal role as one of the key architects of the split within darts and the foundation of the PDC. He gained recognition not accorded to any other player of the 21st century, and would go on to finish runner-up in 2010 to Tony McCoy in the BBC Sports Personality of the Year Awards.

But there is another side to Taylor's trajectory to the top. In 2000, he was charged with sexual assault. The incident had taken place in the camper van that Taylor used to take on the road to save money on hotel bills. The victims, two women in their early twenties, pressed charges against him, and Taylor was convicted. He had tried to kiss and undress them, undoing their bras and fondling their breasts. They resisted him and eventually asked to be let out of the camper van.

It is a story he relates in his ghostwritten autobiography, *The Power*. In his version of events, he seems to accept the verdict of the court. At this point, there is a tightness to the prose that suggests the intervention of a legal read. However, something of his attitude towards this unseemly part of his story seeps through when, on hearing of the relative leniency of his sentence (Taylor was ordered to pay a £2,000 fine), he rather downplays the crime for which he had been convicted.

'I felt relieved. I think a fine of £2,000 puts the case in perspective. It seemed to me like being convicted of drunken driving and not being banned...'

It looked like he had got away lightly on that occasion, what really hurt Taylor was the withdrawal of his MBE. His name had been one of those included on the latest honours list. He was to receive the same medal as his great rival and sometime boss Eric Bristow, a man against whom Taylor has consistently measured himself since their first meeting in the Crafty Cockney. But it wasn't to be.

One by one, other recipients of honours were called to the Palace to collect their gongs, but the envelope containing the invitation to Taylor and his wife Yvonne, who had chosen a dress for the occasion, never arrived. The damage had been done.

Further harm to his image was done in 2015 when the tabloids printed allegations made by two of Taylor's four children that they had been cut off by their father and were forced to live on benefits in hostels that were, according to the papers, 'full of prostitutes and drug addicts'.

And in 2016, Taylor and his wife Yvonne divorced. That court settlement required him to hand over almost £1.5m in cash and assets.

In his own defence, Taylor remains tight-lipped. 'There are two sides to every story and sometimes the devil is in the detail you don't see,' he said. 'I am not going to wash my dirty linen in public.'

Right to the end of his career, he still commanded attention. Even on entering a room, heads would turn. He held court and people listened, which he liked. He was pretty happy with the way things had turned out and saw no need to indulge in great charm offensives or any unnecessary acts of self-justification.

The way it was, in Taylor's wonderland of hotel rooms and dartboards, motorways and television sets, was the way it was. He owned a few nice cars and a property portfolio of modest rental homes in Staffordshire, some not far from where he grew up. Only now he was the landlord calling for the rent.

Once I asked him how many houses he'd got.

'About 16,' he said, adding, 'I think.' One for each world title, then.

'I always thought you were quite careful with your money.'

'No, I'm not really.' With a wave of his hand, he dismissed the notion, well established on the circuit, that Taylor was, shall we say, frugal. 'I keep my private life private, you see.'

He had few hobbies, favoured loose-fitting leisurewear and owned a reasonably extensive collection of trainers.

'I've got about five pairs of these.' He pointed at his feet. 'That'll last me all year.' Not for running, you understand, mostly for pacing up and down in, fetching darts out of a board and returning to the oche.

'Have you got a massive widescreen TV?'

'I've got all that. Yeah. I've got about six of them,' he laughed. 'But I don't waste money.'

'Can you imagine a life without darts?' I asked him.

'Yeah,' he said, without hesitation.

I think he meant it. Enough was enough. 'Right. I'm off to get my dinner.' And he headed away towards the lifts in one of his five pairs of matching trainers.

I wondered, despite the incontrovertible evidence of his greatness, whether Taylor really was the man at the core of the story. There was something in his make-up that suggested a distance to the world, and to the game that had made him rich and famous.

He had played out his career over decades, from the game darts once was to the game it has become. But still he felt oddly peripheral, as if his brilliance had separated him from the simple endeavour of darts: the pursuit of fun. Because without the fun, what was the point?

Perhaps there was someone else who more clearly defined the spirit of darts than the man who played it better than anyone else. Maybe the root of Taylor's brilliance lay in the genius of the man who spotted his talent.

But that would be another story.

Gravesend

He was just a word for me. I did not see the man in
the name any more than you do. Do you see him?
Do you see the story? Do you see anything?

JOSEPH CONRAD – *HEART OF DARKNESS*

A pattern continued for a while. From time to time, I dipped into darts, diving headlong into a three-day tournament with ITV, then emerging at the other end, gasping for air. For days afterwards, the after-image of the game would stay with me, gaudily burnt into the retina of my everyday consciousness till it receded from my line of sight. But, all the while, darts was carrying on without me, and I was dimly aware of its presence. Almost without my knowing, I was being drawn in.

It was fitting that my parallel journey into the *Heart of Dartness* would start in Gravesend, the old town so beloved of Joseph Conrad, who spent much of his time in the towns of the Thames Estuary. Along the length of this unrushing water, the dark mass of the North Sea sweeps into the ever-tightening grip of this stolid land, as London gradually subsumes it, teasing it into its stone and concrete grip, and the river is tamed.

A hundred years ago, these shimmering, grey-and-white waters would have been criss-crossed with the red sails of Thames barges, laden with a huge variety of goods from Hull, Newcastle, Bristol and Ipswich destined for the capital city. The barges also brought into London exotic freight from overseas. Some of these would have been carrying in their flat-bottomed hulls other cargoes besides, nestling unobtrusively in among the bags of coal, the fish and the timber.

It is along this waterway, for instance, that millions upon millions of darts made their way into Britain from their manufacturing base in France; simple fairground toys whose feathery spores would settle in pubs across the land and take root, spreading out from London, Essex, Kent and Sussex ever deeper into the interior, seeding themselves across the length and breadth of the British Isles. It was along these workmanlike approaches that led to London that the game of darts started to burrow a way into the nation's heart. Estuary England: Dartford, Erith, Purfleet, Woolwich... and Gravesend.

I started to delve deeper into the murky past of this most unusual, but at the same time, mundane game. I was coming to the conclusion that any journey into the history of darts would end up in the same kind of disappointing cul-de-sac in which the origins of the name Gravesend are trapped. The word 'Gravesend' itself is consistently misapprehended. I've often heard the theory that it took its name from the mass burial of London's plague victims there in the seventeenth century. Sadly, this is not true. Instead, the word has some obscure Anglo-Saxon origin, loosely translated as 'place at the end of the grove', which is disappointing. The history of darts, I discovered, was similarly embellished and misrepresented.

Yet the lack of evidence has never stopped historians of this unique sport from hashing and re-hashing similarly obfuscated pseudo-histories from website to website, publication to

publication until they pass for truth. From the seafaring passengers on the *Mayflower* amusing themselves with a few legs of 501, through the widely circulated notion that Greek warriors routinely kept their throwing arms in by launching small spears at the ends of wine barrels, to Dutch archers chucking the broken ends of arrows at some sort of wooden target in their non-combative downtime.

This last version of the origins of darts has gained considerable traction, despite the cold water poured on it by Keith Turner in *Darts – The Complete Book of the Game*, who argues that such a practice was impractical. 'If the head is removed from the arrow,' argues Turner, 'the cut-down shaft would not stick in.'

There is only man to have cared enough about the origins of the sport to have genuinely, rigorously, academically scoured literature for references to darts, and this is the estimable Dr Patrick Chaplin PhD of Anglia Ruskin University. In his various publications, he deems it most likely that a dart was always a bespoke object, and not some sort of cut-down mini-arrow.

Chaplin, brilliantly, cites Claude Blair's work on prehistoric weaponry, in which it is suggested that late Palaeolithic man employed a 'light missile weapon'. He also quotes Leonid Tarassuk, a Manhattan-based expert on arms and armour at the Metropolitan Museum of Art, who confirms 'darts... are documented for the Palaeolithic Solutrean period' in the form of cave paintings. That's a frighteningly long time ago. Neither cricket nor rugby nor football can make anything like that kind of claim to antiquity.

Jumping forward nearly 20,000 years, there is a reference (and again I am indebted to Chaplin's masterful research) to the use of 'launces, swerdes, and dartes' in the 1314 English Romance *Guy of Warwick*. And, leaping 200 years further on, it is often written that Anne Boleyn gave Henry VIII a pristine set of feathered darts for a New Year's gift in 1532. The evidence for that assertion comes from the Austrian emperor's ambassador to the court of King Henry, Ernest Chapuys, who wrote on 4 January 1532 that Anne Boleyn had given her husband 'certains dards fais a la Biscayne, richement accoustrez'. What such 'special darts, richly ornamented in Biscayan fashion' might have looked like, and what purpose they might have really served is anyone's guess. It's a harmless enough titbit that no one is really that interested in debunking, except for Dr Chaplin, a lone academic voice of rigour in an otherwise slapdash world.

One by one, the most widely spread and commonly held darting creation myths fall apart under Dr Chaplin's withering scrutiny, including Maurice Ashby's contemporaneous account of the Civil War in which, he claims, a number of royalist soldiers were taken prisoner by Parliamentarian forces on the eve of the Battle of Naseby as they were getting inebriated in an inn somewhere near Market Harborough 'supping and playing darts or quoits'. On closer inspection of the original source for the anecdote, however, the contemporary *Parliamentarian True Informer* newspaper, there is only a reference to the soldier 'playing at Quoits for handfuls of money'.

Small matter. No really, a very small matter.

Dr Chaplin's well-researched contention is that the centuries-old game of 'puff-darts', or 'puff-and-dart', or 'puff-the-dart' had a much more significant influence on the development of the modern game than it is normally credited with. One of the earliest references to this game came in 1467 when the Borough of Leicester banned all sorts of blatantly immoral games, including 'blowing with arrows through a trunk at certain numbers by way of lottery'.

Then there's the banal and often overlooked theory that it all, quite simply, came from the French fairground tradition of throwing darts at targets. Some involved throwing terrifying-sounding foot-long steel-tipped monsters underarm, a sport that has recently celebrated something of a revival with the opening of Paris's Les Cognées; a 21st-century axe-throwing Mecca. But other phenomena resemble much more closely the game we have now come to accept and love. Given that centuries of close trade and occasional blood-mixing had characterised Anglo-French relationships over many generations, the periodic periods of bloodletting and murder notwithstanding, then it would hardly be surprising that the game might have crossed the Channel. Certainly there is a welter of evidence that documents the import of large numbers of handmade wooden darts in the nineteenth century into England, rising to an improbable sounding *10 million* darts, exclusively manufactured for the English market in the Hasnon region by 1900.

So, darts is French, basically. Which is an awkward conclusion.

No matter: most chroniclers of the game, I discovered, simply didn't bother researching its history, or wilfully made stuff up. As late as 1968, for example, in a book also imaginatively entitled *Darts*, Noel E. Williamson wonders out loud whether prehistoric man had 'thrown sharp pieces of stone into a tree at some time or another, and how much farther back than that can we possibly get?' This, as historical research goes, is about as thorough as an attempt to clean the gutters of a three-bed semi with a pack of a dozen cotton buds.

'Of its origins I can tell you nothing,' wrote the unlikely sounding darts aficionado, Rupert Croft-Cooke in 1936, the author of a very entertainingly written volume also, you will by now be unsurprised to learn, entitled *Darts*. This was the first book solely written about darts ever to be published.

'Perhaps before Agincourt,' Croft-Cooke speculates in a shamelessly vague way, 'the English archers set up a target and threw their arrows at the bull's eye; perhaps in the eighteenth century, when labourers worked for a few shillings a week, they forged this diversion from the monotony of their days.' That 'perhaps' occurs not once but twice in that sentence tells you all you need to know about its reliability.

Fast-forwarding to the early part of the 20th century. Puritanical Victorian morality (enshrined in the Licensing Act of 1872) had led to a purging of card games and other vehicles of vice from public houses. Games of chance were banned, and darts (or rather, 'dart-and-target'), was deemed to be a game of chance. Nonetheless, there was no shortage of publicans out there, as court records testify, willing to run the risk of allowing darts to be played on their premises. The beer flowed as the profits soared. Darts was as popular as it was (perhaps) illegal.

But was it a game of chance? In 1908, the Leeds constabulary turned up at the Adelphi Inn on Kirkstall Road where a game of darts was in progress, as it was most evenings. They promptly arrested the perpetrator of this decadence, the landlord, a Mr James Garside. The game of darts, alongside the landlord himself, was to have its day in court.

Called as a witness for the defence when the case was heard at Leeds Magistrates Court, one of the pub's regulars, William 'Big Foot' Anakin, asked for a dartboard to be mounted. He then, according to the urban myth, proceeded to hit three single twenties, followed by three double twenties, if the chroniclers of this case are to be believed, which they almost certainly aren't. With Big Foot's unerring accuracy, the defence built a compelling case against darts being considered a game of chance, unless, that is, an untutored player, chosen at random from the legal profession, could match his score.

Setting aside your rightful scepticism, you can still imagine the scene. Court officials were invited to step up to the oche and either equal or better Big Foot's score. The first court clerk probably hit a seven, a two, and then missed altogether.

'Case dismissed!'

Darts could continue on its merry way, a game to play, according to Croft-Cooke, with the 'golden glow of beer in one's brain, to the sound of tinkling glasses'.

By the early part of the 20th century, darts' stronghold was in the south of England, in a swathe from Wiltshire to Berkshire, Kent, Suffolk and Norfolk. London was, frankly, besotted with the game. And by the 1930s, in the depths of, and perhaps because of, the Depression, it had taken grip, reinvigorating the public houses. The playing of darts was encouraged by breweries and the drinks industry, whose primary interest was in fending off the several threats of the temperance movement, the advent of non-alcoholic drinks and food in the English pub, as well as competition from music halls and other forms of entertainment that didn't involve simply sitting around on wooden chairs and downing flat ale.

At the same time as it was gathering increasing popularity up and down the country, despite the almost feudal patchwork of regional differences between board designs and local rules, it was becoming part of the national sporting calendar. This is where the *News Of The World* enters the story. Long before Rupert Murdoch had turned the newspaper, first published in 1843, into a bawdy grind of celebrity misdemeanours, and long before the phone-hacking scandal finally did for the brand, the infamous tabloid occupied a different, more comfortable space in the national affection. Always salacious, built as it was on a predilection for crime reportage, it had a popular touch that struck a chord with huge numbers of working Britons.

By the 1920s, its circulation had grown to a fulsome 3 million, and ten years later, it topped out at 4 million. The readership was working class, and, in an era when many families could only afford to buy a paper at the weekend, the 'Sundays' had to be worth reading. With its heavy emphasis on sports writing, the *NOTW* had a captive readership, whose numbers they intended to swell. Their first move into sponsorship was golf. But it wasn't long before darts followed.

There is little dispute that the first *News of the World* Individual Darts Championship was held in May 1928 at Holborn Hall in Gray's Inn Road, London. It was won by a chap whose name, if he had been around in the era of the Premier League and the walk-on, would have been a marketeer's dream: Sammy Stone. Not only would the moniker work a treat in the modern age, but his personal background would have made him hugely interesting to the non-darting media: he was a 49-year-old slater, and survivor of the Boer War with nine children to his name.

Thousands of players had entered the inaugural tournament, from pubs and clubs up and down the capital. Stone, representing the New South-West Club, scooped the main prize, then, after vanquishing the best darters that the London Metropolitan area had to offer, became the first *News of the World* champion.

From its very inception, the *News of the World* Championship was a leviathan. Before the Second World War, despite the fact that it was still regionally organised, it nonetheless provided a platform for genuine stars to emerge, many of whom became household names.

There was none bigger than Jim Pike, the South Londoner. In 1939, 17,000 paying punters turned up to watch him lose 2–1 at the Royal Agricultural Hall to Marmaduke 'Duke' Breckon of the Jolly Sailor pub in Hanworth.

Pike went on to fame and was the subject of a stultifying dull Pathé film about his throwing action, in which a man called Harold Lewis drones on about poised elbows and steady gazes over early super-slo-mo footage of a man in a suit throwing darts.

Pike enjoyed a great rivalry with another darter of the era, best known for his antics at early 'exhibition' matches, staged simply for entertainment, a tradition that continues to this day. Joe Hitchcock was his name, and darting trickery of the most audacious kind was his game. His favourite turns involved throwing six-inch nails instead of darts, knocking cigarettes out of the mouths of his assistants or, even more ridiculously, hitting

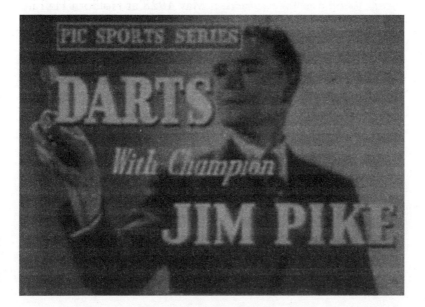

coins from their pursed lips or aiming darts into the middle of a hair band held between the teeth of some unfortunate.

'The idea,' narrates another clipped Pathé voice, 'is to land the dart inside the ring without first going through the lady's face.'

Hitchcock and Pike were big news, and in the post-war years there was considerable clamour for the two darting stars to go head to head to sort out once and for all which of them was the greatest. It was, in some ways, a foretaste of the 'reunification' bouts of the late 1990s between the PDC and the BDO world champions, Phil Taylor and Raymond van Barneveld. The first 'Match of the Century' was held at Acton Town Hall, and covered live on the radio. For the record, Hitchcock, known severally as the 'Marathon Man', the 'Demon of the Dartboard' and the 'Treble 20 Wizard' wiped the floor with Pike, who presumably didn't have enough nicknames. And then, when a rematch was organised, he did it all over again.

Hitchcock, whose charity darts team raised huge sums of money for the war blinded, but whose sponsorship by Watneys Brewery meant that he was classed as a professional, was never

allowed to compete in the *News of the World*, a competition open only to amateur players. His is probably the biggest name missing from a roll call that would go on to feature most of the greats, from Bobby George to John Lowe and Eric Bristow.

The *News of the World* only became a truly national event in 1947–48, when it was reinvented post-war. The first winner of the national (for which, effectively, you should read 'world') crown was a certain Harry Leadbetter from Windle Labour Club in St Helens. The final was played at the Empire Pool, which is now Wembley Arena, and more familiar to fans of *X Factor* and similar. Ten thousand people turned up to watch the players battling it out.

Leadbetter, another man with a considerable hair oil habit, a razor-sharp parting and wearing a three-piece pinstriped suit, vanquished his foe in fairly straightforward fashion. He was clearly not a darter who had to contend with unruly nerves. At the culmination of the tournament, he was presented with a handsome trophy, not unlike the FA Cup, and was promptly thrown aloft by his fellow darts players from his home town,

not all of whom had a full set of teeth, but who had made the trip down south to support their champion. To a man (there appeared to be no women among the travelling party, though many were in the audience to witness the win), they were all sporting heavy woollen suits.

And yet, there were those in Fleet Street, even in those austere post-war years, who could not resist a sniff of disbelief, if not disdain at what darts represented. The tournament preview in the *Manchester Guardian* had concentrated, in time-honoured fashion, on the extraordinary elevation of the game into Wembley's 'blaze of light' from the more appropriate setting of a 'quiet corner of a low-roofed taproom'.

Moreover, in the Olympic year of 1948, as the capital city was gearing up to host the 'Austerity Games', it would be fair to say that the country's press let their attention stray from the oche. The games, of course, were the first to be held since Hitler's showpiece event in 1936, and London had very nearly successfully foisted them on the USA, citing a complete lack of money with which to stage the games. In this blitz spirit of putting on a show for the watching planet, the nascent darts 'world championship' seemed something of an oddity to the national media, who grappled with the familiar problems of how to characterise a game that they still considered, deep down, to be a little infra dig. A *Guardian* reporter noted that whoever ended up winning the prize could hardly be elevated to the same status as a truly international Olympic champion.

'If St Helens goes down it will only be to Gloucestershire or Durham and no cups will go irrecoverably abroad. It may be that America and Australia have not yet fallen in any big way for the double-ringed board and the subtractive joys of "301-up". If we really wanted any more competition from overseas, it might have been as well to postpone tomorrow's finals until the Olympic visitors arrive.'

By 1963, the tournament proves its doubters wrong, was going from strength to strength. Having flirted with Earls Court and outgrown Wembley, it was time for the *News of the World* to put down roots at Alexandra Palace. That switch added lustre to the sport, moving distinctly upmarket. After that, it wasn't long before television started to get interested, and then the whole gig changed for ever.

This competition was the original one which would continue in its evolving guises until its ultimate demise in 1990. It was briefly revived in 1996 so that Phil Taylor could add it to his collection, after Eric Bristow goaded him, claiming that the *NOTW* was the only tournament that mattered, and then it was finally put out of its misery to make way emphatically for what we now know to be the UK Open. Its demise was a definitive break with darts' history. But these were the generally accepted origins of the sport as we know it.

Yet it is also possible, as I discovered, to read in several accounts online (if you dig deeply enough into the darting dark web), that there might have been a kind of pseudo-world championship even before that first tournament organised by the *News of the World*, before 1928. Intrigued, I delved deeper into the story, which seemed to upset the accepted order of darting history. I found a forum in which it was discussed at length.

This semi-secretive landmark event took place, according to some darting conspiracy theorists, in 1927 at a pub in Dartford. The story was that a rogue group of staff from the newspaper set up their own darts tournament, the first of its kind, a year before the first *NOTW*. They were joined in co-sponsorship by the local brewery C N Kidd and Sons Ltd, and they attracted over 1,000 entrants from the London area. The winner, who could probably get away with claiming to be the first unofficial champion of the world, was a certain, totally unheard of, William Jewiss.

Then I spotted a post on the forum in which a man claimed to be the son of the first world champion, the mysterious William Jewiss. A little more basic sleuthing revealed a name and an address. That very afternoon I reached out and touched darts history. In Gravesend.

William Jewiss's son, George, is alive and well.

I had tracked him down, with frightening ease. In fact I just turned up and rang his doorbell.

His wife Hilda had answered and seemed pleased that someone wanted to ask George about his dad. 'Oh, he'd love that,' she'd said, and had promptly closed the door on me, a stranger. 'I don't mean to be rude,' she said from behind the door, 'but I don't really know who you are.'

So I sat in the car, outside on the road, and waited, watching schoolchildren lark about in a timeless fashion on their way back home. Then, after about ten minutes wondering whether or not to continue this stakeout, I spotted a man heading towards the Jewiss front door.

I got out of the car and introduced myself to George. He welcomed me in.

I was the only journalist he'd ever spoken to about the sporting heritage of his family. Over a cup of tea, he pieced together the fragments of memories he had of a father he barely knew. Outside it was a wind-blasted late afternoon. Bright sun lit up his living-room curtains, drawn against the chill, then darkened abruptly, as all the while he tried to remember the story.

They were hard years, and Gravesend has always been a hard place, short on comfort.

William 'Mick' Jewiss, George's father, was a bit of a scoundrel. He lived on the hard margins of the Thames, in a two-up, two-down terrace on Factory Road, Northfleet, a bleak row of a dozen houses on either side. At the end of the road, the ground falls away steeply into the river. Nowadays the view of the far bank is of a forest of cranes, where Tilbury Docks loads and unloads container ships too big for further passage down the river to London.

When Mick Jewiss lived there, he used to keep a rowing skiff moored to the bank, which he and his mates used to race on the treacherous waters of the muddy estuary for fun. Jewiss was a labourer, taking jobs as and where he got them, sometimes in the cement works, sometimes in the surrounding fruit farms. Mostly he used whatever money he could rustle up to drink away in the pub. That's where he became prodigiously good at darts. But that ability in itself was no small wonder. He'd been sent home from battle during the Great War after suffering from gas poisoning, a condition that affected his eyesight.

At least that's the official version. His wife, George's mother, would later confide that she had her doubts, half joking that 'he'd probably poisoned himself on rum rations in the trenches'. George was the youngest child, by a long distance. He was only 11 when Jewiss passed away, already in his sixties. But George has some clear pictures of his father: well turned out, stocky, strict. Unreliable.

'He was a drunk, I suppose you could say. Mother would have to drag him out of the pub to get him back for Sunday dinner.'

George used to be taken along by his dad, and his dart-playing friends 'Dodds' and 'Fox', when they played exhibitions in pubs all around the area. Young George would be bought a lemonade and told to sit quietly in the corner while his father chalked for the others.

Jewiss family legend has it that, in 1927, he entered, and won, some form of dress rehearsal for the first ever *News Of The World* darts tournament. The winner was presented with a smart set of silver darts (only silver-plated, according to George, in whose possession they now are after his dad bequeathed them to him three days before he died) and a little gold medal. It is a quite unremarkable thing. Mick's brother Jack subsequently wore it dangling from a chain as it were a fob watch. Jack, like Mick, is long dead.

Jewiss, according to his son, was always ill. A horrendous case of rope burn he suffered while serving as a Group Leader in the Civil Defence had left him with agonising dermatitis. It affected not only his hands, but, through nervous reaction, his whole skin. 'Every third day, he used to put newspaper down on the floor and scrape all the dead skin off his body.' It's not a pleasant image (though George seems curiously unaffected and almost amused by it). But, in a way, it seems appropriate that the game's first-ever world champion (if by 'world' you mean Dartford, Northfleet, Ebbsleet and Gravesend) was extremely mortal, a little flawed and not entirely savoury.

Darts was never a beauty pageant. It was, from its outset, a non-conformist preoccupation, whose greatest practitioners were, sometimes, Sunday-dinner shirkers and payday wastrels, but whose very brilliance on the oche might well have been born of a neglectful lifestyle, alongside incomprehensible natural talent.

Just as I am leaving, George Jewiss is distracted. He has temporarily lost his father's medal that brother Jack left him in his will. It irks him. He phones his daughter to see if she knows where he might have put it. She can't help, seemingly. Then he hands me some photographs of the memorabilia.

'It'll be there somewhere,' he tells me. I thank him and take my leave.

It was only when I got home from my visit to George that I began to scrutinise Mick Jewiss's claim to have been the first 'world champion'. I looked at the photograph of the little medal the family understood that he had been awarded for winning the tournament. His name was engraved on the back of it, there for all to see: WILLIAM JEWISS.

But the date was bothersome. It clearly states 1928–29, not 1927, as had been claimed. And just as puzzlingly, the initials

S.D.A. have been engraved above Jewiss's name. It was unclear what these meant, though they were not N.O.T.W. or even N.D.A. for National Darts Association. They'd been partially masked by some tape, but were still legible. George had told me that he'd tried to cover them up as they didn't make sense, or tally with his narrative, and they bothered him, too. Perhaps they stood for something else, related to a later tournament his father had won. 'D.A.' does suggest 'Darts Association'.

So, sadly, it seemed unlikely that the medal the Jewiss family all believed their father had won, along with the 1927 *News of the World* title, was indeed what they thought it was. Perhaps, at best guess, the tournament they thought he'd won, in 1927, and therefore not the one for which he had been awarded the medal, was some sort of regional dry run for the real thing the following year. I could not divine any more, and nor could George. An email exchange with Dr Patrick Chaplin confirmed the doubts we shared.

It is a frustrating tale, obscure and riddled with uncertainty and hyperbole. The tide had gone out at Gravesend and had left me to pick over the flotsam and jetsam, which hadn't amounted to much.

Typical darts. None the wiser.

The Viking

I have wrestled with death. It is the most
unexciting contest you can imagine. It takes place
in an impalpable greyness, with nothing underfoot,
with nothing around, without spectators, without
clamour, without glory, without the great desire
of victory, without the great fear of defeat.

JOSEPH CONRAD – *HEART OF DARKNESS*

Woolwich, farther inland and upstream from Gravesend, is where London starts in earnest, and the run of the river churns the tidal waters brown. I lived there for seven years, a five-minute walk from the Thames, where the old ferries, big diesel beasts, snarl and catch in the currents, moving their cargo of cars and trucks from coast to coast. This is Andy Fordham's playground; the streets of SE7 and SE18 are where he has always called home.

This is where I first met the Viking, a long time ago.

On the advice of the bejewelled darting legend Bobby George, with whom I had spent the morning, I had descended on Fordham's pub in Woolwich with a film crew, working on a short film about darts for the BBC's coverage.

In the welcoming surroundings of the pub he ran at the time, the Queens Arms, I was greeted at first with suspicion by Fordham, as he sat for hour after hour on a bar stool at the end of the counter, drinking Holsten Pils. He was well over six foot, with a beard and a long mane of hair, and weighed a truly amazing 31 stone. He drank a lot, all the time, really. Fordham was a colossal drunk. There was no other way of describing him.

'What the fuck you wearing that for?' I distinctly remember Fordham asking me this, with not the trace of a smile. He had simply raised a bottle to his lips and glanced, gimlet-eyed, down at the logo on my T-shirt.

For some reason, best known to myself, I had chosen to wear a white shirt that had the word ARGENTINA emblazoned across it, with a crest from the Argentinian football association. It was the summer of 2002, when the England football team was preparing to fail at the quarter-final stage of yet another World Cup. I had bought the T-shirt in a spirit of what I considered to be playful contrariness. It had only been a matter of a week or so since David Beckham had placed a spot kick beyond the keeper, and England had vanquished the Argentinian foe (which, in turn, had exorcised Beckham's youthful demons of 1998, when he had been sent off against Argentina in the previous World Cup). That match had in turn been a rematch of the Falklands War.

I wasn't that bothered by the rivalry. It wasn't that I didn't like England. I did like them. I just didn't dislike Argentina. Andy Fordham did. And only then did I realise that the wearing of an 'ironic' T-shirt might be a misplaced gesture. I was given to understand that Fordham might have strong, and wildly differing opinions to mine.

'Argentina,' he noted. 'You can fuck off with that, for a start.'

More time passed. Over a decade, in fact, during which I watched Andy 'The Viking' Fordham's career blossom and collapse. From time to time we met, in Dublin once, at the World Grand Prix, and in Wolverhampton. We exchanged numbers; stayed in touch.

It had been months since I'd last heard from him, and 13 years since that first, unfortunate encounter. Another summer had come and gone, and save for the occasional text message, in which he had complained about Phil Taylor, or commented profanely on the football, I had not heard a thing from the Viking.

Then, one warm night I was sitting at home, listening to the white noise of my family's life around me, fiddling around on the internet. It was around nine o'clock that I became aware of a reasonably important darts situation developing at the City Hall in Hull.

Beneath the august Victorian ceiling, a row of boards had been erected. Eight matches were under way simultaneously. The prize at stake in this knockout tournament was a place at one of darts' high tables, the 2015 Grand Slam of Darts. Both finalists would qualify for the prestigious event.

The Grand Slam enjoys a very a special status in the darting firmament. Second only to qualifying for the World Championships, this was a very big deal, promising a week's worth of television coverage, a huge prize for the winner, but a decent consolation prize of £2,500, even if you lost all three of your group matches.

This draw for the qualifier in Hull contained one very special name, a former world champion: Andy Fordham, the 'Viking', was bulldozing his way through the rounds.

One by one, he seemed to be picking off his opponents. In the first round he dispensed with the 54th best female player in the world, Canada's Ivy Weishlow, without losing a leg.

Next he edged 5–4 past the world's 938th best player, Grampian's Craig Robertson (who listed his career earnings to date as '£0'). After that, in an almost endlessly long evening of darting action, he straightforwardly knocked out Neil McDougall, Jeff Smith (another Canadian) and Tim Jones from Wales. That took him through to the quarter-finals.

Here he faced Darren Clifford, a man whose CV had a last eight appearance at the 2012 Turkish Open emblazoned on its list of achievements; a result that earned him a handsome £100. But Fordham did him over too, winning the ninth and decisive leg.

Now just one man stood between him and a place in the big time.

Neil Duff was the Northern Ireland No. 1, and former winner of the Stranraer Mixed Pairs (among other tournaments). Fordham, though, was a former world champion; and that meant that he was entitled to a latent pedigree, or glimmer of remembered class that might just get him over the line. As the clock ticked way past nine o'clock at night, both men had been playing competition darts, pretty much without interruption, for nearly six hours.

Inevitably, it went to a final, and decisive, ninth leg. Now it was winner takes all, with 501 to knock off and no second chance. The big man stood at the oche, his right foot against the wood, his throwing arm extended, one leg away from a remarkable comeback. Even though I was 200 miles away, following the match on a Twitter feed as if watching a game of football on Ceefax, I still crossed my fingers and held my breath and did all those things you do when you fervently want a sporting fairy tale to come true. Fordham was all on his own, in a near deserted hall, a long way from home. And he certainly needed to win. He needed this win more than he had ever needed a win in his life.

But that's not true, really. That's just sporting hyperbole. Andy Fordham's battles were way bigger than that.

'Do you get recognised a lot?'

'Ooofff....'

'Every day?'

'Yeah.'

'By complete strangers?'

'Yeah. Being my size, you stick out don't you?'

If things hadn't got very serious indeed for Andy Fordham, it would have been tempting to dismiss his extraordinary presence on the darting scene as simply an amusingly exaggerated cartoon. He bestrode the oche like a slightly implausible distortion, a one-off augmentation of the regular ebb and flow of the darting panoply.

The Viking was, for many outsiders, the distillation of a darts player. If you'd made him up as a character in some too-clever-for-its-own-good metropolitan BBC2 comedy series designed to lampoon the darting classes, you'd have been accused of heavy-handedness.

Fordham sported the finest of self-cut, silky mullets that cascaded down his back. It was fashioned over many years of careful grooming, and held in place by toxic amounts of hairspray. A grizzly beard sprawled across his considerable face, and his grim-reaper-tattooed throwing arms were of such heft, his fingers of such breathtaking fleshiness, that the little dart (he has always thrown an unusually light 14 grams) simply vanished from view between throws, clutched into invisibility by the Viking's giant mitts.

He spoke, and still speaks (but at greatly diminished volume nowadays), in a very specific South London cockney, strewn with unconscious profanity. He is a supporter of both Glasgow Rangers and Millwall Football Club; a dual association with a certain type of political hue that sets the noses wrinkling of the metropolitan elite. But unlike his London club, which prides itself on being disliked, Andy Fordham is spoken of with almost universal fondness, except perhaps by Phil Taylor. This is not common among darts players; to be virtually enemy-free. But the Viking inspires genuine loyalty. He's gentle and warm, and perhaps a little wounded and a little lost.

We met again in the Blackheath Standard pub in South London one Tuesday lunchtime in the spring of 2015. Even as I chained my bike up to the railings outside, I could make out the shape of his waterfall of hair silhouetted against the lit optics behind the bar. And when I pushed open the door to the pub and walked in, he turned his impressive mane my way, and smiled warmly.

Then I noticed, almost immediately, that he was stirring a hot chocolate. That answered my most urgent question. The night before our meeting I had agonised over the possibility that I might have to buy him a bottle of beer. And I really didn't want to.

In an already heavily alcoholised environment, Fordham had set new, hitherto unreachable levels of daily consumption. A case – 24 bottles – of Pils was just to keep the engine ticking over. The drinking began first thing, and finished last thing at night. One night, as he fell asleep, sharing a hotel room with a darts-playing pal, he remembers seeing a half-drunk bottle of Pils on the bedside table as he drifted off. Then he saw his mate's hand reaching out towards the bottle. Instantly, a ham-sized Fordham fist had grabbed a hold of the offending wrist.

'Don't touch me breakfast!'

But the Pils consumption was just the baseline. He could sit at a table in a Chinese restaurant, eat not a thing, and consume six bottles of white wine on his own. Drinking was like breathing, except that he was good at it. Breathing, he was less good at. In fact, in the end, he nearly stopped doing it entirely.

But he was very, very good at darts. He had a faultless calm at the oche, and a languorous, natural action. He rose slowly through the ranks, growing in confidence and girth with each passing year. His wife and childhood sweetheart Jenny would put his darts shirts through the wash, and he'd struggle to pull them on. 'Jenny! You've shrunk the bloody shirts again!' But she never did. It was just that the Viking's weight gain was totally out of control.

Eight years prior to that lunchtime meeting in Blackheath, he had collapsed, just before a match at the BDO World Championships in Lakeside. They stretchered him out, not without considerable difficulty, and the deployment of two ambulance crews, and he entered a desperate limbo that lasted for days, during which he repeatedly thought his time was up. Over three weeks at Frimley Green Hospital they drained over 18 litres of fluid from his lungs that had been compressed for years, and suffocating him.

Then, when he was stable, they turned their attention to his liver, and found that it was 'ruined. They didn't try to cover up. They gave it to me straight: "Carry on drinking and you'll die."'

He turned yellow with jaundice. He was fighting for survival. The double brandy someone had plonked in front of him to revive him that night at Lakeside was the last drink he'd ever taken.

With remarkable fortitude and resolve from both him and Jenny, who stood by him as he withdrew almost entirely from the world, filled with self-doubt and shame, he held firm to his word and quit entirely. Gradually, and to the amazement of his doctors, his liver recovered sufficiently for him to be taken off the transplant list.

Fordham shed weight, down from his peak of 31 stone. At one point, he remembers being told he had to lose 19 stone, a weight that happened to correspond with that of his best mate, the darter Darryl Fitton. 'Fuck me,' he told Fitton. 'I've got to lose you.'

He got himself down to an unimaginably low 16 stone. But the weight loss left him looking much older, frail, tired. And that was as low as it got. He was alive, but, by everyone's reckoning, no longer quite himself. Then his weight started to come back. Sometime before arranging to meet with Fordham, I had seen him on TV playing, and losing against, Alan 'Chuck' Norris, in a tournament in Holland. He looked big.

I had drawn my own conclusions about what I saw. I had put his spectacular weight gain down to an inevitable inability to stay off the drink.

I was wrong.

We stood chatting at the bar, Fordham leaning on the counter, cradling his drink, with those elaborately tattooed forearms on the bar. I ordered a soda and lime, and some fishcakes, while Fordham opted for fish and chips.

'Do you want your fish with mash, chips or wild rice?' asked the barmaid, punching in the lunch order to the till. Fordham simply looked confused, as if the question made no sense. I intervened on his behalf.

'You're chips, right, Andy?'

'Yeah,' he said. 'Chips, darling, please.' And then I saw him almost inaudibly mouth, 'Fuck's sake.'

'How's your darts these days?'

'Getting there.'

'How hard was it at first to get back playing?'

"The first time I threw a dart, aiming for the 20, I hit the big 19.'

'Did you throw the other two?'

'I think I threw them both at the same time. I don't know where they went...'

This was just one Tuesday lunchtime and it was a long away from where he had once been, when he could talk the talk of a champion. It had all deserted him.

'What a night. It's getting better and bigger!' John McDonald, the MC, is whipping the Grand Slam crowd into a frenzy.

November 2015, a month on from that qualifier in Hull, and it's Saturday night in Wolverhampton. Fordham has made it.

He is about to take to the stage in a televised major for the first time in a decade. These are the early stages, the group phase of the Grand Slam when each player faces his three opponents in his pool. They are quick-fire, short-form games, and, in some ways, they are the best entertainment in darts.

The Civic Centre is bedlam, all because of him. It's the opening weekend of action, and the organisers have scheduled Fordham for the primetime slot: designed to hit that sweet spot of hysteria in the crowd, when the hop-based adrenalin coursing through the veins of the darting public has not yet curdled and turned sullen, nasty or taciturn. In short, the old place is bouncing: everyone is standing, arms aloft and howling with delight, from the stalls to the balcony in this tight madhouse of a venue.

'And now, ladies and gentlemen, a former Lakeside champion, making his debut here tonight...'

Fordham's heart is beating out of his chest. He has not known fear like this ever in his darting career.

'...prepare to welcome...'

He has been a world champion before. He has faced Phil Taylor at the Circus Tavern in a head-to-head showdown of the two codes (a match that was aborted when Fordham started to sweat, in Sid Waddell's words, 'like a hippo in a shower'). But he has never been so scared.

'...The Viking. Andy. Fordham!'

And he has never had to do this sober. The music bangs in. Hundreds of lights gyrate wildly and he is bathed in white spotlight, backlit by lasers.

As he wrote in his autobiography, *The Viking*: 'The pressure is why darts is so good to watch. Add in the characters and the crowd and you have all kinds of drama and tension. The booze... stopped me from being intimidated by anyone. All I needed was the drink to get me going.'

Now in a heightened state of alertness, trapped by a bright awareness of the mayhem around him, he finds himself on the point of bursting into tears.

The walk-on music picks up its beat. It's 'I'm Too Sexy', by Right Said Fred. The place erupts.

In his words: 'I felt myself going. I could feel it all about to break out. I thought, 'Just get through this. Just hold it all together.'

Glad-handing the baying crowd that spills over the barriers, and, welling up at the eyes, he strides forward, not at all in time with the beat. He passes comment on someone's hat. It's a blur.

He stops briefly to exchange a word with one of his entourage in the VIP area. Then he lifts his heavy frame up the three or four steps that lead to the stage.

So sexy it hurts!

To keep focused he stares resolutely at the space dead in front of him, which, as he points out later, was occupied by the walk-on girl Charlotte Wood, who was probably unaware that she was being closely pursued by a man on the brink of losing his composure completely. Once up the steps, Fordham, dressed in a voluminous but sober black polo and black trousers takes to the stage. He goes through the pre-match ritual. He shakes hands, places his darts on the table, waves to the crowd, takes a sip of water, and then watches on appreciatively as his opponent makes his entrance.

Wayne Mardle, commentating for Sky TV takes a breath, then describes the scene. 'This is what sport is all about. This man has come back from death to be here.'

And now, Fordham can hide it no longer. His eyes betray the emotion of the moment, as his name, chanted by the thousands in the hall, ricochets from end to end of the arena.

'If you'd have said to me 12 months ago,' adds John Gwynne, his co-commentator, 'that I'd be watching Adrian Lewis and Andy Fordham at the Grand Slam of Darts, I'd have said, "Go and talk about something you know about. Because you obviously don't know about darts."'

And in the flurry of a few confused moments, the warm-up darts have been thrown, the music fades, and the man on the mic has issued those two liturgical words: 'Game on.'

Lewis steps up, and throws treble one, 20, treble one. Bed and breakfast: 'Twenty-six!'

Fordham raises his hand to throw. The inside of his right forearm reveals the figure of a Viking. The other arm, on the blind side, features Death, with a scythe.

He throws a treble 20. Then another. 'Oh, my word!' from Mardle.

Then another.

'One hundred and eighty!' The place erupts all over again.

'You could not make this up!'

Crying is often Fordham's default mode, especially when confronted with either of life's twin pillars of triumph or despair, both of which he has tasted, repeatedly.

It's not long after picking his way through the cod and chips, leaving much of it on the plate, that he whips out his iPhone to show me pictures of his two blond grandchildren, smiling wonderfully from the digital distance of his touchscreen.

'I need to be there for them. I missed my own children growing up. Now if I'm away on a Friday and back on the Monday, the first thing I'll do is go round to see them.'

I mutter something about how special that must be for them to have him around, and Andy Fordham, the Viking, starts to well up. 'You've got me fucking started.'

He wasn't always known as the Viking. In fact, at the point at which the BDO decided that every player should have an amusing, or at least appropriate handle, Tony Green, the legendary darts commentator of *Bullseye* fame, suggested that Fordham should adopt the nickname 'The New-Age Traveller'. It was the era of Swampy and the Newbury bypass protest. But still, zeitgeist or not, it was not a natural fit.

'I told him he could shove that up his arse,' recalls Fordham. 'Then there was Bluto.'

'Not bad that, I can see that one working,' I chip in.

Fordham shakes his head, and his mullet drifts gently after. 'I like the Viking.'

He's not a man to entertain flights of fantasy for long. And besides, who could argue with his nickname. It's as comfortable as a lightweight easy-fit nylon shirt.

'So do I.'

Fordham came to prominence in the smaller of the two rival darting codes, the BDO, playing in ever-increasingly demanding leagues until he made his World Championship bow in the 1990s. But it wasn't until 2004 that he broke free from whatever it was that was constraining his obvious ability. He vanquished Raymond van Barneveld against all the odds in a Herculean semi-final. And then, in a tense World Championship final against the ultra-competitive and eerily focused Mervyn King, he edged the victory, throwing his last two darts with nerveless perfection, having made a hash of his approach.

Television pictures of that final visit to the oche tell the story of what mental cold blood is required to win a tournament such as that. His first dart misses badly. Wanting treble 15, he throws a treble ten. He steps back, smiles ruefully, recalibrates and throws again. A single 15. Now he just needs double eight. King is lurking behind him, stranded still on 219.

Suddenly, where there should be no thought at all, there is a rush of emotion. If you watch him weigh up the dart in his right hand before the release, you will see that fractional elongation in the throwing rhythm, the half a beat longer before he throws. Into that space roars all that is contained in the potential of fulfilment, all his hope.

'Don't cry, you silly fat bastard,' he told himself. 'You haven't won yet.'

When the World Championship-winning dart landed, a weight lifted from his massive shoulders. He let fall his heavy throwing arm, so that the chunky gold bracelet that had drawn the eye throughout the match now nestled against his wrist. He looked far, far away, a gaze directed God knows where, and he licked his lips. That gesture, a quick dart of the tongue to moisten his lips had become a hallmark of his action, a minimal, unconscious act of reassurance. Now, it looked as if it were the only thing holding him together.

He and King turned to embrace one another. For a moment, the two men, dripping with sweat, talked intimately to each other, almost touching noses. It was a curiously private affair. This moment in darts often is, when one man wins and the other is finished.

King had congratulated him, and told him not to cry.

'It's too late,' you can see Fordham telling him. And then the big man dissolves into tears; a not unusual state for the Viking, who, had he not appeared so physically intimidating, might well have been described as a 'big lummox'.

Eleven years later, back in Wolverhampton, he is once again shaking like a leaf. After that blistering 180 maximum, he holds his nerve. The next visit is OK. Fordham hits 81, his chest visibly heaving as his heart and lungs race to keep his big frame serviced. Lewis is way off the pace, distracted by the mania in the venue, and has yet to hit his stride.

Fordham, whose hands are clearly shaking, hits 135. He

has left himself on a finish of 115: doable, but under these circumstances, hard as it comes.

He hits a perfect treble 20, a dead centred big 15, leaving forty on the board. Then, with 'tops' for the leg, he balloons his 12th dart an inch or two over the double 20. He winces and blows out his cheeks. But he comes back the next time, and with his second dart in the visit, nails the outshot, and takes the first leg, against the throw. 1–0 to Fordham. First to five legs wins.

But then, for whatever reason, the spell is broken. Normality returns, and the difference between the two players in their recent form (since Fordham nearly died, Lewis has been the two-time PDC world champion) now looks like an unbridgeable chasm. Lewis breaks straight back and then holds his throw, breaks again and holds again. Walking off stage after five legs, Fordham finds himself 4–1 down, and a leg away from losing his opening match. And two minutes, 30 seconds after the resumption of play, he has gone down. 5–2 was the final score.

The following day, Fordham beats local favourite and Grand Slam semi-finalist Wayne Jones by 5–3. It's as if the Wolverhampton crowd has forgotten that Jones is one of them as the hall rises to acclaim the Viking. But he still has to beat Michael Smith, an extremely talented player in the form of his life, and 30 years his junior.

On the Monday night, faced with the prospect of elimination, Fordham's nerve deserts him, and his remarkable run comes to an end. Fairy tales don't happen to blokes like Andy Fordham. Sure, the story can soar for a while, but on the turn of a page, it can flatten out into a long, long, hard journey. It is over, for now. But the Viking has proven, albeit fleetingly, that he still belongs.

He saved himself from dying. The game might yet help him with living.

The Viking moniker continues to work, despite his partial incapacity. He's plagued with a 'gammy' leg that is wreaking havoc with his stance. He's worried about a chronic weakness in his left knee, and he's just recovered from a hernia operation. But this is just the top layer of his towering medical notes.

'Not drinking's helping, of course. But the fat's a problem, still.' As he speaks, he grabs a double handful of girth, lifting his excess off his lap to illustrate his point. It's as if he's decided he is no longer subject to the same respect and privacy others enjoy. After all, his slide and demise and struggles have been public property, his flesh a matter of public scrutiny and debate.

Given everything he has endured at the hands of the press and the medical profession, Fordham displays a disarming willingness to lay himself bare. Not literally, unless he's in the hands of his doctors, which he often is. Perhaps it's just that he's so used to answering questions about his weight, about his drinking, about his health. But he betrays no sign that he feels trespassed upon when discussing the latest state of his liver cirrhosis. He is admirably, almost troublingly, open about it all.

The spotlight of the oche is remorseless, and takes no prisoners. No other sport, you might argue, revels to such an extent on the physical imperfections of its protagonists. And it's not just Fordham who plays by these demanding rules. Big 'Rocking' John Henderson, the nearest rival that Fordham has in terms of size, relishes his image and plays up to it, just as Andy 'Pieman' Smith is not known as 'Pieman' for nothing. But it doesn't stop at physical size alone. At the height of his mental health troubles, James Wade, who is a bipolar depressive, used to walk on (somewhat manically) to 'Bonkers' by Dizzee Rascal.

Fordham is in good company.

Granted grandchildren and a life, even if it was deprived of comfort and dignity, Fordham set about rebuilding everything from scratch. He and Jenny drifted from pub to pub, running establishments in ever-less salubrious areas, until a stint in charge of a particularly bleak pub in Thamesmead spelt the end of their tethers. Their hopes of rebuilding a new life, with Fordham no longer drinking nor playing darts, meant returning to the same Charlton street where Jenny had grown up.

The great task is to get back into the game that gave him so much and watched on powerlessly as he took all of it away from himself. 'When you're not born with money, you don't know how to control it, or use it.'

He went through money as if it were in limitless supply, like the little green bottles of Pils that he always clutched. 'I don't know. I didn't control my own money. I had someone else doing it. They stitched me up left, right and centre.'

'So, they took a slice of everything?'

'A slice? I was the one getting sliced. You think it's going to last for ever. It doesn't. Gone. I'm back where I started now. I'm living with my father-in-law, and I live in the bedroom, watching TV. That's that.'

His father-in-law's house is not too far from the branch of Coral bookies where Jenny goes to work every day. Fordham stays at home mostly, hoping that something will turn his way again. And, slowly, slowly, rebuilding his game. Much of what came naturally to him has become frustratingly intangible.

'I don't like it here.' He looks out of the window at the humdrum streets he's known since childhood. A red single decker bus pulls away from a stop with a grind and whine of gears. 'But it's where I know people. Where else was I to go?'

Shortly after the Grand Slam, we meet again at the Six-In-One community centre in Tonbridge, as low-key a venue as they come. He's not playing that night, despite the fact the 'Golden Singles' are in progress, a knockout qualifier, whose finals are in May. He's already been booked to do an exhibition on that date, so there's no point in him entering the competition. Anyway, the place is full of his old mates.

We hang back from the action, while on 11 separate boards, dozens of players go through their matches, their shirts bearing the names of the disparate Kent Superleague teams. A cheerful hubbub of noise permeates the room, while around the boards men of a certain age, with a smattering of younger ones, rotate through their matches, pausing at strategically placed tables every now and again to draw on their lager. Their pints are covered over with the owner's individual darts cases to avoid the inevitable mistaken identity that comes from drinking and spinning round and round in circles.

Here, Andy Fordham is entirely at home. He sits at the side of the hall, smiling, unmoving, with an alcohol-free Becks Blue at

the ready, and a kind word of encouragement for all his mates. They troop past him, shaking his massive hand, enquiring after his health, reminiscing, taking the piss and castigating themselves.

'I played like a prick up there,' says one.

'Yeah, you did,' says the Viking.

'I'm 58 tomorrow, Andy,' says another. 'Can you fucking believe it?'

'Yeah, I can,' says the Viking.

'But I've got a 23-year-old bird, Andy.'

'Oh well, fair play to yer,' says the Viking. 'Fuck's sake.'

'Who're you playing for now?' the Viking enquires of an old teammate. 'Still Snodland?'

'No, West Malling,' he says, ruefully. 'I had to fuck Snodland off.' It's like a rude version of Trumpton.

'You still working?' asks the Viking of another old friend, a tall man in his fifties.

'No, I'm retired. I had to. Through ill health,' he explains. 'I just drink now.'

And they all fall about laughing. The subject turns to boozing, which they all still enjoy, to some extent or other. All except Andy Fordham.

He sits in amused wonder as whole chapters of his life he has entirely blanked out are repeated for him: the time they all went for Polish shots at some bar Fordham recommended in Oxford. The time someone threw someone else through the window of a caravan at Camber Sands. The time Fordham broke a Stannah stairlift on the Isle of Sheppey just by sitting on it. Or the time he suggested that they had a football match, and he volunteered to play in goal. That prompts Fordham to remember how his mate Andy Goram, the former Rangers goalkeeper, had asked him to play in a charity match at Ibrox. 'You can be my back four, Andy!'

And with that I learn that no opportunity to make a joke about Fordham's weight should ever be spurned. That's darts. Their shared history seems so suited to the room, the game, the time, their time of life. As they get further into the past, the gentle thud of darts and quiet mutterings of encouragement and congratulations thin out to a slight background chatter as players are knocked out and go home. The younger ones grab their coats and darts and leave without staying for a pint. The older players bemoan the fact that so many kids only arrive at eight o'clock, which is when the matches are scheduled to start. In their day, they'd have been down there since six.

The subject returns to Fordham's comeback at Wolverhampton. His mate, also named Andy, was watching at his pub near Sevenoaks, where they'd just had a new surround-sound system installed. They'd cranked the new amplifier up to 11, just to make sure it worked. Gathered around the sub-woofers and speakers, the regulars got the fright of their lives when Fordham knocked in a maximum and the Wolverhampton crowd erupted in delight.

'When that 180 went in, the noise!' he tells Fordham. 'Fuck me, it was deafening!'

'You should have been standing where I was.' Fordham smiles at him. 'I nearly shit myself.'

Two Tribes

I couldn't help asking him once what he meant by coming there at all.
'To make money, of course. What do you think?' he said, scornfully.

JOSEPH CONRAD – *HEART OF DARKNESS*

'**Y**ou all right, bud?'
I recognised the voice, and then I saw him, hunched
and facing the marbled urinal, dressed all in black, with super
shiny shoes. A toilet, however well appointed, was not the ideal
place to meet Phil Taylor, a man with whom small talk is not
always easy.

I had sneaked out of the back of the Dorchester Hotel's
ballroom for a call of nature, hoping that no one had noticed
my absence from the after-dinner speeches. Barry Hearn himself,
the mega-promoter effectively in charge of darts, was summing
up another year in which the sport had blown away even the
most optimistic of expectations. 'I don't like swearing,' he'd
said. 'But it's been fucking unbelievable.' The glitzy gala awards
dinner, by now an annual event, had come hard on the heels of
the conclusion of another World Championship organised by
his governing body, the Professional Darts Corporation. It was

a celebration of growth upon growth, millions upon millions, the continuing upward-spiked graph of darts' irresistible rise.

And much of their success was down to the consistent and continuing genius of the man I now stood next to. Neither he nor I looked anywhere other than straight ahead.

'Hi Phil,' I mumbled.

I congratulated him on his umpteenth world title, a victory he'd gained just a few weeks previously. He brushed aside my compliment and muttered something about the toughness of the chicken we'd been served. Then The Power zipped up, and, with a cursory splash of water over his hands, sauntered back to the main event, leaving behind him a typical, cautionary Tayloresque 'you behave yourself, mind'. He had a vague swagger to his gait, almost a strut.

I returned to the ITV table, pausing at the entrance to behold the glittering scene: hundreds of the great and good from the world of darts, dressed to the nines in dinner jackets and ball gowns, the light from a few dozen chandeliers casting a gentle glow over them, and not a darts shirt in sight.

Hearn was launching another withering attack on his great rivals, the British Darts Organisation. I listened to the words of the boxing promoter who'd walked into the Circus Tavern a couple of decades ago and declared that he could 'smell the money'. Well, here was the proof of his instincts, sitting at expensively purchased tables in a five-star hotel in Park Lane. Darts had arrived; or at least, a bit of it had, and a bit of it hadn't.

It's complicated, you see. That Andy Fordham was a world champion is not disputed. That he came off worse when he went head to head with Phil Taylor, who was also a world champion at the same time as Fordham, is also not disputed.

January is a confusing month for the sport of darts. As one World Darts Championship comes to an end, so another one is just starting. The two almost collide in the schedules, much to the incomprehension of pretty much every punter who is not fully steeped in the wrestling match for control of the sport ('think Alan Bates and Oliver Reed in *Women in Love*, only without the flexibility or homoeroticism', according to Sean Ingle writing in the *Guardian*). Rather than D H Lawrence's homoeroticism, I am more reminded of that scene from the *Life of Brian*. 'PDC? Fucking splitters,' seemed to sum up the bafflingly unpleasant schism that has permeated the darting community for the last quarter of a century. 'Yeah, fucking splitters!'

The opening weekend of the British Darts Organisation (BDO) World Championship at Lakeside Country Club, Frimley Green, follows almost immediately on from the final weekend of the monstrously bloated and quite irresistible Professional Darts Corporation (PDC) World Darts Championships at Alexandra Palace. A few years ago, in what I imagined to be a spoiling manoeuvre by the BDO, the two tournaments overlapped by a day, confusing the darting public still further.

The BDO version of the Worlds is a venerable competition formerly known as 'The Embassy'. It has been going since 1978, when Welshman Leighton Rees won the inaugural event in the Heart of the Midlands nightclub in Nottingham. It can justifiably lay claim to being the original, if no longer the best, though that assertion is contentious enough to set online darts forums ablaze with acrimony from either side.

The fact of the matter is that at the highest levels of the two rival organisations, there is an extraordinary well of rancour. They glare at each other from across the pages of the *Radio Times*, and they snap at each other on Twitter, a virtual re-enactment of what should perhaps have been settled a long time ago by a scuffle in a car park at the back of a pub.

The BDO takes every opportunity to appeal to viewers' sense of heritage, referring to their present-day venue, Lakeside, as the 'Home of World Darts'. After all, they have made their home there for nearly 30 years after gravitating south following the closure of the iconic Jollees nightclub in Stoke. By reminding people of their long and uninterrupted heritage, they are also cocking a snook at the young upstarts from the much bigger, much richer PDC. However, with each passing year, as the PDC pile on layers of its own legacy, the BDO's claim to be the custodians of the sport's history loses a little more of its potency.

A few years ago, Barry Hearn tried to buy the BDO for £1 million, essentially to settle the issue once and for all. It took the determined and unbending Olly Croft, Hearn's counterpart in the rival code, a matter of hours to reply but probably only minutes to decide. Later on the same day, Croft flatly rejected Hearn's attempt to unify the codes, which would have wiped out their autonomous culture at the same time. And that was that.

It's worth remembering that the World Darts Corporation, (the forerunner of the PDC), hasn't always had it their own way. The 16 rebel players who broke away to form the WDC were frustrated by what they saw as Olly Croft's limited ambition in dealing with the modern reality of television deals and exploiting the potential of opening up the market. They felt that their livelihoods were being choked. The players were contractually tied to the organisation and threatened with bans if they competed outside its auspices. So the rebels went their own way, triggering a bitter, highly personal legal battle that had the potential to kill off both codes, and annihilate a sport that had sunk to new levels of unpopularity.

One of the BBC's main presenters of the World Championships during the 1980s, the former *Blue Peter* presenter Peter Purves, himself an excellent darts player, describes how the game simply ran out of steam. 'I think I saw it coming, and that's why I decided to bow out.'

In 1984, Purves opted to take up a part in a pantomime rather than present the darts for the BBC, which seemed both eminently sensible, and, with hindsight, rather fitting. 'I liked the game. I wouldn't call it a sport. But I liked the game,' he told me. 'But darts had died. It had run its course.'

Much of darts' demise was linked to the perception that it was nothing more than an oafish game for drunkards. It was an association from which the broadcasters of the time, the BBC and ITV, wanted to distance themselves. Yet the 16 rebels, spearheaded by Eric Bristow's high-profile backing, stuck to their guns and saw it through, at great financial cost in lawyers' fees. And in 1994, darts split in half.

I can testify, from hours spent in the company of some of those rebels, that the scorn for the way they feel they were treated by the BDO sits very deep indeed. Keith Deller, the Milky Bar Kid debutant at the 1983 Embassy, who upset the odds by beating Bristow to the title with a brilliant 138 checkout, is a good case in point. Although Deller can appear delightfully scatty (as someone once pointed out, his eyes are a bit 'Tooting and Mitcham' and he's so clumsy, he'd 'trip over his own feet heading to the table at the bar, then bend down to tie his laces, and bang his head on the way down and the way up'), he is adamant on this one point: the BDO, he believes, tried to ruin them. He's not alone in that belief.

His old mate Eric Bristow has always freely expressed his contempt for the 'others', on occasions choosing to refer to the older, arguably lesser World Championship, as 'Amateur Darts Round One'. Bristow takes to Twitter once a year, during their tournament, to decry the quality on display at Lakeside with ever-increasing fervour. Cliff Lazarenko, another of the original rebels who left the BDO to go their own way, still cannot bring himself to speak their name and talks of treachery. 'They tried to harm me, and I find that very hard to forgive. I'd sooner go to jumble sales to sell things to support my family than to go back there.'

In the beginning, the PDC's World Championship might have featured some outstanding talent, but its strength in numbers was questionable. From 1994 to 2000, five of the first seven finals were contested between the same two players, Dennis Priestley and Phil Taylor, with Taylor winning all but one of those head-to-heads, and 11 of the first 13 titles altogether. At the same time, the BDO was producing genuinely great players such as John Part and Raymond van Barneveld, as well as Ronnie Baxter, Mervyn King and latterly Andy Fordham and Jelle Klaasen. Even the great Michael van Gerwen started out at Lakeside. So there was genuine parity between the two codes for much of the first decade after the split.

But two decades later, the gap has widened. Most darts fans picked sides long ago, and are entrenched in their positions. Like the rivalry for the public's affection between Seb Coe and Steve Ovett, Oasis and Blur, or Nike and Adidas, you have to take your pick and stick with your choice.

Culturally, there are significant differences between the two events. Whereas the PDC events have been overtaken by swarms of beer-maddened loons in spandex costumes gurning at the camera, most of the Lakeside crowd opt for sports leisurewear for their evening out; a polo shirt, perhaps, or a V-neck pullover. In fact, as Wayne Mardle warned me, if you happen to be sitting at one of the tables nearest to the stage, you are advised to bend at the waist when popping out for a call of nature, with an arm raised in apology, so as not to obstruct the view for those seated behind you.

There is, however, a not inconsiderable gulf between the two championships in terms of the quality of the darts, if three-dart averages are a good measure of talent. These days, from the quarter-finals onwards, the PDC competition would expect to record averages of over 100 across all matches. In the 2018 PDC World Championships alone, there were 25 'ton-plus' averages (the very definition of an ultra-high-calibre performance). This compares with the total of 21 averages over 100 recorded in the entire 40-year history of the BDO's event.

The BDO, drawing its pool of qualifying talent from lowlier and more disparate ranks, and unable to offer anything like the PDC's frankly pornographic prize money (£2 million as opposed to £300,000), often sees winners get through to the second and third rounds with averages in the seventies and eighties. In fact, as some PDC aficionados unkindly observe, it's as if they are actually playing in the seventies and eighties.

The game now revolves around the winter solstice and has found its seasonal apotheosis in the fug of yuletide excess. For those who follow the fortunes of The Flying Scotsman, Mighty Mike and The Power, Christmas is when the magic happens. And it happens not with a light sprinkling of angel dust, but in great sugary dollops of darting drama. Its sheer mass and proliferation is enough to induce the TV equivalent of type 2 diabetes.

The PDC World Championships is a beast of an event, and has breached the all-important '1 million viewers' mark over recent editions, which for a subscription channel showing a minority sport is a huge success indeed. Only football does better numbers, as Barry Hearn is always keen to remind us, licking his lips at each contract renewal with the satellite channel. 'That's people talking with their wallet! It's a conversation that you can't ignore.'

Before Christmas, darts is shown pretty much wall-to-wall on Sky Sports, with the interludes between play propped up by repeats of the action you might have missed while out shopping. Then there are biopics of darting legends, rambling chats between players of yesteryear perched on high stools, and retrospective documentaries about classic encounters, such as Kevin Painter's submission at the hands of a bottle-blond and extremely portly Phil Taylor in the final of the World Championship in 2004.

And you can follow the live action in glorious high definition, each bead of sweat over Adrian Lewis's eyebrows glinting in the arc lights.

For weeks leading up to the big daddy of tournaments, promotional videos pushing the darts World Championships start to pop up in the commercial breaks between football matches; moody fist-pumping mini-masterpieces of cinematography featuring cheek-blowing, eye-popping celebration, wild jubilation and tungsten hitting the target in machine-gun rapid sequence, relentlessly, perfectly and irresistibly. Then, as their coverage finally gets under way, the viewer is treated to a massive shock wave of bumping, grinding beats and sped-up shots of night-time London; the Eye oscillating at breakneck speed, traffic shooting past the camera in a tracer blur of red and white lines, Big Ben flashing past at warp speed, until....

... finally the montage settles on an aerial shot of the glorious venue.

Lit up like a gargantuan gingerbread house against the gloom of the surrounding landscape, the grandest of darting houses pulls splendidly into view. The cameras turn and turn again to offer shots of the illuminated façade of Alexandra Palace, the People's Palace, glowing in the darkness of the winter night.

Alexandra Palace stands on the first ridge of high ground overlooking the north of London. The views from the front are immense, spanning the sweep of the capital, from Canary Wharf in the east with its fungal cluster of banking towers, to the banks of the river Thames at Westminster, flanked by London's heritage architecture and marketable assets. They light up, as if seen from the air.

It was 1963 when darts first took over the ornate surroundings of the Grand Hall in Alexandra Palace, swaddling it in the fuggy atmosphere of a giant snug. A stage was erected in front of the great showpiece of the auditorium, completely masking the colossal Henry Willis organ, the centrepiece of the lavish hall, which was rebuilt after the original palace had burnt down just 16 days after it opened in 1873.

The Palace, rebuilt and retouched by successive generations and repeated fires (it burnt down again in 1980) is a fantasy of Victorian kitsch: a semi-baroque riot of plasterwork and pastel colours, featuring pastoral murals of splendidly naked and near-naked mythological whimsy. Just the place for a bacchanalian festival of darts, you might think. And you'd be right.

To this day, the PDC organisation takes over the various gilded ante-rooms and below-stairs lounges that surround the principal venues of the palace.

The press room features a vast mural of a giant hunter god, who has triumphed over a six-breasted monster, or a 'dragon with a row of tits' as one respected commentator in the press room observed. And the fan zone, a giant atrium of fried food, is constructed under the soaring porticos and domes of Palm Court. The burgers are flipped and the pints sloshed in the most glamorous of settings in the darting world. It's a fit and proper use for the self-proclaimed 'People's Palace'.

At night, and I have only ever been there after dark, the old place comes into its own. It is beset by groups of young men and women in polyester-padded clothes. They stagger up the access roads, their novelty hoods and wigs and glowing antlers pressed flat by the cold December wind as they seek the warmth and carousing comfort of a night at the arrows. Fleets of taxis, strung out along the approaches to the palace disgorge their cargos. Men and women sing as they canter up the steps: 'Stand up if you love the darts!'

From mid-December until New Year's Day, London resumes its rightful place at the heart of the game its pubs gave rise to a century ago. After a year trundling up and down the motorways of Great Britain, from Bolton to Blackpool, Milton Keynes to Minehead, with occasional forays overseas, the game has returned to the centre, just as the Tour de France always seeks out its fulfilment amid the glory of Paris, the tennis world doffs its cap to Wimbledon and snooker is synonymous with The Crucible. Alexandra Palace is a proper stage for darts to reflect on another year of growth, of smashed records, or continuing over-achievement.

Back in the Grosvenor House Hotel, I slipped a finger behind my bow tie and surreptitiously undid my top button. It was hot and people were flushed with wine and good news, as if they'd been to a particularly decadent Eucharist. Barry Hearn, the High Priest of the Oche, had just finished his rabble-rousing sermon and was now heading back to his seat, shaking the hands of the invited guests, many of whom were standing in ovation. It was as close as darts ever gets to spiritual.

He exuded satisfaction and beamed with delight, in tune with both the everyday origins of darts, and its long pent-up desire to be taken seriously. He had found a way to turn lead into gold and was churning out the precious metal for all it was worth. Hearn's alchemy was impossible to resist.

'When we first staged the World Championships, at the Circus Tavern in 1994, we only took £45,000 in ticket sales, and paid out £64,000 in prize money,' he'd said. 'Next year the winner'll get £500,000.'

The million-pound darts match is surely just a matter of time. In just over 20 years, the money has increased 30-fold. As Hearn sees it, darts has an identity all of its own that has fuelled this rush to riches.

He once asked me, 'Where else would you get Prince Harry sitting next to a scaffolder? Fuck me! It's not croquet and it's not mud-wrestling. It's somewhere in the middle. It's world-class sport in an entertaining environment. There is no limit to where darts can go.'

Smashing

His very existence was improbable, inexplicable and altogether bewildering. He was an insoluble problem. It was inconceivable how he had existed, how he had succeeded in getting so far.

JOSEPH CONRAD – *HEART OF DARKNESS*

Heading out into Park Lane that night, I had walked on my own across Mayfair; south, then east, then turning right, then left, until I had zigzagged all the way to Charing Cross. Self-consciously undoing my bow tie and stuffing it in the pocket of my dinner jacket, I found, to my own private amusement, that I had inadvertently slipped into the lead male role from the archetypal Volkswagen advert from the 1980s, the one in which the man leaves the casino, having gambled away his money, to find his faithful VW Golf, which starts first time. *If only everything in life was as reliable as a Volkswagen.*

One thing had become abundantly clear to me as I burrowed back through the decades in search of the beginnings that would guide me onwards: none of the high-rolling of Barry Hearn's 21st-century Moneydart era would have been possible if the foundations for the game hadn't been solidly laid some 30 years previously, in the 1980s. And there was nothing more 1980s than *Bullseye*. If only, I thought, everything in life was as reliable as *Bullseye*.

It had been surprisingly easy to get an invitation to Jim Bowen's house. I simply rang him up.

A matter of days later, I made the trip up to the North West to pay him a visit. But I had arrived too early, so had stopped on the way and bought a cup of tea and an Eccles cake, considering that an appropriate combination of things to eat and drink while I waited for the clock to tick over to the appointed hour.

Staring out through the dirty windscreen of my car at the stone-built village set into the heart of Lancashire, I bit into the pastry, allowing the sugar crust to fracture and fall to the upholstery. As a kid, growing up a long way from Lancashire, I loved Eccles cakes, unwrapped from their see-through cellophane bearing the proud legend 'Real Lancashire'. The packaging proclaimed that they are made 'containing pure butter'. They were a fusty old confection, from a bygone age, and one that I had stopped eating from about 1990 onwards.

So it was out of a certain whimsy that I was enjoying an Eccles cake again. I experienced something of a Proustian moment, allowing their sweetness to work on me as the madeleine cake of *In Search of Lost Time* had worked on Charles Swann. The intensity of the raisin filling took me straight back to my early adolescence in Bedford, weaned on a conforming and comforting diet of the New Romantics and whatever happened to be on TV. I used to buy an Eccles cake on my way home from school from the corner shop on Stanley Street, the same shop from which my mate Jim Briscoe once nicked a pint of milk, causing us all to scarper. This act of petty theft had been my Theresa May 'in the wheat field' moment; peak naughty.

Of course, darts featured on the TV often back then. Not ironically, or in the context of some smart-arse nostalgia, but very much at home, comfort-fitted to its age. Darts, and darts players, were the subject of much attention, and the thud and roar of the game constituted the background noise to millions of dozing Britons during the long Saturday afternoons waiting for *Final Score*'s typewriter to start clacking out the football results.

But, occasionally, the game of darts was allowed to break out of its pen. It joyfully burst into other genres, cross-pollenating its nylon spores into light entertainment, *The Generation Game* or *Little and Large*.

There was, for example, the infamous appearance of Jocky Wilson's chubby features in that much-cited episode of *Top of the Pops*. Mention Jocky Wilson to almost anyone born before 1975, and you can be fairly certain that this particular picture of him springs to mind: Jocky smiling, his famous lack of teeth revealed by a playful grin, and with a frond of lank black hair fallen over his forehead. From this black-and-white photograph he looks down on the scene below him, where Kevin Rowland, the frontman of Dexys Midnight Runners, is limply gyrating and flailing his arms around to the strains of 'Jackie Wilson Said (I'm In Heaven When You Smile)'.

For years, the urban myth persisted that the use of Jocky's, rather than Jackie's, image had been a mistake, perpetrated by a dim-witted, musically unschooled *TOTP* producer. The following morning, Radio 1's Mike Read went so far as to lambast them on his breakfast show. 'Bloody *Top of the Pops*,' ranted Read over a nation's cornflakes. 'How could they mix up one of the great soul singers with a Scottish darts player?'

But that's not how it actually happened. Twenty years later, Rowland admitted that it had been his idea all along. It was a famous prank, juxtaposing the dungaree-wearing folk-pop outfit declaiming their musical homage to the great American singer with the unreconstructed beaming face of Scotland's humble darts world champion. Everybody seemed to think it was hilarious, except for me. As a kid (I was 12), I knew well enough who Jocky Wilson was, since his presence – nylon-shirted, grinning impishly as his classic bomber darts peppered the board – was a staple of *World of Sport* Saturday afternoons. But I had not the faintest idea who Jackie Wilson was. So the joke fell a bit flat, at least on me.

And yet, that amusing collision between darts and music was as nothing compared to the seismic effect the renowned darts sketch by Griff Rhys Jones and Mel Smith from *Not the Nine O'Clock News* had on the sport. This simple joke, played at darts' expense, genuinely altered the course of the game's history.

The sketch features two increasingly drunken darters (given the less-than-subtle monikers Dai 'Fatbelly' Gutbucket and Tommy 'Evenfatterbelly' Belcher) stumbling around a table groaning with alcoholic drinks, taking turns in draining their glasses. Over this rather broadly painted comedy, Rowan Atkinson, affecting a Geordie accent, is commentating, rather well as it happens.

'*It's a good start. Double vodka. Single pint. Double vodka.*'

In the end, Rhys Jones's character, chasing the game, opts to gamble and goes for a big checkout. He downs a triple brandy and throws up.

And that's it.

To this day, the darts world is peculiarly obsessed with this sketch. It touched a nerve. The booze culture of the game was laid bare for all to see. For so long it had been a shared, but tacit understanding between viewer, broadcaster and player, passed on with a nod and wink. Darts, this sketch seemed to holler, was a pissed-up, chauvinistic dinosaur, played by northern working-class degenerates. At least that seemed to be the view of the three Oxbridge-educated stars of *Not the Nine O'Clock News*.

However much they might have been privately amused by the parody, the sport's administrators at the BDO, charged with chasing increasingly scarce sponsors and signing ever more meagre television contracts, failed to see the funny side. Darts felt sneered at, principally because it *was* being sneered at. And, beneath it all, there was an uncomfortable truth behind the comedy: dart players drank huge amounts of alcohol.

The sketch set the tone for the way the sport was viewed, and, perhaps more significantly, the way the sport viewed itself. There is barely a darts autobiography that doesn't mention the sketch. Eric Bristow saw how it spelt danger for the game: 'OK it was funny,' he acknowledges in *The Crafty Cockney* 'but it didn't do the sport any favours, especially with the media luvvies who ruled the BBC and the other channels.' John Lowe, writing in his autobiography *Old Stoneface* is clear that 'its long-term damage to the sport of darts at that time was unimaginable, and became irreparable'.

Bobby George, in *Bobby Dazzler: My Story*, while claiming the sketch was 'very clever and very funny' also noted that 'within the game, that sketch was blamed for being the catalyst that turned darts into a laughing stock'. But, later, George bemoans the way the game has visibly cleaned up its image in this regard, accusing the sport's guardians of 'crumbling under the pressure', when 'beer and fags were banned from televised darts tournaments'. To his knowledge, 'not one TV organisation, venue or sponsor put pressure on darts' chiefs to change the rules and alter the game's image. They just did it.'

The late Sid Waddell, darts' greatest commentator, and the clear inspiration for Atkinson's Geordie voiceover, was even more certain that the sport had been panicked into denying its roots. He found the sketch hilarious and disagreed profoundly with the view of the autocratic BDO chief Olly Croft that the image of the game had been damaged. 'I was of the opposite opinion. I thought the boozing – and fagging – counterpointed the skills of the players marvellously. It made them human, ordinary, familiar.' For good or ill, the sketch's resonance was profound, and it's remarkable, 30 years on, to find that it's one of the first and most important cultural references that anyone over a certain age will draw at the merest mention of the word 'darts'.

Yet, as Smith and Jones were ripping into darts, another show was taking to the airwaves. Two men in a Chinese restaurant, somewhere in the Midlands, dreamt it up on a napkin. It could hardly have been more straightforward: 'A man throws a dart at a dartboard and scores points to get questions.'

It was a show that celebrated a different side of the game; something altogether more wholesome, gentler, more lovable, and it was destined to become one of the most extraordinary and unexpected successes of British broadcasting history.

Bullseye was first broadcast on Monday, 28 September 1981.

I drained the rest of my tea, finished the last bite of Eccles cake, and, with a glance at my watch to see that it was just after the appointed hour, started the car and pulled away. A few minutes later, I rang the doorbell of one of the most popular game show hosts this country has ever produced.

These days, Jim Bowen has a device fitted to his legs that helps him to walk. In November 2014, at the age of 77, he suffered from a third stroke that left him with impaired mobility and speech.

I don't notice his walking aid at first. It is only when he stands up, taking the arm of his wife Phyllis, to walk from the kitchen to his favourite armchair, that I become aware of a beeping noise coming from his trousers. Something with a battery and flashing lights is strapped to his waist, and every time there is a beep from within his slacks, his knee seems to jerk, as the muscles are jolted.

'It sends an electric impulse to his nerves, and helps him to take a step,' Phyllis explains, as Jim's trousers beep again, and his right leg reacts.

'How amazing,' I say. Beep!

'Bloody thing,' adds Jim. Then there's another beep. It's slow progress, and it looks painful. It's also a bit like Wallace and Gromit's *The Wrong Trousers*. I can't help thinking that, even in deteriorating health, Jim Bowen has stumbled upon the slapstick. In much the same way, after a terrible start to his professional life, he had stumbled on a career that ended up turning him into something approaching the status of a national treasure. He became, for darts, what Henry Blofeld was for cricket and Boris Johnson was for politics: everyone's favourite buffoon.

Settled in his most comfortable armchair, with his beeping legs switched off and a Lancashire morning wind blowing noiselessly outside his double-glazed windows, Bowen is back in the moment. Despite his faltering speech and repeated need to reach for a sip of water, he is capable of recalling in rich detail the genesis of this iconic game show, conceived in a Chinese restaurant and then honed in the passenger seat of the director's car.

'It was a Rover 75.' His eyes light up. 'Funny how you remember things like that.'

This was how television got made back then. For the lucky few, simple enthusiasm for a project could lead directly to a lucrative commission. Bowen, who'd worked as a binman before becoming a teacher, was a little-known comedian on the northern circuit. He'd made himself something of a reputation as a (by his own admission) 'second-division' stand-up on the Friday night entertainment show, *The Comedians*. But this was his project.

It didn't start well. In fact, when they shot and edited the first two pilot episodes of *Bullseye*, they were so bad that the executive producer Jon Scoffield burnt the film. That isn't TV jargon or a metaphor: he literally took out a box of matches and set fire to each episode, incinerating a £46,000 investment.

'Well, that's you finished,' he'd told Bowen. 'We can't put those out. It would lose us millions of viewers. It would set the industry back 20 years.'

Bowen's style was esoteric (for which, read chaotic and incoherent), the very antithesis of the doyen of TV game show hosts, Bob Monkhouse. At the time, Monkhouse was the benchmark of smooth broadcasting brilliance, hosting with olive-skinned, debonair charm such glitzy blockbusters as *Celebrity Squares*, *Family Fortunes* and *Bob's Full House*. His salesman's features, ennobled with a single, perfect mole, were the very opposite of Bowen's uncultured chops, his pit-fallery and clownish gurning.

'I wasn't a Bob. Bob was all tits and teeth. He was immaculate, groomed. In control. I was quite the reverse. People could identify with me because I was fragile, fallible,' Bowen recalls.

'Is there no beginning to his talents?' Monkhouse wondered in return.

As Bowen recalls, 'People watched the first series when it went out on Monday nights at seven o'clock, and I think they must have gone to the pub every Monday night after the show and said, "Did you see that rubbish? That bloody Bowen on that thing? It was bloody awful." Then they'd watch the next week, and they'd say, "It's got worse!" And by the third week, they were saying, "Christ! It's still on!"'

'He had a great deal to do,' was the withering verdict of the show's co-host Tony Green (who wasn't part of that bumpy first series). 'And he didn't do it very well.'

Bowen would stumble on his words, forget his cues, address the wrong camera, say the wrong thing. In one early episode, he asked this question of the guest professional darts player:

BOWEN: It's amazing how the image of golf has altered over the last five years.
PLAYER: Golf?'
(Audience laughter)
BOWEN: Darts, I should say.
(Blank look at camera)

Even when he managed to fumble his pre-prepared jokes out, they were often clunky and embarrassing. Take this example of some warm-up chatter with a contestant who happened to be a tax inspector.

BOWEN: You play football?
CONTESTANT: I used to play a bit of football, yeah.

BOWEN: Did you play in defence?
CONTESTANT: Left back, yeah.
BOWEN: I'd have thought, being at the Inland Revenue,
   you'd have been into attacks.
(Blank look at camera)

The contestant looked confused. Bowen turned first to the camera, then to the audience. 'Look. Help me out here, folks.' It was a desperately low-rent game show, and Bowen's vulnerability was its secret alchemy, even though, at the time, no one understood this. At the time, Bowen simply wanted to be as good as Monkhouse.

'I said to him, "I'm crap at this, Bob." He said, "Yeah, you are." I said, "Fuck. What do I do now?" He said, "I'll take you to lunch."'

Great game show hosting wisdom was imparted over that steak and chips, because 16 years and 400 shows later, 'Bully' was still rampaging across British TV screens, driving his big cartoon bus, full of big cartoon versions of the top darts players in the world, from the cartoon pub, The Bull, to the studios, into which he would descend on the back of an outsized cartoon dart, holding on to the cartoon flights, all this, of course, to the accompaniment of that famously jaunty fairground music. *Bullseye* attracted, at its peak, a staggering 17 million Sunday afternoon viewers. For context: around 5 million watched *X Factor* in the same slot, on the same channel in 2017.

To anyone with any memory of life in 1980s Britain, Bowen is a familiar figure, a kindly uncle, a friend for Sunday afternoons. Darts wasn't the beloved plaything of the chattering classes back then, and it still isn't. But it had started to punch through into the national consciousness. And this show placed the game centre stage.

Bowen's understanding of the strength of the game that made him famous is unambiguous. 'Darts has always been there. It has always been in the fabric of society, low-tech, downmarket, highly accessible, and it isn't an intellectual stretch. One of the big points of contact in society for the working man was darts. It cost a pint of beer to play. You didn't have to buy any kit. You didn't have to be clever.'

In *Bullseye*'s DNA was its forerunner, ITV's *Indoor League*, hosted (often drunkenly) by Fred Trueman, the former England cricket legend. This series, first screened in 1972 and produced by a young Sid Waddell, showcased pub sports. Darts was prominently featured among a menu of arm-wrestling, shove ha'penny and bar billiards. *Indoor League* constituted the first time that television had started to embrace the game with any regularity. Darts was suddenly recognised, and had begun, albeit with faltering steps, to move out of the snug and into the big time. Ten years later, *Bullseye* gave it a leg-up a social rung or two.

'I can't really describe where the game was in society. It wasn't down in the sandpit,' recalls Bowen. 'It wasn't down in the grit and dust of the workplace. It was just coming into the office level. The bottom third played darts regularly. The office worker played every now and again, but the intellectuals never went into the taproom. The show helped us climb over that mountain where it became the thing to do.'

The vast size of *Bullseye*'s audience continued to grow into the second, third and fourth series. The big-name darts players all clamoured to get a slot on the show, where they would be required to throw nine darts for charity: the more they scored, the more was donated. Not all of them enjoyed the experience, though, and many complained that the board was not mounted at the right height, and the oche was mis-measured. Also, the show's producers had imposed a moratorium on drinking, one which Alan Warriner-Little flouted by necking a can of lager before the show. Eric Bristow and Keith Deller went one step further, refusing to record the show until they'd spent a couple of hours in the pub. Bristow, in particular, had a nightmare cameo on *Bullseye*, and according to Bowen, pleaded with them not to broadcast his disappointing performance.

'Bristow was Bristow, the Crafty Cockney: a very arrogant man. Nobody was more delighted than I was when he got 36 with nine darts. There was a side to him that could be quite good, but he had an arrogance that overrode it. He'd say, "C'mon, Jim, don't fuck about," half joking. But it wasn't nice. It had an edge to it of an unpleasant arrogance.'

It wasn't the star darts players, though, that made the show work. They were not its charm. It was Bowen, and his affable incompetence. 'He was absolutely shocking,' recalls Warriner-Little affectionately. 'It was take after take after take.'

Bullseye will always be best remembered, though, for the prizes.

Like almost all game shows, *Bullseye* was recorded. At their studios in Nottingham, they would shoot two episodes back to back. This meant that they could always stop the recording, and reshoot, if they needed to. The opportunity to stick or twist was key to the game show's success. At a certain point in proceedings, contestants were asked if they wanted to gamble everything or stick with what they had. In one episode, a pair of Irish friends had collectively accrued £50. They were offered a chance of going for 'Bully's Star Prize'. They chose to stick, not wishing to jeopardise the money.

This was not in the script. Recording was stopped while Bowen patiently explained to them that, in order for the show to work, they really needed to gamble. 'I'll give you the £50 out of my own pocket if you want. Just say you'll gamble.'

They started to record again. 'So, lads, will you keep what you've got or gamble everything for a chance to win the star prize?'

'We'll keep the £50, thanks Jim.' There was no budging them.

Bullseye had a £7,000 pot of cash for prizes on each episode, which the producers regularly splurged on the star prize. One in four shows would feature a car, which blew the budget to bits. If the contestants failed to win, then they'd be shown the car to the accompaniment of a remixed mournful version of the theme tune and Bowen's famous, conciliatory/salt-rubbing 'Let's have a look at what you could have won.'

But the fact is, that with a few exceptions, the car was never up for grabs. The show couldn't afford to give it away every week. So, when the winning dart went in, behind the scenes the stagehands would wheel in another prize altogether, like a fitted kitchen or a set of dining room chairs, or indeed, a speedboat.

The hard economics of balancing the budget had led the show's director, Peter Harris, to do an exceptionally favourable deal with a local speedboat company. So speedboats it was, for any pairing of contestants who could throw 101 with six darts. Bowen remembers discussing how this part of the show might work when they were drawing up plans.

'I remember worrying about it and asking Harris, 'How are we going to tell them they've lost?'

'Just fucking well tell them. Just tell them,' said Harris. 'I'll get their faces. Make sure I've got a clear camera to get their faces. You say 'Ooooh. Look at what you could have won.' And then I'll get straight into their faces.'

'Just watch the last three or four minutes of any episode,' Bowen suggests. 'When there's a gamble, just watch their faces. All they needed was 101 in six darts, which any dart player can do. But you could feel it in the studio, the pressure was enormous. And when they lost it, they were struck with disappointment and incomprehension, and not being aware of where they were.' Bowen shakes his head. 'Their world had gone.'

The glorious incongruity of the speedboat is one of the enduring charms of *Bullseye*. Of what possible use, to most of the contestants, could a speedboat be? To this day, people continue

to amuse themselves by reminding us of the sheer dissonance of the speedboat, with its hint of James Bond on the Côte d'Azur, offered as a prize for throwing some darts. In 2017, two decades after the show's demise, a photo of a rustling vessel was posted on Twitter with the caption 'Speedboat outside the home of Barry and Sue Jenkins, Bullseye Champions, 1991'. It went viral.

On another occasion when a contestant in a wheelchair was throwing for Bully's Star Prize, Harris realised with a sudden dread that hidden behind the screen was a three-piece suite; inappropriate, perhaps, for a man who could not leave his wheelchair unassisted.

'Peter was screaming in my ear, "Don't let him win the star prize! He's got a chair he can move and we're giving him a grand's worth of immovable leather."

'I said to him, "Sorry, Jack, we've got a technical problem." I went round the back of the set and we decided to swap the prizes.'

It was a simple enough solution: for the next episode, the star prize was a holiday. It was a simple switch as they hurriedly removed the furniture from the set and resumed the filming.

The contestant duly went on to win the prize to everybody's delight and relief. The problem, as they found out when the prize was revealed, was that it was a skiing holiday.

And then there was the famous occasion when Bowen asked a contestant what he did for a living. When the man told him he was unemployed, Bowen, unfazed, replied, 'Smashing, super, great.' I had always taken this to be an urban myth, but when I ask Bowen about it, he confirms that he did indeed say just that.

'I didn't listen. I wasn't listening to his answer. I was looking at the cameras like a demented shepherd.'

Thirty-five years on, the show's host takes a sip of water and grins with schoolboy cheek. 'It turned out that we'd invented a phenomenally rich game, rich in content: greed, envy, fright, panic.' Rickety, at times ill-conceived, *Bullseye* lurched through its long life. 'It was like a struggling puppet that was scrambling to its feet. Hang on, it's got legs. And eyes and ears. It crept up on the nation.'

By the late 1980s, it was less of a hapless puppet, more of a ratings juggernaut, setting its host up, financially, for the rest of his life, and popularising darts to hitherto unforeseeable levels. And it held its wobbly head high until Bully was finally put out to graze in 1996.

Few television programmes are remembered with such universal affection. My own unremarkable childhood was punctuated, one day in seven, by its chirpy theme tune rattling around in the plastic and glass box in the corner of the room. It was that dread time of the week, a darkening late afternoon Sunday, where thoughts turn, for adults, back to the rigours of the Monday to Friday, and, for children, to unfinished homework. The something-and-nothing scheduling, neither daytime nor primetime, allowed for the snag of guilt to fester and grow within. If I were to start the maths homework now I could have it done before *All Creatures Great and Small*.

On the other hand, here was Jim Bowen, jauntily stepping down through the crowd and onto the stage, and welcoming us to half an hour of the familiar shtick: 'Keep out of the black and in the red, nothing in this game for two in a bed.' Tea sets, carriage clocks, video recorders and the chance of walking away with a speedboat. The drama of the gamble, laced with the menace of total failure and Bowen's dreaded 'BFH', standing for 'bus fare home', for those hapless few who left the *Bullseye* studios empty-handed.

'When people hear the music, even today, they smile.' Bowen smiles.

I have kept him talking too long, and I sense that he is tiring. So I prepare to take my leave.

The show's legacy endures. It brought the simple game of darts out from the back room of the pub and into people's front rooms. People recall the show with great fondness, Bowen rightly claims. Instinctively, it cheers them up.

'It's not a dismissive smile. It's... Oh, yeah. That was good. Nice and warm. It never acquired the kudos of a gold star. It was always a tin star. Like an old faithful black Labrador running through the streams of television.'

'Bloody hell,' he sums it up. 'That was good.'

Flight Club

Paths, paths, everywhere; a stamped-in
network of paths spreading over the empty land...

JOSEPH CONRAD – *HEART OF DARKNESS*

I said my goodbyes to Jim Bowen, smiling to myself. It had been infectious; his palpable, mystified delight at the way his life had turned out.

Darts had not been part of Bowen's master plan as he was growing up, just as it hadn't been part of mine. Yet here I was now, many years later, carefully reversing up his drive and away from his bungalow, with my very own 'Bully' key ring dangling from the ignition of my very own Renault. This is what adulthood was all about, then.

I wound down the window. 'Cheers, Jim!' And as I waved and the car window closed up, I just about heard him shout, 'Take care, son!' I caught a glimpse of him in my rear-view mirror, turning slowly back towards his front door, with his trousers beeping.

The motorway stretched before me, a ribbon of suspended time, where travel puts life on hold.

HEART OF DART-NESS

We all come from somewhere. Where we end up is another story altogether. And while some of our lives run smoothly along their narrow gauge tracks, others find themselves tossed and turned, buffeted through events way outside their control, or simply guided by an unseen, fickle hand through a series of joints in the rails they didn't even know were there, with all the busy, senseless huff and puff of a model train on a mission beyond its comprehension.

Some lives sometimes find their way to darts, but very few begin there. Darts is not often a launch pad. Darts goes looking for no one; it just waits in the wings to be found.

The game is not often cited as a 'childhood dream', for instance. Few young children fall asleep with their hearts full of imagined glory on the stage of the World Grand Prix. This is not the grammar of a darting life, however you might want to spin it. It seemed increasingly clear to me that darts tended to be where you ended up, a game of second, and sometimes last, resort. A refuge.

Jim Bowen was a case in point. He had been born in 1937 to an unmarried woman on the Wirral. As a baby, he was surrendered to a children's home across the water in Liverpool. In 1938, he was adopted by a kindly childless couple of a certain age, Joe and Annie Whittaker from Clayton-le-Moors in Lancashire.

Bowen's adoption meant he escaped the Liverpool Blitz. In the summer of 1940, the city was lit up by the Luftwaffe as a stream of bombers tried to destroy the ports of Liverpool and nearby Birkenhead. Outside of London, nowhere in the country was hit as badly as Liverpool. A total of 347 children under five, Bowen's cohort of infants, lost their lives during the bombing, but he had been spared that fate. The Whittakers had picked up his model train and plonked it down on a branch line, heading for the safety of the countryside. He had jumped ahead of the millions of others whose lives were uprooted.

These thoughts stayed with me as I headed south. I slid in the CD he had given me; Jim Bowen, reading Jim Bowen's autobiography. Accompanied by Bowen's trademark smoke and syrup vowels, I drove on, ever further away from the lands that had given rise to his voice and his character.

His voice spoke to me across the decades, of a time when a Britain that still looked, felt and smelled post-war was emerging into modernity, like a forced plant in a greenhouse. The 1980s saw the industrial heart of the country in slow convulsion and a generation of baby-boomers, who had been weaned on war but hadn't fought, rose to power.

Darts stood its ground in the midst of this tectonic shift, welcoming those for whom the reassuring thud of dart on board was the equivalent to the crack of leather on willow; one of those irony-free eccentricities that are the hallmark of our culture. And those others, who would start to pack out the seats at venues such as Jollees nightclub in Stoke, flashing their extra cash from doing double time on the shop floor, a night at the darts was a brash, noisy two fingers at the status quo.

Darts looked both backwards and forwards, representing something for everyone. Jollees itself was a brick-and-mortar expression of this great lurch forward, doubling up as a modern, spangly darts venue, while at the same time serving as one of the very last of the old variety halls. It was a building at a cultural crossover, undergoing the same uncomfortable metamorphosis that would befall the cinemas that became bingo halls in the nineties, the warehouses of the Thames into the aspirational penthouses, and the banks turned into pubs.

The spray of thundering wheels announced the proximity of the M25, the vortex in which London's freight circled the capital. I was returning to the cradle of the game, heading south again. The grime-coated lorries bore the names of the age: Stobart, Morrisons, Argos. Happiness, and the pursuit of freedom, lined out in single file along the slow lane of a motorway. Peace in our time.

At the same time that *Bullseye* was reaching and passing the zenith of its popularity in the early 1990s, and the war child Bowen was entering his early fifties, another part of the world erupted into conflict. The Balkan Wars prompted another wave of refugees, the biggest movement of people in Europe since the Second World War. One of those men on the move, it turned out, went on to make a home in a game he had barely known existed; another life whose kinks and twists no one could have predicted, but whose routes led unexpectedly to a dartboard.

During one of my earlier stints working for ITV on a darts tournament in Frankfurt, I first came across an extraordinary player called Mensur Suljović, a Serbian who had fled to Austria. He was, in a word, odd; unusual to behold in almost every sense. He has since shot up the rankings and now sits comfortably in the top ten, but at the time was a virtual unknown. Not only that, but his entire appearance was unorthodox. Nothing about him seemed right. No one could recall ever seeing anything like Suljović at the oche.

He fidgeted his way onto stage, shooting forth elbows without warning, and lifting legs in sudden, donkey-kick twitches. His throwing of a dart was no less unusual. It involved him reaching forward, seemingly wildly off balance, and spinning the dart through his fingers about seven times in quick succession. And without fail, win or lose, he would maintain a steady flow of muttering. He chuntered incessantly to himself, in self-reproach or for encouragement.

But he was unusually good, and though nothing about his game suggested he would be able to throw a dart straight, the fact of the matter was that he could, and did. Despite, or perhaps because of, his seemingly clumsy technique, he won his way through to the latter stages of that tournament in Frankfurt where I first came across him.

The first time I ever spoke to him was live on TV, and in German. He spoke no English. He also spoke slightly unusual German, with a heavy Serbian/Austrian accent. The painstaking process of live simultaneous translating back and forth of questions and answers between me and him, German and English, was, with hindsight, ambitious.

The following morning, in the breakfast room of the Novotel near Frankfurt railway station, where the crew and players were billeted for the tournament, two men were overheard discussing my televised interview with Suljović. A colleague later delighted in recounting the conversation to me.

''Ere. You see that fucking interview on the TV yesterday with Mensur?'

'No, go on.'

'It was in fucking German. That ITV bloke did it in German.'

'Fucking tart.'

And, with that, Mark 'Walshie' Walsh, the Watford-based 2005 UK Open runner-up, had apparently shaken his shaven head in disbelief and disgust, and continued spreading his toast.

Suljović's background, much like his unique throwing action, obdurately refused to conform to the standard darts narrative. For one thing, the name Mensur is derived from Arabic, an ethnography that is hugely under-represented in the darting world. Mensur, often also transcribed as Mansoor, means 'the one who is victorious'. I told him this a few years later, expecting him to know. He had been unaware of the origins of his name, and was delighted. The next day he went on to lose to Simon Whitlock.

Mensur is also, curiously, but unconnectedly, the fifteenth-century Latin term that gave its name to the practice of *Mensurfechten*; the Teutonic duelling with swords, leaving the cheeks of the opponents scarred. This was commonplace in German and Austrian universities, most notably in Vienna, where Suljović would eventually settle. I told him this, too, and he pointed at a scar on his neck, where he'd had a lump removed. Then he roared with laughter.

Tutin, Suljović's place of birth, is a remote town in the west of Serbia, hard up against the Montenegro border. These days, in a remarkable twist, it is home to around 150 refugees, principally young Afghans, who have made it through the 'Balkan Route' from Asia in the hope of getting into the European Union via Hungary. Tutin, in common with so many other towns in this complex part of the world, has always been a place of flux and flight.

In winter it is bitterly cold, but in summer, the town is surrounded by high prairies and meadows. Its population of 30,000 is still predominantly Bosniak, the Muslim ethnic population in the region, whose ambition for self-determination ended with them being dragooned or hounded by the forces of Serb nationalism, and suffering some of the worst abuses of the Balkan Wars. Though peace has returned to the region, the Bosnian War saw hundreds of thousands of Bosniaks living in Serbia displaced by a policy of ethnic cleansing and genocide. Many thousands were killed.

The Balkan Wars were beyond the understanding of most Britons. This series of bewilderingly belligerent mini states, steeped in ancient grudges, presented us with a conundrum we failed entirely to decode. But the starving men of the camps, dressed in rags and looking with dull expressions over barbed wire fences at their rescuer, they were real enough. They were in need of refuge.

Serb forces led by Radovan Karadžić swept through these lands and on towards Sarajevo, where they lay siege. In Tutin, Bosniak men of serving age were forcibly conscripted. Mezid, one of Mensur Suljović's three elder brothers (two were already in Austria) disappeared overnight, press-ganged into the military to fight for Serbia, first against Croatia and then against Bosnia. For months at a time, the Suljović family didn't know if he was still alive. That was when Mensur, aged 19, was smuggled out of the country, taking a bus over the border into Macedonia.

Stopping the transport at the border, Serbian soldiers pulled all the men of fighting age off the bus, leaving the women behind. When they came to Mensur, he showed them a letter in which he had undertaken to join up with the army at a later date. It was something of a bluff, but, with his heart beating wildly, it got him out. He spent a year in Skopje, before continuing his journey through Turkey and into Austria, where he joined his older brothers. He was one of the lucky ones, who got away in time. But there are many others, relatives, old school friends, fellow townsfolk, who died in the war.

'All my childhood memories are Tutin,' Suljović told me. 'My father was a forester and our mother brought us up. As a child I played football and basketball, which I was really good at. Perhaps I'd have turned professional. The war had a huge impact, of course. If it hadn't been for the war, I'd never have come to Austria. Most of my friends are still there.'

On arriving in Vienna, he gravitated to the coffee shop run by his brother. For hours on end, he'd sit at a table, reading a book on German grammar. From time to time his natural garrulousness took over and he'd talk to some of the other customers. In that manner, within six months he'd mastered the language.

There was a soft-tip dartboard in the café, one of those electric ones rarely seen in the UK that do the counting for you. This was in itself unusual, Austria being somewhat of a darting hinterland. But darts has a curious way of intervening in lives, as if the blank eye of the board was winking at the young Serb.

At first he didn't want anything to do with it, but his brother persuaded him to throw. The occupants of the café watched on as Suljović took them to the cleaners. He gambled rounds of drinks and soundly beat allcomers. He had never played the game before, but he was instantly transfixed by his own ability.

'If I lost, I'd go home and practise for hour after hour, just on the double that I had missed for the checkout.' Unconventional from the very inception of his darting career, Suljović used to spurn the number 20, opting instead to focus solely on 19. It was as he rose to the top of the Austrian rankings that orthodoxy took over and he started to aim for twenties. When I first encountered him a handful of years ago, he was hitting them with frightening regularity, despite having to overcome a crippling case of dartitis, the equivalent of the yips, which nearly nipped his career in the bud.

Austria may have offered Suljović a cold welcome at first, with its baroque walls and marble halls exuding a kind of exclusivity that so many migrants have had to battle with, but darts, the narrow yet broad-minded church, flung its doors open to Suljović and welcomed him into its beery midst. He joined Austria's premier darts club, the strangely named DC Darts-Control, whose constitution is, according to their own documents, 'built on values rooted in the tradition of the basic principles of the democratic republic of Austria' and whose motto is 'Steeldarts mit Excellence'.

For many years he ran a pub in Vienna called, weirdly, The Gentle. Presumably, it is a misconstruction of 'The Gentleman', but its origins have been lost in time and the fug of post-war Viennese history. The name of the pub may be a curiously maladroit anglicisation, but Suljović's flowing darts shirt bears the eponymous legend in capital letters.

More importantly, Suljović likes the word. 'Aber, das bin ich, doch,' he protested, when I once suggested his nickname was misconstrued. '"The Gentle". But that's what I am!'

Mensur Suljović's obvious otherness has found a home. Viewed with a little scepticism, and largely dismissed as an oddball, The Gentle's gentle rise to the top has been broadly and widely celebrated. In fact, his not-so-much-broken-as-shattered English and gobsmacking array of ticks and quirks, both verbally and facially, have made him something of a cult hero.

In the autumn of 2017, he made his debut on the BBC's inaugural *Champions League of Darts*, smashing his way to the title by claiming the significant scalps of Peter Wright, Raymond van Barneveld and Gary Anderson. It was a stunning achievement, and though it doesn't put him right at the top of the game, it suggests that on his day, he is the equal to anyone.

'I'm feel... perfect,' he fumbled with words during his live TV interview after his winning double 14 finally went in. 'I never denk I win Gary Anderson, das ist... I'm happy.' Then he finished by simply shouting uncontrollably for joy.

'I didn't know whether I was going to cry or not,' Suljović told me when we sat down to talk in a dimly lit bar one January lunchtime. 'I didn't know what I was supposed to feel. But I slept with the trophy that night, and in the morning it was still there.'

Week after week, it sank in, that nothing could take that achievement away from him, and that it was his for ever.

'When my father died five years ago, I expected him to come back every day. And every day he didn't come, it started to hurt more and more, until the pain became real.

'Grieving is the same as happiness. It's the same process.'

Olive Byamukama had come even further than Mensur Suljović. It was at Frimley Green in 2017 that I witnessed her first-round exit at the BDO World Championships, marking the premature end of a journey that had begun in Uganda. The story of how an Inverness resident from Kampala ended up in the opening round at Lakeside is haphazard, bizarre and, in that respect, completely darts-like.

'I'd never have thought I'd have ended up playing in the World Championships,' she told me as she prepared for the match. Tall, slim, elegant, and in her early forties, she was one of only two black players in that year's tournament. 'I never put much effort in. It's like cheating, really. I just arrived.'

She smiled, fleetingly, as she shook her head in disbelief at the sequence of events that had landed here there. 'I'm like, why am I here, you know?'

Her opponent was a young player making her second appearance at Lakeside, but already highly rated. Fallon Sherrock, just 22 years of age, was keeping her throwing arm in motion, loosely peppering the practice boards. Blonde hair piled high, she was impassive, in the zone. Sherrock was a strong favourite to win.

Byamukama did not seem so composed as the two players waited to be called to the oche. In fact, she was at the opposite end of the spectrum, chatting nervously with the clutch of friends who were there to support her through her Lakeside debut. But even the glass of red wine from which she sipped had little effect. The truth of the matter was that she was terrified. She'd rather have been anywhere else.

'Olive. Smile, for God's sake!' Mandy, her friend and county teammate from the Highlands, implored her. 'Just enjoy yourself out there and smile.'

'I would have to pin my lips behind my ears,' replied Byamukama. And she gave a look that suggested she meant it literally.

When the time came for her match, she walked on through the crowd, rather improbably, to A-ha's 'Take On Me'. Byamukama entered the arena as if she were in a nightmare, striding jerkily towards her opponent, her eyes fixed in horror on what awaited her. After the match she told me, 'I didn't even hear my walk-on music. I was shaking, I was so nervous. I was trying to smile and I felt like my lip could have gone on top of my nose. I am the most nervous person on the planet.'

Although she got off to a decent start in her match, taking the first leg on a double 16, and then missing tops to check out 125 and break the throw in the subsequent leg, Sherrock was too good for her, as you might expect from a player who had 14 BDO ranking titles to her name. Before too long, it was over: an undramatic first-round defeat, which hadn't even been close. The crowd had willed Byamukama on, sensing that she needed support and painfully aware of her nerves, but the contest had never really ignited.

'You've seen me crying.' I offered her another glass of red wine, but she politely declined, explaining that she only drinks alcohol before a match. 'I am such a bad loser. No one wants to lose. Most people are fine with it when they lose, but me? I'm just, "Noooo!"'

The simple challenge of throwing darts at a target should have been a breeze for Olive Byamukama, who had spent five years defending some of Uganda's most notorious killers.

She was educated at the rigorously old-fashioned Namasagali College in Uganda's capital Kampala, whose motto is 'Strive Regardless'. It was a good school, supported by aid from overseas, and it spared her and her schoolmates the dreadful consequences of the famine that swept through the land in 1980. Starvation and disease killed one in every five in some parts of Uganda, including 60 per cent of all infants.

She went on to study at the prestigious Makerere University, where, after a strait-laced upbringing, she let her hair down in time-honoured student fashion. But her education came at a cost for her father, a school caretaker, who invested every spare penny in his daughter's future. At one point, she accrued debts that could only be solved by a phone call home, and a plea to her father for funds. He sold a cow to oblige his daughter.

At university, darts took a hold. But it would not have happened without an enlightened minister for sport in the Uganda of the early nineties, who, in an effort to foster grass-root participation in the game, hung dartboards in the Makerere University halls of residence: one board in the women's block, the Mary Stuart hall, and one in the male students' residence.

The men quickly wore their board out, so they moved into the women's hall and started to monopolise their board. This was an intolerable imposition and caused the sports minister to personally intervene on behalf of the female students. She decreed that henceforth, darts could only be played on 'neutral' ground at the junior common room. So a board was moved there. And that is where Olive Byamukama met and fell in love with both darts and her husband-to-be. 'I don't even know how it happened. I loved it. I was just so committed. And I met my husband because of the darts. I thought, *Oh! He's interesting.* Just like that! Stupid!'

Jacob was, in Olive's words, a 'city boy, brought up in Kampala'. 'He used to take me around to the big hotels, and they all had dartboards. I think he realised that I really loved the darts. I couldn't give it up. It was just that extra thing I had to do.'

Soon, she was representing her country at darts. 'I went to the World Cup in Durban in 1999,' she recalls proudly. This tournament was the pinnacle of the sport and pitted her against the likes of the great Trina Gulliver, who would go on to win. Byamukama acquitted herself admirably, narrowly failing to beat the experienced American Stacy Bromberg, a former private detective. 'I was well ahead of her, and then the crowd gathered around and started to cheer for me and I started losing. To win [Bromberg] had three darts for double 16. She put two down, and, with one dart, checked out. She beat me.'

This defeat was, to date, her best moment on the oche, and still a source of pride. 'She [Bromberg] gave me a small badge from the USA. But I lost it. I don't know where.' Her face clouds over as she leans on the Lakeside bar, suddenly looking like someone who is a long way from home. 'I lost it,' she almost whispers. 'I lost it.'

Byamukama studied hard at Makerere, graduated from the university with a post-graduate qualification in law and joined the Public Defender Association, working on the hundreds of hopeless cases that commercial barristers would never touch. It was tough work and it ground her down.

'They were all guilty, but they were always looking for a way to get out of prison. And because you had that attachment to them, you had to find a way to get them out. It was hard.'

'Going to the prisons was another thing,' she recalls. 'You have all the prisoners looking at you. They'd be weighing you up. You had to dress in a certain kind of attire. You really had to cover yourself up. You have all this protection, but your safety is not guaranteed. Anything can happen – because these are people who are living in the wild. As soon as you walk in there, they are watching you. If you got close to them anything could happen.'

As a mandatory defence barrister, she didn't often win the cases she was handed. But when she did, the victory felt huge. It took an immense reserve of mental strength, resolve and a degree of fearlessness, but it played with her nerves.

So, appearing in front of a Tuesday night crowd at Frimley Green should have been easier than it was for Byamukama, especially given her history. She puts down her darts on the counter of the players' bar and stares at them. 'You go to sleep thinking you have to get this person out. And then the person is in the dock, you're representing them. If you get them out you're smiling and everything is fine. But when things go wrong... it's so personal, you just can't believe it.' She looks back up at me. 'I did that for five years. It was hard.'

After five brutal years spent defending the most notorious criminals in the country, she drifted into litigation where she became ruthlessly good at extracting debt from multinationals. But her husband Jacob's career in civil engineering was gathering pace, too, and the best opportunities lay overseas. At first he moved to Leeds, and then in 2005, the couple left Uganda for good when he accepted a position in Manchester, and, a few years later, in Inverness. They were now, officially, a long, long way from home.

Emigration to the UK spelt the end of Olive Byamukama's professional career. 'I had to swallow my pride. I am a lawyer by profession, but as soon as you open your mouth in England, no one is going to believe in you as a lawyer.' She now juggles a home life that includes caring for her young family with a job as a care worker that she, like so many other migrant workers, is ludicrously overqualified for, but which she adores.

'Working as a care worker is like a blessing in disguise. I am so happy. I am not stressed. No one is telling me what to do.'

It's only the darts that stresses her. Darts, the simultaneous source of her discomfort and joy, a game she can't leave alone. 'When I have a match, I dread it. I pray and pray. "God help me out of this, please, please."'

Deep down, she knows she'll be back for more. Darts reminds her of Kampala, of her youth and courtship, of the fun of it all. It's woven itself into her story.

An extraordinary life, in which the gentle game of darts, translated across two continents, has played more than a cameo role. Darts is good like that. Three lives bound up with one game, and a curiously eclectic final destination in the heart of little Britain.

Byamukama sums up her arrival at the oche with a simple expression: 'That's life.'

And it is all just that: life. The chorus of Mensur Suljović's awful walk-on music, performed by the Austrian band Opus, rings in my ears:

'Live is life!

Whatever that means.

Home

The tranquil waterway leading to the uttermost ends
of the earth flowed sombre under an overcast sky

JOSEPH CONRAD – *HEART OF DARKNESS*

I shook Olive Byamukama's hand, leaving her to join her friends in the players' bar. She was met with a wave of concern and consolation. Some players, warming up for their matches, broke off their preparations to throw an encouraging arm around her. Her friends from Inverness hurried to her side. Officials from the BDO, passing in or out of the venue, stopped to offer her some comfort.

She had fallen into the right arms. This was Lakeside, the self-proclaimed Home of World Darts, with the emphasis on the word 'Home'. At least, that was the impression I gained when I had first set foot on its hallowed tarmac and muddy verges. It had been my first visit to the 'other' code, having been weaned on the excesses of the young upstart PDC.

It had not disappointed.

When I had approached the Lakeside hotel complex at Frimley Green that evening, the dark drizzle of an early January evening had been unrelenting. Nevertheless, I had a warm feeling, born from the downbeat, unpretentious familiarity of the scene, an unassuming small town on London's unlovely border between Surrey and Hampshire.

Perhaps it was a function of the name of the town, Frimley Green, Trumpton-like in its promise of nostalgia. Or maybe the walk itself, two winding miles from my hotel in Farnborough town centre ('Proud to be the birthplace of British Aviation') pacing dead silent suburbs, smelling of pine trees through whose black branches I glimpsed the pre-curtained evening routines of those who called this place home. Children were idling on couches and mothers wearily gathering in dry laundry. A dog padded twice around a basket and then slumped into it.

The route took me across two pedestrian level crossings, along whose shining tracks the dew was settling, caught in sodium orange light. I caught a whiff of wet-railed danger, a tiny thrill on an ordinary walk. There was something gently adventurous about opening and shutting a series of white picket fence gates and then striding across the mainline to Waterloo.

Frimley Green, I discovered to my delight, actually had a village green, albeit fringed with slightly shabby estate agents and restaurants. They were odd relics. Chinese food served in mock Tudor terraces, above whose doorways hung signs that still insisted on the use of the word 'Peking'. This anachronism, perhaps perpetuated through neglect rather than wilfulness, gave a hint at the heyday of Frimley Green: probably 1976.

On a side street and up a slight rise, invisible from the green, was my destination, Lakeside. And yet, the iconic location, which uniquely accorded Frimley Green its moderate fame, was keeping a low profile, allowing access only to a trickle of taxis, indicators winking into the sour, diesel-black steaming air.

The Lakeside Country Club is the personal fiefdom of one of the key figures in the darting landscape. Bob Potter

OBE is a son of Hampshire farming stock who, after a brief amateur drumming career, made it reasonably, if locally, big in the business of music promotion. He booked the Rolling Stones and the Beatles before anyone knew that one day people would be writing about how remarkable it was that Bob Potter booked the Rolling Stones and the Beatles to play at his club in Camberley and only paid them £55 each. His business acumen slowly fattened into wealth. Lakeside was built in his image.

Potter is widely understood to be the inspiration for the character Brian Potter from *Phoenix Nights*. Peter Kay's fictional Potter, wheelchair-bound and permanently clad in caramel-coloured nylon knitwear, is a local nightclub tycoon whose venues mysteriously flood or burn down, and who is engaged in a turf war with local rivals.

In real life, Bob Potter has published a fabulously self-aggrandising memoir, written rather awkwardly in the third person, titled *One Man's Dream* (yours for £20 via the Lakeside website). In the introduction to this work, he unwittingly adds to the impression that he is indeed the inspiration behind Peter Kay's fictional nightclub owner by recalling how 'lesser men might have given up when his showpiece club was razed to the ground in 1978 but Bob rebuilt Lakeside, raising it like a *Phoenix* from the ashes, and then carried on with "business as usual"'. The book goes on to detail his many brushes with fame, celebrity and even royalty.

I had been warned that Bob Potter wasn't a man to be messed with. There was, I had read, a tougher side to him. 'He does not suffer fools gladly and has been known to flare up in temper but then buy that person a drink shortly afterwards,' writes Potter's biographer. 'Success so often breeds envy and Bob has found himself on the receiving end of the jealousy that such success can produce in others.'

And here was the nub of my disquiet. With scant regard for how the self-made octogenarian property tycoon and philanthropist protected his margins, I had decided, with the kind of grotesque sense of entitlement in which the media specialise, that I didn't have to actually buy a ticket to the darts. I had another way in. I intended to get into Lakeside by stealth, and by the fact that I knew the TV presenter hosting the coverage that evening for BT Sport.

This association with BT Sport represented a huge break with the past for the BDO residency at Lakeside. For nearly 40 years, the BBC had stayed loyal to the BDO World Championships as they grew less and less potent, next to the PDC juggernaut. But the BBC stuck to their task, broadcasting the event free-to-air, and ensuring that their final was consistently the most watched darts match anywhere in the world on TV, comfortably exceeding anything that Sky Sports could offer. Besides, it was a distinct and different kind of tournament, with a more armchair-friendly vibe, less hung up on statistics and empirical proof of talent. The presence of the perma-chained, red-faced Emperor of Bling, Bobby George, imparted to the watching public a feeling as warm and familiar as if the game had been frozen in time in 1983.

Now into his seventies, George is a direct link with a simpler age, if that's not a strange thing to say about a man who made his name from walking onstage in a black cape clutching a candelabra. But his television style was no frills, despite the presence of vast layers of frills, ruffs and high-blend artificial silk blouses on display. I remember being so amused by one comment Bobby George made on the BBC's Lakeside coverage that I grabbed a pen and made a note of it.

COLIN MURRAY (for a long time the host of the
    BBC's coverage): Bobby, some people say that Dennis
    Harbour is a rather deliberate player. Would you agree?

BOBBY GEORGE (without hesitation): No. He's boring.

MURRAY (trying to mediate the harsh judgement meted
   out to the player we were about to watch): I'm sure
   you just mean he's methodical.

GEORGE: No. He's boring.

In fact, the Harbour Master (for that was his nickname) was
indeed a wonderfully soporific player to watch. Nodding off in
front of the telly during an afternoon session at the Lakeside can
lead to confusion upon waking up, as if you've been transported
back in time. It can be a wrench to discover that the Mini Metro
is no longer the pride of British Leyland, and that *Bergerac*
hasn't been recommissioned for a fourth series.

But it was a slowly diminishing return. After 39 years,
the BBC lost heart in the BDO and pulled the plug on their
broadcast operation, dumping the great Bobby George onto the
scrapheap at the same time. So when in 2017 the BDO hooked
up its future to a combination of the much more niche Channel
4 and BT Sport, Sky's main pay TV rival, a brave new world
beckoned for the ailing, but senior darting body.

Approaching Lakeside that night, I was looking forward to
immersing myself in the BDO's otherness. But, that afternoon,
a rather worrying exchange of texts with the man who was to
smuggle me in had put me on notice that Potter might not be
best pleased with my freeloading presence at the venue.

'Bob Potter being weird about passes,' warned BT Sport's
presenter Matt Smith. 'Shout when you get here. I have a
different plan.'

Arriving at the rear entrance of the main venue, I made
contact with Matt, who lent me his accreditation and he spirited
me inside. There was no sign of Bob Potter, and, with my bogus
identity swinging like a medallion in front of my best darting
shirt (a perfectly normal shirt but open at the neck one button

further than usual), I strode though the TV production area and immediately into the players' bar, under a false identity. Nobody stopped me. I was in!

What a scene. The room held enough space for three quite tightly packed practice boards, complete with a clutch of players happily throwing and chatting to their friends and family. The practice oches were rudimentary constructions and had the appearance of being knocked together from offcuts of two-by-four timber. There was a small bar, padded on the outside, so that with one simple swivel, pint glass in hand, you could face the room, while resting the upper portion of your buttocks against its cushioned sides. All the while, bottles of beer and the occasional glass of something fizzy with lemon and ice were being handed over the counter. It had the feel-good normality of a pub on an otherwise unprepossessing Sunday night.

It took me a while to process the fact that I was looking into the hallowed locker room of a world championship event. It looked like a venue in which one might idly flick beer mats in the air and scoff crisps. It was a pub, for heaven's sake! And, as such, it struck a different chord to the cavernous backstage areas of the vast PDC events, held in arenas whose normal function was anything from hosting rock concerts to ice hockey matches. This, the beating heart of the BDO's flagship event, was much more intimate.

The walls were covered from skirting board to ceiling in hundreds of photographs that bore witness to decades of darting talent. I examined them more closely, trying to pick out individual players, and was struck by the array of faces that met me. We have yet to witness a generation of players who have risen straight through the ranks of the PDC without first enjoying a weaning period enveloped in the warm bosom of the BDO. Until the sensational arrival of the PDC world champion Rob Cross in 2018, all the previous stars of the game, across

both codes, had played at one time or another under the rules of the BDO.

There was among that gallery of talent a photo of an unrecognisably young and matinee-idol glamorous 'Snakebite' Peter Wright, long before the Mohican took over. John Lowe, hair combed to within an inch of its parting, vied for space alongside Eric Bristow, Phil Taylor, John Part and everyone else who'd ever thrown a dart at the Embassy, as this venerable old tournament was formerly known.

Even the unmistakable Michael van Gerwen, still the world number one and greatest talent on the PDC circuit, was there, pre-baldness and pre-brilliance. The pictures were hung with less than a millimetre of clear wall space between them, like the locked together shields of a Roman legion defending themselves against arrowheads. What a slice of history. Each frown or grin or vacant stare into the lens told a story of a life lived with the glass half full.

I fetched a pint and headed for the main hall, slipping out through the same door the players were using to gain access to the stage. I tried not to look too self-conscious, nodding at the surprisingly elderly security guards, splendid to a man in their BDO blazers, crested at the breast pocket with the organisation's tri-darted emblem. I opted for the obvious tactic of looking utterly like I belonged and hoped that such a brazen message of belonging would deter any of them from looking too closely at my accreditation. An over-egged, 'Evening gentlemen!' appeared to do the trick, and before I knew it, I had taken my seat at the very front of the first row on the raised VIP section to the right of the stage. From this very special vantage point I had an unobstructed view, not only of the board and the players, but of the walk-ons too.

The crowd were filing slowly back in for the evening session. A lone man with a hat shaped like a dartboard was devouring half a roast chicken with chips. He paused after alternate mouthfuls to suck all the fingers of his right hand clean of fat and salt, before repeating the operation with all the fingers of his left hand. Pockets of people in fancy dress were limbering up for the evening's fuzziness, including a group of ladies on a hen night, bedecked with all the usual accessories such as spangly pink cowgirl hats and learner plates. Their T-shirts were bespoke: Leanne from Lancaster, Mel from Morecambe and Ann from Anywhere. Every now and again, an occasional shriek would be heard. They were befriending a man in a Queen of Hearts costume who seemed intent on taking a selfie with everyone in the hall; any stray players, the Dutch match referee, the security operatives, the cleaners, his pint, his chips… everyone and everything got the Instagram treatment. The whole function room, low-ceilinged and hung with chandeliers of dubious quality, smelled pleasingly like school Christmas dinner was about to be served. Predominantly, I noted, the odour of the BDO was gravy.

On either side of the stage, itself a riot of 1980s neon geometry, hung screens featuring images of the two men soon to be engaged in the preliminary round clash. Up against the Eastern European qualifier, Poland's Krzysztof Ratajski, was the 'former winner of the Turkish Open', Willem Mandigers from the Netherlands.

The music started and the MC, 'Little' Richard Ashdown, bow-tied, BDO-badged, and fairly short (hence the nickname) introduced the first players, but not before he'd drawn a few laughs at his own expense by encouraging the audience to join him in a chorus of a dwarfish, 'Hi, Hooooooo!'

Then there was a thud of something techno and Ratajski walked on, awkwardly high-fiving one or two of the fans along the way, fists pumping and elbows jabbing in an approximation of syncopation with some impenetrable Polish rap. About seven seconds later, he'd reached the stage and the music was faded out, much to everyone's relief, including Ratajski's by the look of him. The musical choice of his Dutch opponent was hardly any less obscure, and equally brief; but it confirmed a trend I had observed in the PDC as well, namely, that continental darts players haven't got a clue how to choose a proper walk-on song. They seem to confuse the music they listen to for the music that gets the hall to its feet.

Soon both men were busily throwing their warm-up darts. That was the next shock. When each dart landed in the board, the loudspeakers in the hall gave off a loud and slightly comedic 'Boing!'.

This was most unsettling. In the PDC events, the sound of the dart landing in the board is amplified massively. Relayed through sub-woofers the size of small cars that hang from the ceiling, this is one of the great sounds in sport, like the crack of a cricket ball being cut to the boundary for four, or the wallop of a serve going down the line on Centre Court.

That's why the BDO's slightly silly sound effect came as such a shock to the system. It upset my perception of what the game was. I couldn't help wondering how off-putting it must be for the players. I imagined it would be like running the 100 metres accompanied by the Benny Hill theme tune. I glanced around to see if I was alone in finding this funny. It seemed I was.

The crowd were settling down to watch this intriguing clash of Poland and the Netherlands. A hush descended. Both men were now ready to go.

Ratajski threw first. 'Forty-one!'

Then Mandigers stepped up. 'Forty-one!'

I watched the opening few legs and then drifted off. I sensed that the match could go on for some time. In fact, it took well over an hour, including the breaks after five legs, when the players briefly disappeared.

Only as late as 2017 did the BDO introduce music into the hall during the commercial breaks when the players left the stage. During the BBC years, there had been no such entertainment on offer. Whenever the players left the stage, as they had to after five legs, the hall simply used to go quiet and the punters would resume their polite darting chatter.

Now, with amplified singalong music bursting over them, they all stood up and swayed to perfectly chosen crowd-pleasers like 'Green, Green Grass of Home' and 'Hi Ho Silver Lining'. But even these totemic tunes were more akin to a knees-up at the local than the Sky Sports-induced nightclub frenzy of the PDC events. Less fist-pumping, more gently swaying.

The accepted wisdom in the darting world is that Lakeside is patronised by 'real darting people', the salt and vinegar crisps of the earth. The attribution of these virtues implies, by its very existence, that there is another kind of people who are unreal.

This distinction is drawn in many other sports, and is related to the kudos gained in the football world by supporting a non-league team. The Premier League is all very well and good, so the sentiment suggests, but the Combined Counties Evo-stik South-Eastern Division Three is where football is still real: £10 to get in and a pie for £1.50. Plus you can have a pint with the players afterwards. What I now saw laid out before me was the tungsten equivalent of the home support for Sutton United on a Tuesday night watching a third round match in the FA Vase, which just happened to call itself the World Championship.

After 20 minutes my pint was empty, and that gave me all the impetus I needed to get up and go for a walk.

Back in the players' bar tucked away behind the stage, the next darters were warming up, and, strikingly, they weren't blokes. The BDO World Championships runs a parallel women's competition alongside the men's. It is a different approach to fostering greater equality in what is a very male sport, and many think that it is the fairer way of developing the women's game.

While the PDC events are technically open to women, there is currently not one woman playing the game who could hold their own in the company of the best men in the world. There is no reason at all why women should not be able to compete at the highest levels, but a paucity of opportunity and a much smaller talent pool have meant that, as yet, none have made it.

That's not to say that women cannot match the men. I witnessed the first ever televised defeat of a man, Vincent van der Voort, by a woman, Anastasia Dobromyslova, a Russian player resident at the time in Ellesmere Port. Van der Voort had been genuinely mortified when I interviewed him afterwards. The shock of his perceived humiliation was so great in the darting world that you could be forgiven for concluding that his career has stalled ever since.

The BDO do it another way, and for better or worse, they separate the sexes. This has resulted in the making of a few legends. There is no bigger name in women's darts than Trina Gulliver, a fact recognised in the addition, in 2013, of the letters MBE after her name and the mapping of the 'Trina Gulliver Trail' in her Warwickshire home town of Southam. The walk traces the landmarks of her career including the Bowling Green pub, where her father was the landlord, and where she honed her early darts skills, and the school she attended.

Gulliver has won Lakeside ten times, and was widely tipped in 2017 to win it again. She is a level-headed, even-tempered winner, widely respected among the players for her considerable achievements, and the author of an extremely matter-of-fact sporting autobiography. *Golden Girl* begins with the line, 'I was born at 3:15am on 30 November 1969 at the Warneford Hospital in Leamington Spa.' And it continues in much the same way, ending with the statement that Gulliver is 'not prepared to… hand over [her] world title any time soon.' What happens in the middle is testament to a no-nonsense approach to life that has seen her support her husband (though eventually they divorced) through the profound effects of Guillain-Barré syndrome, as well as a bizarre accident with a cross-saw which saw him cutting off three of his fingers. Put it this way: she's tough.

Then there's the multiple major tournament winner Deta Hedman, who I watched throwing some practice darts, even though she wouldn't be competing that evening. The former girlfriend of Colin 'Jaws' Lloyd, Hedman is a Jamaican-born first-generation immigrant who has been at the very top of women's darts for a couple of decades. Arriving in Witham near the Essex coast as a teenager in the mid-seventies, she followed her brothers down to the pub where she watched them play darts. She recalls the kinds of long Sunday lunchtimes where the landlord had laid out pickled silverskin onions and cubes of cheddar for people to nibble on. Originally stepping out under the nickname 'The Dark Destroyer', she has since rebranded herself to a more politically safe, (but worryingly close to my book title), 'Heart of Darts'.

Of course, just as Gulliver has had to show stoicism in her private life, not everything has been easy for Hedman. She's had to deal with racist heckling every now and again, and the inequality of financial reward has meant that she's had to work long shifts at the Central Post Office in Farringdon to make up for the huge disparity in prize money between men and women in the game. The men's winner at Lakeside takes home £100,000, while the winning woman has to be content with just £12,000.

My lager replenished, I left Hedman busily chatting away in the players' bar and carried my second pint cautiously back inside, avoiding eye contact with the elderly steward, who I sensed had started to wonder about my credentials. I sat down once again in the best seat in the house, just in time to see Ratajski dispatch Mandigers 3–2, with both men averaging in the high eighties. And so the evening proceeded, as the games came and went. At one point I fell into conversation with a player from Newcastle, who had come to watch the darts on his night off. He was in action the following evening, he told me, before going into considerable detail about how he was going to approach the occasion, drink-wise.

'Just need to get there,' he held his half-empty beer glass in front of him, as if it were a dart about to be launched, and kept it steady, while he fixed it in his gaze. 'Just there...' he said again. 'And hold it there.' We both stared at the motionless half-drunk lager, admiring its poise.

Shortly after that, I was rumbled.

'Could I ask who you are, sir?' the elderly steward said, extremely politely.

Unable to think on my feet, and increasingly unable to stand steadily on them either, I simply answered, 'Ned,' and flipped over my accreditation that said 'Matt'. Then I grinned at him and said, 'No, Matt.'

'Well, Mr Potter wants you to leave the VIP seating, sir.'

'Yes, of course,' I replied. 'And thank you, sir.'

I relocated to the main body of the hall, finding one of a very few empty seats. The evening was drifting towards a conclusion of sorts. At one point, at a table next to ours, a security officer approached one of the spectators who had fallen asleep with a full pint in his drinking hand.

'Try and stay with us, sir. Or I'm afraid I'll have to ask you to go home.'

'Sorry!' The sleepy drinker sat bolt upright and took a colossal gulp of lager. 'Sorry. Awake now.'

At that point, I dropped my false ID back with my colleagues from TV, bade farewell to Lakeside and pushed out into the night, leaving the World Championships to carry on without me.

Frimley Green, Lakeside, the BDO: a holy anachronism, where the absolute pursuit of excellence is only optional, and plays second fiddle to tradition and simple pleasure. Inclusive, appreciative, humble and enduring, the BDO may soon be an obsolete acronym, like the TSB, the WI or the SDP. But when it hands over, as hand over it surely must, to the market forces that drive the game to ever-greater noise and money, something of its magical night-time charm will have gone with it, and, like a sober wintry dawn breaking over the Lakeside complex, we will perhaps see its cracks and flaws illuminated, its chipped plaster and cracking paint. We will see its era for what it was, and how it can no longer be. And we will miss it, most of it.

I walked on, watching my beery breath rise into the black night with each step I took. At one point, I laughed out loud to myself.

'Hold it just there,' I said to the receding lights of Lakeside. And I held out an imaginary pint. Then the darkness closed around me, unthreateningly.

Different Class

The worst that could be said of him
was that he did not represent his class.

JOSEPH CONRAD – *HEART OF DARKNESS*

The game returned me to the centre. No matter how far away my journey took me, I seemed to be drawn back to the capital. The London Eye turned slowly, the glinting tip of the Shard, an upended arrow. Here I was in Zone One, the Bullseye.

I turned my back on the Thames, heading away from the South Bank, with the tide high and lapping at the concrete embankment on which London's cultural heritage was housed: the Hayward Gallery, the Royal Festival Hall, the British Film Institute, the National Theatre. I left them all behind me as I slipped through the tourist crowds heading the opposite way, past the Archduke Restaurant, over York Road. And before I knew it, I was mounting the pigeon shit-spattered stone steps of Waterloo Station.

The departures board lit up with the names of England's homely past: Winchester and Fareham, Gosport, Frimley. Here, the lines from Hampshire and Surrey converge as they rush towards the capital through the New Forest and the Surrey Hills towards the moneyed outer districts of Twickenham, Richmond, Teddington and Putney. I hurried on to the café at the end of the concourse, where Justin Irwin had installed himself. I apologised for being late.

Irwin is an articulate, affable, middle-aged man. He is a very good darts player. He is shortish and baldish and English. And he works as a freelance consultant to the charity sector. Ten years ago he was the chief executive of the charity Childline. The work ground him down, slowly but surely, and one evening, leaving the pub after post-work drinks in a state of pleasing inebriation, he decided to jack in his job and become a professional darts player.

As we cradled cappuccinos in our hands and gazed down on commuters rushing through automated gates, Irwin recalled the story he tells so well in his memoir *Murder on the Darts Board*. It all started with that aim of turning professional within a year. In his words:

> I had never thrown a competitive dart and I knew that currently I was rubbish. So, I would commit myself to practising for four to six hours a day for the next four months... My overall goal would be to qualify for the World Championships within a year.

No one believed he meant it, but he was absolutely serious. But at the risk of spoiling the book, he didn't make it to Lakeside. From the moment he cannot figure out where to hang the dartboard in the flat he shares with his girlfriend (somewhere that won't ruin the furniture), to the time he accidentally stabs himself in the face with a dart during one of his early, and doomed, competitive matches, his quest grinds towards failure with all the weight and horror of a Greek tragedy.

When the hour of his darting hubris arrives, it plays out in Hull, and he has to split the petrol money to get home. This is a fittingly humdrum denouement for a less-than-epic finale.

In fact, despite hitting his first competitive maximum 180, he ends up losing his match in the World Championship Qualifiers 4–0. He accepts defeat with humility and a newfound respect for those players he had hitherto only marvelled at from afar.

My admiration for professional darts players had never been higher. Against a backdrop of stereotyping and mickey-taking they put their careers and their livelihoods on the line on a regular basis. I had gone to pieces in front of 16 blokes in a pub in Angel. The pros play darts for a living in front of millions of people. They sure have some balls.

'Do you still play?' I ask him.

'Oh yes. Got a pub game tonight.'

Since returning to the world of work, he curates a website in his spare time that lists and celebrates the dwindling number of darts pubs in London. He has been tracking the decline of the dartboard, as they are taken down from the walls to allow for more tables (pubs serve food in a way that they never used to) and perhaps to encourage a different clientele.

That's his concern for the game he loves, that darts has started to disappear underground at the same time that it is considered to be booming, thanks to its sudden ever-presence on the TV screens. There is a contradiction here that worries and confuses him.

'It's totally hidden away. That never used to be the case, even ten years ago. In the last five years about a quarter of London's darts pubs have shut or taken the board down. And if you think almost every pub used to have a dartboard 50 years ago, it's quite logical to presume that in 20 years' time you won't find a dartboard in Central London.'

The result of this stripping away of the game from the visible surface of London's drinking life is that it has shrunk back to its heartland, a marginalised place where the middle classes are unlikely to venture. Irwin plays in a league that visits the many working men's clubs that proliferate, perhaps anachronistically, across the sprawling width of the diverse capital city. These places are a far remove from the welcoming inn of the folkloric imagination, where the landowner might rub shoulders with the labourer over a jug of mild as they battle on the oche. The game is still there, but it's played, increasingly, in the shadows.

'The darts world does exist, but it's bits of society that you don't see often anywhere else. It really is. It's white, working class, very, very poor.' He describes how all the sandwiches and sausage rolls that are put out on platters get either consumed or spirited away. 'The food comes out,' he says, 'and it's rubbish food at darts matches. But it'll all disappear. Half of the food gets put in plastic bags and carried out. It all gets used.'

The encounters that playing darts has fashioned in his life have changed his outlook permanently. The game has drawn together disparate lives in a capital city that divides ever more savagely down socio-economic lines, lives that might never otherwise have crossed paths. In post-Grenfell London, this seems a worthwhile testimony to hear.

He feels the difference keenly, between his own middle-class upbringing, as well as that of his teammates, and the rest of the darts world, drinking and throwing and conversing in the Chiswick Memorial Club, for example, where he often plays. 'You wouldn't go into those places unless you were a member. And you wouldn't go into those places if you were middle class. You just wouldn't find them. Our team are posh and tall and speak with loud voices. They're totally different from everyone else, who are almost like an underclass in London, people who I don't see anywhere in the rest of my life.'

Then his phone rings. It's one of his teammates in his darts team, crying off the match. While he talks on the phone, with one hand raised apologetically towards me, I think about what he has said about class.

For me, there has always been the issue of fitting in. Like the Englishman Marlow, the narrator of *Heart of Darkness*, I was both thrilled and alarmed at the unexplored otherness of, in my case darts, in his case, Africa. Marlow was drawn on by the lure of the landscape and that long snaking river, and so too was I, navigating my uncertain route to the interior of a culture I was reaching out to understand. But at the same time, I knew that I would always be a foreigner to its senses, an alien, a bit other, like Marlow.

Never had I been more troubled by this dissonance than during the prolonged fallout from the removal of the walk-on girls from televised darts. It had been a decision that had been coming long before it was enacted, and perhaps was hastened by the welter of sexist scandals and the accompanying soul-searching that were the result of Harvey Weinstein's disgrace. Across huge swathes of public life, things changed, and darts fell into line.

Yet the resistance to change was loud. A petition for the reinstatement of the walk-on girls raised 40,000 signatures in no time at all. Players campaigned, fans were vocal. I watched Charlotte Wood and Daniella Allfree, the models in question, appear regularly on television, decrying what they saw as interference by busybody outsiders who had no feel for the game.

I raised the subject over breakfast one morning with my non-darting, non-male family, and suggested that, while it was clearly the right decision, it 'wasn't entirely black and white'. I continued to spread my toast in the silence that followed.

Then a knife was dropped on a plate. 'No, sorry,' came the response. 'It is completely black and white.'

I backed down instantly. 'Yes, of course. You're right.'

And perhaps I had been guilty of bad faith after all, of deviating from what I believed in order to fit in, while making assumptions about what other people stood for, or didn't: a kind of class traitor, almost.

Despite my familiarity with the game, built up over a good few years, there was something uncomfortable about full immersion into the obdurately working-class world of darts. For all its joyful innocence, darts unsettled my Conrad-reading middle-class sensibilities. Try as I might to ape the language of Estuary English, the native tongue of a game which took hold 100 or so years ago on this very coastline, it withered and died on my self-consciously middle-class tongue. And the surrounding jungle merely put that awkward otherness in me into sharp relief, for as Marlow said of his surroundings:

> It seemed somehow to throw a light on everything about me – and into my thoughts – not extraordinary in any way – not very clear either. No, not very clear. And yet it seemed to throw a kind of light.

But Justin Irwin is speaking from a different position of some authority. It is he who will be playing darts in Chiswick that evening, not me.

When he's finished making his arrangements, we change the subject. I tell Irwin that I have been trying to get hold of Stephen Fry to hear what he has to say on the subject of darts. Irwin looks sceptical, but understands why I might be keen on hunting down the finest of cut-crystal voices in the darting firmament. After all, Fry is about the poshest, genuine darts fan the sport has known since Rupert Croft-Cooke wrote that remarkable tome *Darts*.

Fry's evaluation of darts, although differently framed from Croft-Cooke's, is born from the same kind of detached fascination for the whole scene with which another writer, Martin Amis, painted a picture of the game and its players in his 1989 novel *London Fields*, a book which has played an intriguing role in Irwin's intriguing life and education in darts.

London Fields is a dazzling story of desperate lives in a visceral London setting and has darts woven through its fabric in ways that romanticise it and sometimes brutalise its players. Despite, or maybe because of, the violent poetry of the language, there is a deep and genuine love of the contest that saves *London Fields* from simply being nasty.

Amis's anti-hero lead character, Keith Talent, is a darts obsessive, and a thieving, abusive cheat to boot. He lives a low kind of life on the margins, but comes into his own when he has three darts in his right hand.

The darts in his blood coursed through him, feeding his darts brain. A darts brain, that's what he had: darts nerve, darts sinew. A darts heart. A darts soul. Darts.

In Waterloo, Irwin tells me that he and Amis's novel share a curious connection. By a curious twist of fate, he had written a dissertation on *London Fields* for his English degree. This was not because of his love for darts (in his words 'I had no interest at all back then'), but more because, being something of a corner-cutter, Irwin decided that Martin Amis would be a good writer to focus on since no one had really written much about him, and therefore there would be less secondary reading to plough through. But he could never have imagined, as he studied the intense prose of *London Fields*, that he might one day work with one of the biggest stars of his generation on a Hollywood adaptation for the big screen.

It happened like this. In 2013, he was contacted by some mysterious folk who wanted to take him out to lunch. It turned out that they were film producers, working on a screenplay adaptation of Amis's story of degradation in the 1980s.

The producers explained that they needed someone to help them with a bit of location scouting and some darts coaching for the star actors in what Irwin fondly imagined would be a low-budget, low-rent kind of film, a supposition only reinforced when he discovered the meagre sum of money they were prepared to offer him for his services. But, intrigued and flattered, he agreed to become the film's 'darts consultant', and in the process staking a claim to being the first of his kind ever, in the history of cinema. At least that is what I suggest when he tells me about his employment, and neither of us are in a position to contradict.

'Keith Talent is played by Jim... oh, what's his name? He's really famous, but no one's ever heard of him.' I later discover that he means Jim Sturgess, who, as he'd rightly guessed, I'd never heard of.

Irwin was hired to go round to Sturgess's house and practise with him until he got good enough to throw his own darts in front of camera without the need for judicious editing and/or a body double, although the former BDO world champion Scott Mitchell was drafted in, at Irwin's recommendation, to throw the darts so they landed in the right place for the close-ups. That said, Sturgess got so good at it that he took a leg from Mitchell during filming, which was roundly celebrated by the film crew.

Johnny Depp had been booked to play the part of the mysterious champion darter Chip Purchase. But with Depp, the same kind of interest in learning how to play wasn't forthcoming. Indeed, the first time Irwin met his famous student was on the sound stage, with all the crew watching on, waiting to shoot the final scene.

'We were meant to do some practising offstage, but it didn't happen. So it was onstage that I went up to him and said, "Hi Johnny, I'm Justin. I'm the darts consultant on the movie."

'He leant in towards me, carrying a stick and covered in scars, and leered, "I know exactly who you are."'

Irwin was impressed. 'I was thinking, "*You're quite famous.*" I've met some quite famous people. I've put him on my list now.' Then he tells me who's on the Irwin list: 'Depp, Stephen Fry and Robert Mugabe.'

The film of *London Fields* was beset with problems, almost from the outset. What started off as a low-budget adaptation got steadily grander in design and budget as it pulled in such Hollywood names as Amber Heard and Depp. But even after filming was complete, its release stalled as Heard, in the middle of a fraught and upsetting divorce from Depp, reportedly demanded that certain of the more provocative sex scenes were cut. This in turn led to the film's producers contemplating legal action against Heard for damaging the film's prospects of release by embarking on a 'concerted campaign of disinformation'.

Nonetheless, during filming, Irwin was also introduced to Martin Amis, who came to the set to see how shooting was progressing. He told Irwin how his inspiration for the character of Keith Talent had come from a meeting with the Milky Bar Kid, Keith Deller, winner of the 1983 Embassy World Championships. In 1988, a year before the publication of *London Fields*, Amis had written a profile of Deller called 'Darts: Gutted for Keith' for the *Observer*. In many ways, it was a rough sketch for what he would flesh out a year later across the pages of *London Fields*.

Some of the descriptions of darts that Amis conjures up are unimprovably vivid:

A 20-stone man threw a 20-gram nail at a lump of cork, while the crowd screamed for blood. Tiddlywinks in a bearpit.

For anyone who has never witnessed a Friday night at the Wolverhampton Civic with Ted Hankey on the stage, it comes mighty close.

It is safe to say that Amis felt a fascination with the salacious underbelly of the game, and seemed to mythologise it with an outsider's respect and awe, as well as that faintly squeamish writerly distaste for the primeval passions he ascribes to the game's unwashed practitioners and supporters. The percussive sound of darts, so unlike the BDO's Lakeside 'boing', reverberates through the book:

> ... solid thunks followed by shouted numbers against a savage background of taunts and screams.

But there is also space for Amis to enjoy the celebrated vagueness, lack of rigour and playful obfuscations that swirl around the history and origins of darts. For a while, Talent becomes immersed in reading up on the ancient traditions of the game, buying into a lineage of English darting folklore.

> 'It is thought by some,' read Keith, 'that the secret of Stonehenge lies in darts. The circular stone ruins are shaped in a circle, like a dartboard.'

And the board itself, through the eyes of Talent, becomes an object of transcendental significance.

> From time to time he would stare up at the swimming beauty of the dartboard: the kaleidoscope of every hope and dream.

Justin Irwin, whose literary contribution to the darting opus is less ambitious but much more rooted in real life, would have found himself, surely, nodding along with some of Amis's elaborately worded conclusions. When literature and darts collide, you might as well cut and paste the content straight into *Private Eye*'s 'Pseuds Corner', the gap can appear so unbridgeably wide. Much of this failure to meet in the middle can be traced back to the stratification of the British class system, so stubbornly resistant to social engineering.

'Society is much more snobbish than it was,' Irwin contends, with a sigh. 'The working classes are looked down upon. There's a national dislike of people who don't have proper jobs, of the benefits culture.'

This is, he suggests, a continuing process that began when darts first started to decline. 'That's the reason darts went off the radar in the late eighties. It was the result of Thatcherism, I'm convinced about that. I don't think the producers who took the decisions would say that. But that's really the reason.'

Darts may be globalising, but its spread in its mother country, in sociological terms, seems to be far more horizontal than vertical. True, there is a chain of extremely upmarket darts-themed pubs in the City of London now called *Flight Club*, in which besuited and high-heeled young City workers hire Hawk-Eye camera-equipped dartboards for £20 an hour. But this is at the expense of innumerable 'old man's pubs' in the Square Mile that have been gentrified or simply demolished. It seems the tectonic plates are moving further away from one another in London, and darts is being pulled underground.

There is an encounter in *Murder on the Darts Board*, deep into the failing trajectory of Irwin's attempt to qualify for the World Championships, between Irwin and Keith Deller himself that strikes a chord with me. It happens at a caravan holiday park in Great Yarmouth where he is staying for a weekend's tournament. Despite his familiarity with the darts world, it is the sheer concentration of 'dartness' here that starts to unsettle him.

When it came to it, regardless of how affected my accent became, I didn't quite fit.

At one o'clock in the morning, as the dance floor seethes with life, an inebriated Irwin spots his idol bopping away to 'Too Much Too Young' by the Specials.

There he was. My inspiration, Keith Deller.

He made his way over to him and tapped him on the shoulder.

'Keeef.'
No response.
'Keeeeef!' I tapped him a bit harder.
'Wot?'
'Keeeeef. You're the reason I play darts.'
And on that note I hugged the 1983 Embassy World Darts champion.'

And so he did just that, as Amis might have put it, 'in fateful synergy, drink and darts'.

But for all that Irwin has returned to the fold of *Guardian*-reading middle-class sensibility, he has certainly not cast aside his love for the game that sparked his partially Guinness-sodden mid-life crisis, played out to the calculated chatter of chalking down from 501. He still plays the game every Wednesday night. In fact, he's constantly checking his phone to see if anyone on his team has managed to unearth a replacement for someone dropping out of the pub team for that evening's match.

'It's the school holidays. This always bloody happens. Half the team's gone missing.'

While we talk, he does in fact receive a text message, but it's not the one he anticipated. Instead, it's from Scott Mitchell, the world champion, texting him to let him know that he's appearing on *Countryfile* that evening. He's been filmed throwing a 180. Irwin texts him back with a cheeky question.

'How many takes?'

The answer pings back. 'Three.'

'Well that's bollocks.'

The game, the culture of the game, has been joyously diverting and gloriously welcoming to Irwin, yet at the same time, a quite unobtainable, distant, inaccessible dream.

That is to say, the mastery of the game, his stated aim, has revealed itself to be a frustrating chimera, elusive to the point of maddening. He never quite got to grips with that crucially important bit that involves scoring treble twenties each and every time you step up to the oche. And it's not as if he hasn't tried.

It provoked in him the addictive fascination of whittling human endeavour down to the obsessive pursuit of an almost entirely pointless objective. The strange passions that a missed treble or winning double can arouse, no matter how grand or humble the stage.

Ten years after his chastening, but delighted, foray into the world of the professional darter, Irwin is much more comfortable in his skin. He has returned to his high-flying, ethically unimpeachable career of working with charities.

But a love of darts opens surprising doors, and can lead you down unexpected paths. No one knows this more acutely than Justin Irwin. His life's span has a kink right in the middle of it, for which the game of darts is wholly responsible, and which influences him to this day. Without darts, there's no way he would have met Johnny Depp.

We shook hands and went on our ways. I continued my journey on foot.

And he jumped aboard his Chiswick-bound train, thinking no doubt about his match that evening, and opening the gate to the platform with his standard-class ticket. Justin Irwin was certain of his destination. Me? Less so.

Naming Rights

Your own reality–for yourself, not for others–what no
other man can ever know. They can only see the mere
show, and never can tell what it really means.

JOSEPH CONRAD – *HEART OF DARKNESS*

Leaving Waterloo, I walked past the tiny statue of Sir
Laurence Olivier as Hamlet, who stands outside the
National Theatre lifting his little sword aloft to the skies, all
four foot six of him. Not for the first time, I chuckled at its
size, wondering why he was so small. I decided, to my own
satisfaction, that his darting nickname would have been 'The
Dithering Dwarf'.

'This above all:' Polonius had told Laertes, in *Hamlet*, 'to
thine own self be true.'

I considered those words in the context of Justin Irwin's
involvement with the game, envying him his ability at darts.
The fact that he threw so well seemed to buy him access to the
game's culture that I, for all my exposure to it, still found to be
frustrated by my middle-class roots. Irwin's three-dart averages
seemed to circumvent his background.

I was also somewhat envious of the fact that he had met Stephen Fry.

Sometime later, though, I finally got a response from Stephen Fry. He sent me an email just as he was about to disappear into what he called 'writer's purdah', but he had time to tell me how he had once been asked to commentate alongside Sid Waddell during a Premier League event for Sky Sports in 2010, a heady cocktail that mixed the treacle of Waddell's Northumbrian scattergun poetry with the Wildean prose of Fry's cultivated tongue. It had been, he told me, 'spellbinding', and an 'inestimable honour' to commentate alongside the 'legend Sid Waddell'. Comedy being never far away from Waddell's orbit, it had also been entirely fitting that the night's action had been 'rather hilariously called off due to a power cut, and we all returned the next day'.

'It is still primarily a game that working people are mostly associated with,' Fry continued, 'and I wouldn't want that to change. If it becomes gentrified that would be a shame. But what is so notable is how warm, friendly, witty and good-natured the crowds are. There's none of the lager-loutishness that people ignorant of the game might assume.'

He went on to tell me how he was an obsessive viewer, a big admirer of the game. And 'game', for him, was the important word. 'I don't really like sport as such. I like *games* and darts is a supreme example of why I enjoy them so much. It's the human drama, the tension, the rhythm, the whole "narrative" that plays out over the course of the legs and sets of a tournament.'

Underpinning all the pantomime, there was, according to Fry, a heavy-lidded, knowing wink; a wry and clear understanding that this was all just a monstrously overgrown giggle. The parade ring of professional darts was a remarkable place, a stage on which to celebrate the very contrast between their assumed identities and their real selves. 'The true personality is always revealed on the oche,' Fry wrote to me when we swapped opinions about players we both admire. 'There is room for a discontinuity between the stage persona and the real character. I like that Peter Wright, for example, can wear the armour of Snakebite, but is clearly, underneath it, a gentle and even shy soul.'

Fry was correct about Wright. If ever there was a man less snake-bitey than Snakebite, then that man is Peter Wright, who reinvented himself a few years ago, bursting forth from his darting chrysalis to become the game's most multicoloured totem. So Polonius was wrong, in a darts context, where authenticity plays second fiddle to fun.

Wright is a shy man, almost painfully so at times. And on Armistice Day, 11 November 2017, he was a gentle, shy soul with a glittering poppy and silhouetted soldier kneeling with his rifle at the grave of a fallen comrade lovingly painted onto the shaven side of his head, along with the legend, 'We Remember'. There is room for great themes to be explored on the blank canvas of the Snakebite scalp.

Nothing, in darts, is to be taken at face value. Like in a grotesque masked ball, strange connections are forged and surprising associations can suddenly run deep. I cannot, for example, hear 'Eye of the Tiger' without conjuring up a mental image of an Amsterdam postman with his eyes rolling back in his head. Nor will the gorgeous syrupy strains of 'Sweet Caroline' ever be entirely free of their connection to Daryl 'Superchin' Gurney (he has quite a pronounced chin) conducting the crowd into ever-greater ecstasies of delight. And a strong Norfolk accent will only ever make me think of the diminutive Darren 'Demolition Man' Webster ferreting his way through a leg of darts.

'Does he work in demolition?' I remember asking Alan Warriner-Little, when I first saw Webster playing.

'No,' he replied. 'He's a builder.'

I nodded as if that explanation made perfect sense, though building was surely the opposite of demolition.

The familiarity, the humility, the lack of pretension, the repetitive nature of the experience, the gentle punning humour and the fuzzy warmth; all these things make darts a welcome and harmless addition to the nation's portfolio of pleasure. And at the centre of it are the players themselves, styled to suit their own image, conforming willingly and relentlessly to the characteristics expected of them.

The chief protagonists appear to be ageless, or at least ageing infinitesimally slowly, so that the process happens invisibly to the viewing eye of the spectator, who is barely able to discern a change in their heroes from year to year. So, in their array of different physical traits, from the height of Vincent van der Voort, the lanky, loping Dutchman, to the rippling pectorals of ex-Rugby hooker Gerwyn Price, they are paraded across the stage for our pleasure.

These men are cardboard cut-outs of flesh and beating blood, condemned for ever to be paraded in a fake world. It's a wonder that speech bubbles don't emerge from the corners of their mouths, and thoughts don't float up, cloud-like from their furrowed brows: '137 minus 60 leaves 77, which is treble 19, double 10.' It's astonishing too that they don't lose a grip on their own identity amid all the artifice. Although perhaps some do.

Spending time in their sphere, whether face to face or through the God-like medium of television that created them, is like inhabiting the pages of a well-thumbed comic book. Looking at the order of play in the opening rounds of any tournament, you might find yourself flipping hastily through the stories that don't interest you – I could never get worked up about Billy Whizz in *The Beano*, for example – and heading straight for the pages that really hit the spot. Roger the Dodger, for example.

There is a playfulness and gentle irony at work here, when grown men with often ultra-macho trades behind them get to dress up as fantasy characters, just as the granddaddy of them all, the great Bobby George, did when he walked onstage with brazen insouciance and a borrowed candelabra.

Prior to George inventing the glorious silliness in 1980, it had never crossed anyone's mind to dress up daft in order to throw darts. But Bobby Dazzler changed all that. First came a sequinned shirt, (modelled on that worn by a singer he'd admired in Torremolinos) which disgusted the autocratic BDO head honcho Olly Croft. 'You can't go out like that!' he'd protested before George's first round match at the Embassy. 'Don't you realise the pressure you'll put on yourself if you play in that shirt?'

But it didn't bother the big darter from North London, who counted Liberace among his role models. 'The glitter and the sequins had nothing to do with effeminacy,' George later wrote. 'They were about looking good onstage and putting on a show for the crowd. If a man my size and from my background couldn't get away with it, who could?'

What wasn't in doubt was that the crowd loved the show. Women wolf-whistled and the 'beer-swilling blokes with fags in their mouths' quickly got in on the joke, too.

The Liberace theme was then amplified after George's quarter-final win against Leighton Rees when one of the BDO officials handed him a candelabra as he left the stage in homage to the American crooner, Liberace. They'd borrowed it from a pub across the road, and had even tried to get hold of a piano, which, much to George's relief, they never managed to obtain or, George feared, he 'would have been carrying that around for the last 25 years as well!'

Bobby George is still mucking around. Most recently he has reinvented himself as a staple component of a certain type of reality TV show. He played a big part in *The Real Marigold Hotel*, a series that introduced his particular form of avuncular darting roguishness to an audience more accustomed to watching the *Antiques Roadshow*. Latterly, in the winter of 2017, he also appeared alongside a bunch of other late-middle-aged celebrities (George is now in his early seventies) in a show called *Gone To Pot: American Road Trip*. In one memorable scene early in the series, which 'documents' their Ken Keseyesque journey through the USA marijuana belt, he is seen to be vomiting raucously alongside Christopher Biggins after over-indulging in some hashish-filled ice cream. I think he's enjoying his retirement.

Some images are more enduring than others. Recently, I was prompted to shout out loud when I saw a road sign with Hastings written on it. 'Voltage!' I found myself pointing at the sign. Then I informed my family that Rob 'Voltage' Cross lived in Hastings.

There followed the sound of the wind passing over the car, and the rubber tyres on tarmac.

'Why's he called Voltage?' came the reluctant reply.

'Because he used to be an electrician,' I said. There was another long pause. 'He lives in Hast—'

'Yes. You said.'

We drove on in silence. 'He's the world champion.'

I first met Rob Cross during the UK Open in 2016 when I was working for ITV. Nothing more than a pub player at the time, he had won through a regional heat at a branch of Rileys snooker halls to take his place in the first round of the televised finals. This was already a considerable achievement.

Cross had arrived at the UK Open an almost total unknown, even to many in the darts world; a perfectly commonplace tradesman from a perfectly workaday town. He was a pleasant,

unassuming bald man in his mid-twenties, who didn't have a walk-on song, didn't have a special darts shirt and didn't have a nickname. Having won his way through the first three rounds on the 'multi-boards' (the equivalent of the 'outside courts' at Wimbledon), he then drew the top seed and world number one Michael van Gerwen in the round of 32. This meant that, for the first time in his career, his match would be played in full on the main stage at Butlin's Minehead, in front of thousands of fans on live TV.

'What do you want to walk out to, Rob?' he was asked by the PDC officials on the eve of his big match against MVG. He had never before been given the full 'walk-on' treatment.

'Oh, I'm not that bothered,' he replied, phlegmatically.

This, in itself, baffled me. I had thought that there was not an amateur player in the land who had not decided what their walk-on track would be, given the chance. After all, on our production team, we were constantly discussing what we would choose, given the entirely fanciful opportunity of taking to the stage through a seething mass of cheering, dancing darts fans. I'd always wanted Stevie Wonder's 'For Once in my Life', the same song I've chosen for my funeral.

But Rob Cross had genuinely never given it the slightest thought.

'Well, what music do you like?'

'I'm not really into music, to be honest.'

So it fell to us to choose something for him. We took his trade as the starting point in our quest, and began to search for music with a vaguely electrical theme. John Rawling, the commentator, came up with 'Electric Avenue' by Eddy Grant. But I won the day with my powerful suggestion of Phil Oakey and Giorgio Moroder's 'Together in Electric Dreams'.

In the event, my choice didn't really work. The lilting 1980s chorus hardly ignited the lunchtime Butlin's crowd, and Cross

himself, shuffling awkwardly forward seemed reluctant to embrace the moment (although he did confide to me, when I met him a year later, that he'd 'quite liked' the music I'd chosen for him).

Cross has subsequently turned pro, and continued to get better and better at an unprecedented rate, reaching the finals of the 2017 European Championships and losing to Michael van Gerwen. He also took better advice than I was able to offer him and soon sported the nickname 'Voltage', walking on to 'Danger! High Voltage!' by Electric Six. But by the time the 2018 World Championships came about, he had changed his choice once again. Accompanied by the totally un-electricity-related strains of 'Feeling Hot Hot Hot' by the Merrymen, he stormed to success, lifting the Sid Waddell trophy after accounting for van Gerwen in the semi-final and then trouncing Phil Taylor in the final. It was arguably the greatest rags-to-riches story darts has ever told. He was already halfway to being a millionaire after one piffling year on the circuit.

Darts players, like Cross, reluctantly enter into a Faustian pact with their trade from the minute they start to appear on the television. The UK Open in 2015 featured a run all the way to the fourth round of a certain Paul Hogan. This Paul Hogan did not have much in common with his Australian namesake. In his early fifties, and a delivery driver from Dudley in the West Midlands, this Hogan was a cheerful gangly chap, unused to such public attention, and bashful as a result. He also stuttered, not during normal speech but when called upon to give the TV cameras his thoughts. I liked him a great deal and spent a good few hours in his company drinking tea and watching his unfolding delight at his continuing progress in the tournament.

Nevertheless, he was duly, inevitably, unavoidably, dubbed 'Crocodile Dundee', just for the simple coincidence of his name. He didn't so much embrace the nickname as reluctantly accept it, hoping that it would simply go away. He was to be disappointed. What he needed, I persuaded him after his third round win over Benito van de Pas, was, at the very least, an inflatable crocodile to take onstage with him.

That afternoon our production manager duly scouted the out-of-season seaside resort we found ourselves in for a blow-up amphibian reptile.

The following day, blushing from head to toe, Hogan took to the stage clutching a five-foot crocodile. He looked deeply uncomfortable and I was hit by a short, sharp stab of guilt.

But the truth is that 21st-century darts players need an image on which they can build a fantasy; a nickname that demands an accompanying image and potted biography that stands up to scrutiny, in much the same way that a comic character's byline defines the parameters of his personality. And so it is fated, to a certain extent, with the darters. They get a name, and then the name must stick.

Some players earn themselves pretty strait-laced names, Phil Taylor's 'The Power' probably being the most po-faced of all. A player of his all-engulfing, ruthless magnitude would have been poorly served by a lesser nickname, such as the one he was cursed with for the first half-decade of his career, the 'Crafty Potter', a nod to Taylor's home town of Stoke and its ceramics industry. It would have worked better if he'd played snooker, of course.

But 'The Power' came about, as many others have done, on the instigation of television. A junior producer at Sky Sports had decided that a particularly irritating hit, 'The Power' by Frankfurt-based Eurodance project Snap! would be a great walk-on tune. And, on the all-important visual level, Power began with a 'P', like Phil. Just about.

But others' names are more playfully framed. In his great rival and friend Dennis Priestley's case, his identity was literally cartoonish, since he branded himself as 'Dennis the Menace', thereby boxing himself immediately into a sartorial corner that involved wearing red and black striped shirts for the rest of his professional life, a not insignificant concession for a middle-aged coal merchant from Mexborough in South Yorkshire.

Terry Jenkins, a veteran player from Ledbury in Herefordshire, first got really good just as the darts started flying on Sky Sports in the early part of this century. An antiques dealer by profession (although, having visited his overflowing house, filled in every crevice with interesting collectibles, the term 'antiques' is loosely applied), Jenkins had neither a name that could be excitingly riffed on, nor did he have an identifiable physical characteristic that might lead towards an identity.

For example, Simon Whitlock arrived on the scene dressed like a ready-made nickname, with a long, bizarre dreadlock/mullet home-made haircut. That, coupled with the fact that he hailed from Australia, meant with total assuredness that he would for ever be called 'The Wizard of Oz', since all known wizards have haircuts that are a cross between a mullet and dreadlocks.

Jenkins was not so lucky. However, a slight reddening of the cheeks gave another tuned-in Sky Sports producer an idea. Living, as he did, in Herefordshire, it was ordained that Terry Jenkins would henceforth be known as 'The Bull', and would take to the stage to the tune of 'Wooly Bully' by Sam the Sham & the Pharaohs. Once planted centre stage, he stamps his hooves and places both darts on the top of his head, as if they were horns. The crowd adore this more than they adore the actual ensuing darts match, and in some cases, more than life itself. They are sent into raptures. 'I don't mind it,' admits the softly spoken Jenkins. 'I quite like it, really.' Terry Jenkins is 55.

The fashion for a well-chosen nickname shows no signs of giving way. The top players mainly enjoy well-crafted images, most notably Adrian Lewis, known as 'Jackpot'. There's something perfectly fitting about this name, as it calls to mind a cascade of good fortune, effortlessly chugging forth its reward. This fits hand in glove with the public's well-founded perception of Lewis as a happy-go-lucky, untroubled soul, whose latent talent is uncontainable.

The story behind the genesis of the name is just as fitting. In 2005, and still just 20, Lewis joined the party of senior pros who flew over to Las Vegas to compete in the Desert Classic tournament. He was under the informal tutelage of Phil Taylor at the time, who had long since identified the big youngster as his natural successor. But, for all that he was there to help the kid out, Taylor could do nothing about the predicament Lewis found himself in when a fruit machine he had been playing suddenly coughed out the maximum jackpot of $72,000. However, in the eyes of Nevada's questionably inconsistent laws, Lewis was too young to have been playing the machines in the first place and was denied his winner's prize. In fact, only judicious intervention by the men in charge of the tournament prevented the youngster from being arrested. The money slipped through his fingers. A hefty blow, you would imagine, but the nickname and the legend were born. And the £2 million he's won in prize money alone since then must have gone some way towards mitigating the pain.

'Jackpot' is not alone in sporting a first-class nickname. 'Rocket' Ronnie Baxter, with his cryogenic liquid propellant personality is a good fit, given that he is liable to ignite and soar vertically through the ceiling at the slightest provocation. In fairness, Baxter's immolations were normally reserved for late-night fireworks, and he rarely exploded onstage. But one would be well advised to be wary of 'The Rocket'.

Colin Lloyd, aka 'Jaws', struck a chord with the public, too. Touted as a genuine threat to the Taylor hegemony of the mid-nineties and early part of this century, 'Jaws' was a likeable stable lad turned darts pro from Essex, who once confessed to me an improbable fondness, bordering on obsession, for quiche. He had acquired the shark-like nickname simply by virtue of his ragged incisors, whose sharpness, I felt, was wasted on quiche. That in turn led to his choice of walk-on music, 'Monster' by the Automatic. It brought the crowds to a point of frenzy. They shouted the chorus back at Lloyd as he made his way to the stage. 'IS IT A MON-STERRR?' Lloyd, by no means a natural athlete, obliged with a trademark pirouette, arms outstretched. I once tried to copy this simple-looking move, under his instruction, in a hotel suite in Dublin. I failed repeatedly, tripping over my own feet, unable even approximately to mimic Lloyd's fluency of motion, and my respect for 'Jaws' grew commensurately.

Two-time PDC world champion 'Darth Maple' John Part (he's Canadian, you see) is by any measurement a standout weird nickname in a world populated by oddities. Part has publicly admitted to not really being that bothered about *Star Wars*, and he doesn't walk onstage in a cape, nor with a black mask obscuring his benign matinee-idol features. He just wears a black shirt and a pair of sensible strides. Nevertheless, it somehow fits. He's a huge, spooky-looking figure, vaguely intimidating, with perhaps a hint of the dark side. He's actually an extremely affable man, and is one of the game's great thinkers as well as commentators, full of philosophical distinctions and nuanced psychological observation. But, there you have it: 'Darth Maple'. It doesn't even rhyme with 'Vader'.

The retired pro Denis 'The Heat' Ovens, on the other hand, provides an interesting counterpoint. His unusual surname cannot pass uncommented on. After all, he is the only man I have ever met who is literally named after a kitchen appliance, and in that regard, I guess 'The Heat' is as good an option as any other. And his walk-on to 'The Heat Is On' by Glenn Frey was a joy to behold, especially when the ever-increasing urgency of Frey's *'Tell me can you feel it'* was answered simply by a raised eyebrow from the extremely muted Ovens. And that's where the metaphor disengaged with reality. For I have never met a more stolid, unflappable, dry character in all my life, a man who managed to bring the audience to their seats rather than their feet during his profoundly un-thrilling approach to the stage. Ovens looked like he was walking to the local branch of Wickes to collect a few lengths of two-by-four and a litre of undercoat.

A builder in his late forties at the time, Ovens spent the first few years of our acquaintance trying to pitch for my business when he found out I was having some double glazing replaced. Sometimes a year would pass since I had last seen him, but that didn't stop him from enquiring, 'Got those windows done yet?'

'Not yet, Denis.'

'How many do you want to do? I can do you a price...'

Then there are the nicknames that should never have been chosen. Some players have got off to a bad baptism and never had the guile to change their image. Paul Nicholson, a young, slim, exceedingly thoughtful Geordie, decided to market himself as a villain. However, by nature, he simply isn't a villain. But now he's stuck with being a villain, which is tough.

His New Age beliefs, and predilection for crystal-based meditative energy-gathering led him misguidedly to believe that it might be a good idea to walk onstage wearing a pencil tie, shades and a poker face, broken only to sneer at the audience. This he coupled with the dreadful nickname 'The Asset', based on some dastardly character in a third-rate film that no one seems to have seen. This led to a cacophony of abuse from the crowd, wherever he went and whoever he played.

After a few good years, including winning the Players Championship at the Circus Tavern, he has lost his way in professional darts and is instead turning into an excellent commentator. But he still clings to the misguided name when he does play. Were I him, I would have opted for something less provocative. And I certainly wouldn't have walked onstage and pretended to shoot the audience, Columbine-style, with my two fingers, and 'blown the smoke' from my fingertips.

Even more established nicknames do not always stand up to close examination. Joe Cullen, young, good-looking, very decent at darts and eminently marketable, has taken the nickname 'Rock Star'. I once quizzed him about it, with perhaps needless persistence.

'Do you sing, Joe?'

'No'.

'Can you play an instrument?'

'No.'

'So, why...'

'Don't know.'

Ian 'Diamond' White is another nickname that amuses me whenever I think about it, because Ian White, in his early fifties, from Stoke, is almost the only non-drinking player on the circuit. And he's the one named after a premium-strength cider.

He also amused me greatly by losing a final to Gary Anderson and then stomping through the back of the shot while Anderson was giving an interview, carrying a plastic bag with his coat on. He later told me that it was a homage to Eric Morecambe, and that the next time it happens, he's going to wield a broom and start sweeping up behind the victor.

Then there is the case of Wes Newton, 'The Warrior'. There is little warrior-like about the slightly nervy but cuddly lad from Fleetwood, whose darts career hovers just around the margins of viable. How he became 'The Warrior', I do not know.

One year Newton arrived to play the UK Open having helped his wife give birth the night before. The baby had come early, and quickly, and Newton had been there to help deliver it. And scarcely 24 hours later, he had shown up at Butlin's in Minehead to play darts; priorities, and all that.

'You should change your nickname, Wes,' I suggested to him after his first-round victory.

'What to?'

'Wes Newton: he delivers...' I thought out loud. 'The Deliverer'.

Newton looked at me sceptically. The Deliverer was a crap suggestion, and we both knew it.

'No, even better...' and then I hit upon it. 'The Midwife!'

And we imagined him walking onto the stage with a plastic baby doll and a pair of forceps.

'I think I'll stick with The Warrior, Ned.' And he went off to the bar to get a drink.

I watched the former accounts assistant stroll up and politely order a lager in his red darts shirt, with the gothic 'Warrior' logo dripping blood on his back. I could see where he was coming from. I let him off the hook.

So you see, in darts, as in life, you take what you are given. Make your peace with it and settle for what works. And don't ask too many questions; it doesn't have to stack up. And don't pretend to be something you're not.

Unless you think it's funny, in which case, on balance, you probably should.

Cliff Edge

The wooded banks slipped past us slowly, the
short noise was left behind, the interminable miles
of silence – and we crept on, towards Kurtz.

JOSEPH CONRAD – *HEART OF DARKNESS*

During my journey into darts' hinterland, I was discovering that burrowing further into the history of the sport meant turning your back on the future. The shape of the game to come would take care of itself. I was increasingly filled with a sense of urgency about its vanishing past, slipping away round each successive twist and turn in its fluid timeline, and disappearing out of view as one by one the men who had defined its spirit passed into retirement, or simply passed away. Jocky Wilson had led the way; Sid Waddell had gone. More would follow, as follow they must.

Often, eating breakfast in some hotel during a darts tournament we were covering for ITV, I listened, slightly aghast, to the likes of Chris Mason, Alan Warriner-Little and Keith Deller talk about the old days of the circuit.

For the most part, that talk meant celebrating and complaining about Eric Bristow: Bristow cutting people down; Bristow walking out on obligations; Bristow sneering. Bristow, brilliant before he lost the ability to throw. The closer I seemed to get to him, the more he drifted away, taking on the shape in these ever wilder stories of something supernatural, a kind of darting shaman. His peers spoke with awe. They couldn't help it.

I knew I'd have to face up to Bristow's overpowering legend one day. But the closer that moment came, the harder it seemed. For some reason I felt unwilling to ask Keith Deller for his number, and still less could I entertain the possibility of ever dialling it. Something was blocking me.

I treasured these breakfasts. These were our lingering mornings, before the darkness of the darts venue would obliterate all sense of time once more. I never tired of listening to these old friends talking about life on the road. Their tales, each one trumping the next and growing in implausible decadence,

seemed made up purely for our listening pleasure. But the thing that made them irresistible was their stunningly unlikely basis in truth, underpinned by the knowledge that they were stunningly true. This really was what it had been like: boozing, darting, womanising (a word that has fallen correctly into disrepute), laughing, darting some more and then boozing. In fact, all the while, there was the boozing. That was the constant.

'Who was the biggest drinker of them all?' Sometimes, looking up from spreading marmalade on toast, I'd ask that question, knowing already what the answer would be. Every time, in fact, it was the same. And never did it disappoint.

'Big Cliff.'

I never got bored of asking, and seemingly, they never tired of answering.

'Cliff.' They'd all nod. 'Definitely Lazarenko.' Then they'd shake their heads.

'No one, but no one, could fucking touch him when it came to drinking. I tried once or twice. Nearly killed me. He was made of... fuck knows what.'

It seemed impossible to articulate the name of Cliff Fucking Lazarenko without its customary fulsome, X-rated elaboration. He probably merits the full expletive, and he usually gets it. But, when his old acolytes remember him, his memory is graced with unusual and universal admiration, such that the swear word is not used out of spite. It is an affectionate F-bomb, deployed with a kind of awe-filled respect. Lazarenko is less a name, more of a notion, gargled back from memory with delight and wonder, and some horror.

The horror.

Big Cliff filling up a bathtub in his hotel room in Jersey with 40 bottles of white wine, and helping himself to gallons of the stuff by dunking in the tooth mug. If they were playing in the morning in a World Cup match, Lazarenko would set his alarm for 5:00am, and crack open a can as he put the kettle on to boil for a morning cuppa. Somewhere in the gloom of his hotel room, his room-mate (it was usually John Lowe) would open an eye just in time to see a can of cider winging its way through the air towards them. 'Get that down yer!'

Or the time he got on a plane to Canada with Eric Bristow. The details of this particular journey, recounted lovingly by Bristow himself in *The Crafty Cockney* are so extraordinary that I'd assumed they were all exaggerated.

The gist of it, according to Bristow (no mean drinker himself), is that after a 'good four or five pints' in Gatwick airport before the flight, he and Lazarenko then consumed 12 bottles of champagne between them en route to Toronto. Bristow's fame had resulted in them being upgraded to first class, even though the stewardesses thought they were about to welcome Cliff Thorburn, the suave snooker player, instead of Cliff Lazarenko, the ever-thirsty darter. Once the champagne was done, Big Cliff hit the Cointreau, followed by Baileys on ice, and then Southern Comfort, refilling his glass every ten minutes. During a four-hour stopover in Toronto, they calmed down a bit with a few beers, then got on a small connecting flight to St John during which Lazarenko broke wind with devastating effects, and the inebriated pair dissolved into helpless laughter. They landed, went straight to their hotel, 'had a couple' at the hotel bar before heading out for the British Legion, where they spent a few hours downing pints with spirit chasers. After visiting 'a couple of late-night bars' and 'a few more drinks' they returned to their hotel, and even though Bristow now attempted to crawl upstairs, he was summoned down again. It seems that it wasn't time for bed.

Big Cliff Lazarenko went and sat down at the bar. They did not leave the place until they had worked their way from left to right across the row of optics on display: vodka, brandy, whisky, gin, rum... there were a total of 18 bottles. They both had one shot of each.

Only after a late-night takeaway curry, they went to bed. Bristow was not seen for days after that. It nearly killed him.

The horror.

'Is that even half true, Cliff?'

We are drinking tea in his immaculate front room at his home in Wellingborough. I was expecting him to deny it, or at least shake his head and pour cold water over Bristow's artistic licence. But instead, he cocks his head at me and a smile plays over his features.

'Bang on. Yeah, it's bang on.' He roars with laughter. 'Eric didn't get out of bed for a day and a half.'

'So, everything is true?'

'About 98 per cent.' And I am left wondering where the missing two per cent lie. Perhaps one of the pints at Gatwick airport.

The Lazarenkos live in a very tidy 1960s house situated in a modest, very quiet estate on the outskirts of town, in a county that is neither here nor there. The brickwork is grey, the carpets are soft and cream, the photographs of the grandchildren are on the TV, and the kettle comes to the boil in a spotless, almost spartan kitchen. It is not the house of a hell-raiser.

Cliff Lazarenko sits in the main armchair in a blue pullover. He is rather bald and slightly baby-faced, a very tall man, still corpulent, his giant legs outstretched into the centre of the small living room, and his hands folded contentedly across his belly.

He has the same giant's build as his dad, a Canadian of Ukrainian descent from Winnipeg, who arrived in Britain with a false date of birth and the intention of joining up for a bit of action in the war. After doing his bit, he stayed on in England, handsome, tall, tanned and ready to step into the breach when he met the future Mrs Lazarenko and became stepfather to her three daughters, as well as, subsequently, father to young Cliff. Another son died in infancy at the hospital in Great Ormond Street.

They made their home in Liss in Hampshire, a village Lazarenko sums up as: 'Two pubs, one British Legion, surrounded by potato fields.' His father worked on the railways, and for 30 years his mother picked potatoes. Sometimes, when money was tight, his dad would switch to night shifts and join his wife in the fields for a few hours. It was back-breaking work. When the spuds were out of the ground, she'd go into giant barns to sort them and bag them.

Little Cliff grew into Big Cliff. He'd join his dad from time to time in the local and watch him playing darts, treasuring the golden taste of his semi-illicit shandy, swilling around in a tankard. At some time in his non-education, Cliff left school for good and started grafting on building sites.

But it was darts that captivated him. The game. There were three boards at home: one in the bedroom, one on the side of the garden shed and the main one in the sitting room. After his dad had finished his tea, and popped out to fetch a couple of bottles of mild, the entire Lazarenko family would settle in to play darts for two or three hours before bed.

He'd play almost every night of the week, and when there were no games to be had at home, he'd take his darts down to the Crossing Gate pub, home to the Maguire brothers. They were two Irish labourers who dug the irrigation in the low-lying potato fields in the valley. Coming home covered in thick, sticky Hampshire mud, one of them would bathe while the other practised on the dartboard with their precocious young friend. Then, when he was cleaned up, they'd swap over and the other Maguire brother would wash. As soon as both men were clean, young Lazarenko, reluctantly, had to leave them to tuck into their dinner.

But he had a good enough eye to know that he'd found his game. By now, in his late teens, nothing else mattered. It was, for Lazarenko, simply about the buzz of the booze, the thrill of the game, and the endlessly repeating cycle of winning, sometimes losing, but always drinking.

'By the time I was 18, I was playing four nights a week. And then I'd be down the pub on Saturday lunchtime playing darts. Saturday night, playing darts down the pub. Sunday morning I'd be sitting on the doorstep outside the pub with the old man, waiting for them to open.'

He started to win the local tournaments, then graduated on to bigger things. He took on the 'townies' in Portsmouth, where he was known as the 'boy from over the hill'. That hardened him up, but he had to wait a while for his big break.

Monday lunchtimes at his parents' house were an appointment to view the *Indoor League* on ITV. He vowed that within two years, he'd make an appearance on the show, a promise he kept. Lazarenko still clearly remembers the trip in the winter of 1976 to Leeds to do the filming for the series. It was the first time he was introduced to Sid Waddell, the show's producer, as he was back then. But his most vivid recollection is of the free drinks trolley that was wheeled into the players' practice room. Some things are just more important than darts.

It was 1976. Seen from the present day, it looks like a time of brown ale and brown wallpaper. The cars of the age, caught on the surviving sun-bleached 16-millimetre footage of the day, look breathtakingly old-fashioned, their chrome noses glinting at an uncertain future and away from a past that was fading like the ink on a Polaroid print: the burnt-out end of old Britain.

But there the darters were, booked into a city centre hotel, about to appear on television; an unimaginably glamorous opportunity, planted firmly in the middle of an increasingly embittered political and social landscape. All was not well in the country and Yorkshire Television was no exception.

Lazarenko recalls how his appearance on the show coincided with the three-day week and the power strikes. There was, he recalls, a dispute involving various different workers in the studios. Some of the set builders carried the dartboards from the van to the studio floor but refused to put them up, since that fell outside their job descriptions. To a labourer like Lazarenko, used to working outdoors on building sites, this must have appeared precious, to say the least. To cap it all, a power cut disrupted the filming of one of the final matches when all the lights in the studio went out. Everyone had to reassemble the following day to get it finished.

Later that year, his country called. In May 1976, Eric Bristow, John Lowe and Cliff Lazarenko all made their national debuts at the Tottenham Royal in the West End of London. In total, he would go on to appear over 50 times for England, but this was the first time of all.

Lazarenko's first opponent was John Assiratti, making the match-up an attractively exotic-sounding Assiratti versus Lazarenko. 'We were introduced as two ice-cream salesmen!' Actually, it was England versus Wales, at the time the greatest rivalry in the game of darts. Wales boasted Alan Evans and Leighton Rees, two of the very best, whose talent had held sway in the fading years of pre-televised darts. They were still major stars, even if they were about to be superseded by the rising tide of English talent, spearheaded by Lowe and Bristow. For Lazarenko, this sudden elevation was nothing short of mind-blowing.

The players were bussed into town from Camber Sands, where they'd all been playing in another tournament. They were joined on the bus by a group of supporters that included his mum and dad as well as his future wife Carol. This was her second date with Lazarenko. The first time he'd taken her out had also been to a game of darts, a local Superleague match in Portsmouth.

Neither Cliff nor Carol had ever seen anything on this scale before. There were 1,500 lager-swilling, fag-ash-sprinkling spectators in the venue, ratcheting up the national fervour. It was not uncommon for the crowd to get unhelpfully involved, as they did during an England v Scotland game, in which Eric Bristow was hit by an airborne, and still surprisingly full, can of Tennent's. These clashes were not for the faint-hearted. Even now, Lazarenko blanches at the memory. 'I didn't know whether I wanted to be sick or pass solids. I really didn't.'

He chuckles and adjusts himself in his seat. A clock ticks. This Cliff Lazarenko could hardly look any less like the Cliff Lazarenko of legend.

It must have been a fine life, full of plenty of highs, and a few lows, that could be easily self-medicated into amnesia. The oche was his stage, the spotlight, his natural environment. His career, much like that of Bristow and Lowe, spans the era when darts went from mainstream entertainment to ridiculed sideshow and then back into a more polished future. His tournament successes passed through four decades, starting in the late 1970s and only just beginning to fizzle out in the opening years of this millennium. But it was the eighties and the early nineties (he was one of the 16 rebels, a founding member of the PDC) that defined the Lazarenko years.

He was made for the circuit, as if perfectly designed from his DNA to his nylon slacks for the limitless time spent in average hotel rooms, gazing out of unopenable, slightly mildewed, double-glazed windows on to unlovely courtyards or car parks. He could swallow miserable hours frittering away the time in airport departure halls. He had a method, and no one executed it better than Big Cliff. He and John Lowe, in particular, the somewhat aloof thrower from Chesterfield, were joined at the hip. They shared a room, more often than not, and became a standing fixture of the circuit. If people wanted to know where the action was away from the competition, they simply found out what Lowe and Lazarenko were up to. Sometimes that might involve tearing the bar to bits, sometimes they might just find a blues club. Sometimes they'd go out for a bite to eat and a bottle of wine. Or three.

But, mostly it involved lager. In fact, few things didn't. If for Bristow, it was about the fags, then for Lazarenko, it was the lager. And the fags. As Phil Taylor recalls, the advent of Sky Television, with its commercial breaks every seven or eight minutes, was a boon for Lazarenko, who would 'sup on a lager' in the three minutes or so before the action resumed. Purpose-built for the big man to remain topped up.

Lazarenko didn't belong to the absolute elite. He wasn't part of that select band of players who jostled, and continue to jostle, for the status as 'one of the greats'. According to some records, he never won a 'major', by which is meant a televised world title of some description. But the subject of what, exactly, constitutes a 'major' is entirely contentious and continually debated in the darts world, and Lazarenko maintains that his

1977 victory at the nationally organised Marlboro Masters was just that. He also made something of a habit of winning the curiously named, and weirdly designed 'Dartsathlon', a defunct multi-disciplinary competition designed for the sport of darts to tap into the extraordinary popularity at the time of decathlete Daley Thompson. No one has been able to tell me what the other skill was, except for darts.

He has one third place finish in the 1981 Embassy to his name, and was a beaten quarter-finalist 18 years later, at the 1999 PDC World Championship. That was about the scale of his achievement: he was one of the world's best, without ever challenging for the very biggest honours. But the game he played afforded him a comfortable life, and took him around the world.

Cliff Lazarenko's photograph albums are a precious resource. They impart a concentrated dose of what the time was like and what the man was all about, where he did what he did, and when he did it. There's no great chronology to them, but each photograph has been neatly labelled by Carol.

SKEGNESS 1984
BOTSWANA 1986
QATAR 1985
STOKE 1987
SAN DIEGO 1981
LUTON 1985
TOKYO 1982

The pages are already fragile. Photo albums from the 1980s, up and down the land and in the living rooms and attics of people who were young then, and are now parents and grandparents, share certain traits. They resemble rare parchment manuscripts and must be treated extremely delicately for fear that the transparent sheathes that hold the photos onto the page, whisky-brown with age, will crackle and disintegrate when they're touched.

The photos, never fully in focus and often restricted to a colour palette that ranges from burgundy through magnolia to brown, tend to drop to the bottom of their page and slip onto the table. Glue has a shelf life. Each page turn becomes an exercise in restraint.

Big Cliff, with his big hands, is drifting through the pages. Each photograph, after a slightly myopic frown at Carol's lovingly applied caption, sets him off on a tangent: the Danish Open, the British Gold Cup in Warrington, the Dry Blackthorn in Oldham, the Jersey Open (which he won three times), the Matchplay, and the faces from faraway years, characters with whom he shared the road. He was a travelling act in a global circus.

'Ah, now. See her? She was a white witch, from New Zealand,' he says, pointing at a picture of a middle-aged lady who couldn't have looked less like a witch if she tried. 'She put this weird sort of spell, a kind of blessing on me, started sprinkling me with all these leaves from this little pouch.' A couple of days later, an engine caught fire on a 747 he and Eric Bristow caught from Wellington. He's wondered ever since if it was her dark doing. And so too did Bristow, apparently. Repeatedly, and loudly.

The names are coming thick and fast now. 'There's Stefan Lord. His father was big in Swedish airlines. He bought him a nightclub for his 21st birthday.' Lord was a fixture of the scene in the eighties, as well known to the British public as most of the others, but anonymous back home. Such was the fate of the overseas player. 'He used to be a massive gambler.' He turns the page.

'There's Conrad Daniels. Oh, he was a hell of a man. A tough man to play.' Lazarenko describes how slow the American

'Conny' was on the oche. In between every shot he used to light a fag, take a drag, put it down in the ashtray, wipe his hands, have another drag, and then throw the second one. 'I played him on the floor once. I reckon five people must have gone to the bar to get me a drink in those seven legs.'

Then he points at a man with a cowboy hat on. 'There I am again, look.'

There's Cliff with a trophy in a nightclub; Cliff with a group of friends at the table of a Chinese restaurant on the Southend Road in Basildon; Cliff posing in front of a plane; Cliff with John Lowe by the pool in Las Vegas; Cliff on a cliff in Botswana; Cliff at the top of the Empire State Building, where, to his delight, he happened upon a Yorkshire TV sticker on the wall.

Then there's Cliff and Eric on a yacht in Qatar, the personal guests of the cousin of Sheikh Maktoum ('I will get you drunk, Mr Cliff, so that you will lose to Mr Eric. It's good business for me'). But, in most pictures, Cliff with a smile, a handshake, another smile and always a drink on the go.

He was quite a physical specimen, still is, in fact: six foot four inches tall, olive-skinned, high cheekbones and clear blue eyes. In a way, he's more boxer than darter.

He was pugnacious, too. What remains one of his most enduring moments on the darting stage was caught by the ITV cameras at the MFI tournament in Slough in 1983. He checks out to beat Jocky Wilson in the sudden death decider of a tightly fought contest. Wilson visibly tells him to 'fuck off' and refuses to shake Lazarenko's outstretched hand, walking off stage to leave his opponent stranded.

'Jocky!' Lazarenko calls after him. What follows is an almost cartoonish, 'up yours!' gesture, complete with right hand clasped to the left bicep as the middle finger of the offending hand is thrust skywards. The intent is clear enough, but if there were any room for doubt, Lazarenko clearly mouths the accompanying obscenity. The commentator interprets: 'That suddenly has soured the whole occasion. Lazarenko is clearly unhappy.'

The whole incident, reducing darts to an unseemly squabble, was watched by a massive Saturday afternoon audience on *World of Sport*.

But on the Monday, as if nothing had happened, they were sitting on a flight together en route to the next weekend of drinking and throwing somewhere else in the darting firmament. Jocky Wilson was no doubt indulging his habit of sucking the coating off dry roasted peanuts and handing them round as if they were ordinary salted ones. It's hard to hold a grudge for long, hard and not much fun, which defeats the point of playing darts.

'You boys were superstars, weren't you?' I say. 'You were on the telly all the time. Everyone knew who you were.'

'I guess we were.' Memory clouds his expression then he smiles. 'I guess we were.' And Cliff Lazarenko laughs loudly and scratches his chin ruminatively. He takes a noisy slurp of tea.

'You see, people could relate to us. They couldn't really relate to golf players. You had to be at a certain level of society to get into a golf course, I suppose, not that I really know. I don't play the game. Anyone can play darts. From nine to 90.' He thinks again. 'It was nice to get that attention. It still is nice. It's still happening now.'

From time to time, someone will come through the doors of the little pub that Lazarenko still frequents, and ask him about the good old days. They hang on his every word.

'I found it difficult at times, though. Because I always believed it was "only darts". I'm only a dart player. I found it difficult when someone changed their behaviour, when they tried to be nicer because I was in their company. I used to tell them to drop all that crap. Just be you! When I fall over I don't bleed blue, you know? I'm not royalty or nothing!'

He's 66 now, and that fact alone takes some explanation. Much of his survival, he credits to Carol. 'You ask Eric, he'll tell you. If I hadn't met Carol, I'd have been dead. She put up with a lot of shit. She's been by my side ever since.'

It was returning to the flat one night after a few years on the circuit that the penny dropped with Lazarenko. He would need to have Carol by his side to temper the worst of his excesses. If he didn't do that, the lifestyle would almost certainly kill him. 'I told her she'd got to learn to drive and come on the road with me. I wasn't coping. I wasn't going to survive.

'The problem was I didn't know when to stop. You shouldn't be proud of what your intake is. You shouldn't be proud of that. The three drinks that you need at the start of your career is no longer enough. Then it's four, then it's five…'

His long sessions were extremely long, though. As well as the legendary binge with Bristow, he once tried to match Canadian snooker player Bill Werbeniuk pint for pint. Werbeniuk was also, curiously, from the same stock, a Winnipeg descendant of

Ukrainian ancestry, whose father, in his own words, 'was one of the biggest fences in Canada' and 'committed armed robberies, peddled drugs, every larceny in the language'.

On that particular evening they celebrated their shared ancestry by each downing 'about 25 pints' ('only Heineken, mind'). This was not particularly unusual behaviour for Hampshire's most famous Ukrainian-Canadian darts player.

Yet, it was not entirely out of control, as the physical presence of the man I am sitting opposite testifies. Despite appearances to the contrary, he had his limits. Even the famously cavalier drinker Lazarenko drew a non-negotiable red line.

'I always said, if I was touring, I'd never take a bottle of liquor to my hotel room on my own.' He allows that principle to sink in, and then qualifies it somewhat. 'I'd go and get a six pack,' he adds.

'Of course if I was sharing with somebody, like I shared with Lowey for 20 years,' he continues, in a more cheerful vein, 'we'd always have a bottle of brandy on the go. And some beer. And that.'

He once took a guest from America on the road to experience it. He was a very dapper, well-heeled character, who was nearly ruined by a few days living the life of John Lowe and Cliff Lazarenko as they stumbled across the country, clocking up the miles, churning through the takeaways, idling at bars with total strangers, chucking darts and sinking pints. What started in Eastbourne ended six days later in a tiny back-street bar in Liverpool. The following day, they simply couldn't get the American out of bed. 'How do you do it, Cliff?' he asked his host in awe. 'I mean how do you do it?'

A while ago, he had a scare when he started to get a pain in the back of his leg. He had just come back from a 'boys' weekend' in Great Yarmouth. Thinking nothing of it, he carried on his normal way of doing things, as darts players are wont to do, until it became slightly more critical, and the doctor diagnosed cardiac arrhythmia, and immediately put him on a regime of beta blockers.

'Do you binge drink?' the doctor had asked.

'Yes.' Nothing like a bit of honesty.

'Right. Lose some weight.'

'So, basically, I just shut the doors. I cut myself off.'

He stopped with the booze completely, and within months he'd lost 30 pounds. But when he went back to see the consultant, expecting a pat on the back for his efforts, was rather curtly told that, 'That would be entirely what one would have expected, given how much you drank.'

This was not what Lazarenko wanted to hear; the schoolmasterly tone incensed him. Under the table, Big Cliff's right hand had formed a fist. The doctor might well have found himself with a cracked nose, had Carol not shot him one of her rebuking looks. Big Cliff left the surgery, with his health intact, but no real intention of mending his ways for ever.

It's been about seven or eight years since Lazarenko stopped playing darts for money, save for the very occasional opportunity.

'It must have been quite punishing, as well, I suppose,' I suggest, thinking back to his long career, and the countless pubs along the way.

'Yeah, but...' There is a long pause. Long enough for the tiny metallic sound of carriage clock on the mantelpiece to fill the carpeted space. And as I wait for Cliff Lazarenko to answer me, I can feel the presence of his old mate somewhere in the moment, perhaps in his thoughts, perhaps sitting in a pub somewhere thinking about the passage of time, recollecting Big Cliff. Bristow, I thought. Eric.

'I loved every minute of it. I was just in it. I was enthralled in it. And the money was great!'

And does he still drink?

'Oh yeah. There's a case of 'bow in the garage out the back.'
Strongbow.

The Point

Arrows, by Jove! We were being shot at!

JOSEPH CONRAD – *HEART OF DARKNESS*

One day, playing darts barefoot in my front room, which, unlike the Lazarenkos', has a dartboard, I managed to nick the fleshy part of my right foot, just behind my middle toe. The dart had bounced out of some unremarkable berth, probably a double three, when I'd been aiming for twenties.

'Ow,' I said. To no one.

But the incident served to remind me: the dart is a weapon. It has a pointed end and is designed to fly in the direction of a target, which it then pierces. Every single history of the sport aligns it with some hunting or warfaring origin. That fact shouldn't be entirely overlooked when examining with headlong, hedonistic admiration the sheer frivolity of the game: the dart is a right nasty bastard.

I considered again Conrad's narrator Marlow, navigating the Congo, ever deeper into the jungle, drawn on towards the grim spectral figure of Kurtz, when his riverboat is ambushed by a native tribe, and his helmsman is impaled through the chest by a spear.

It's remarkable, I thought, swabbing a little Savlon on my tiny wound, that given the pressure, the stakes and the sheer intoxication of darting competition, A&E isn't awash with comedy admissions from middle-aged men with darts sticking out of their heads at jaunty angles. I resolved, in future, to wear shoes while playing darts.

On closer examination, It appeared that I was not the first person to think about this, as the search engine algorithm completed my sentence before it was even halfway: 'can a dart…'. In fact, in answer to the vexed question, 'Can a dart kill?' one user has replied, rather fulsomely, on Yahoo Answers, that 'the chances of a dart hitting your jugular and actually making a large enough hole to lose blood is slim to none. Poison-tipped darts and darts dipped in human faecal matter are really the only ways to kill someone with a dart. Other than that, there is not really a chance you'll die from a dart.' He goes on to add, 'Unless it's rusty, and you don't get treated for tetanus and get lockjaw, then you'll die.' Darts folk have a penchant for straightforwardness.

But, nonetheless, the risks associated with darts are not negligible. In 1989, close to the height of darts' popularity in mainstream culture, Dr B.C.K. Patel of the Manchester Royal Eye Hospital published a medical research paper titled 'Penetrating Eye Injuries', in which he analysed the causes of all admissions to his unit over a four-year period starting in 1982, two weeks before Jocky Wilson was crowned world champion by beating John Lowe in the final. The period of research ended on the 31 December 1985, just 12 days before Eric Bristow won his fifth world title.

During that period of time, 68 children from Manchester were treated for penetrating eye injuries, and the leading single cause of injury was identified as darts, narrowly edging out glass, knives, airgun pellets, stones, twigs, bicycles, scissors, pens, forks, needles and coat hangers, as well, mysteriously, as radiators. A dart thrown by another person caused four of these injuries, of which two cases were the result of a brother with a bad or possibly malicious aim. Two more were 'bounce-outs' and there were a couple of cases of stabbing, presumably, although not necessarily, with the flights rather than the tips, after pulling the darts out of the board.

'In two major studies of penetrating eye injuries,' writes Patel, 'between 1950 and 1960 *none* were caused by darts… The game of darts was until recently an adult sport played largely in public houses. In recent years, the sport has received extensive television coverage and has therefore become very popular.'

Even a cursory glance through the collective memory of a nation's image bank will remind us that darts have, historically, been used as, well, darts. In the heady days of unfettered football hooliganism, and in those longed-for innocent days before all-seater stadia and the Taylor report, it was, for some, *de rigueur* to go the match with a ready supply of brass 'bomber' darts to be unleashed against the foe. Since darts were popular and readily available weapons, they were easily grabbed by the fistful from the half-pint jug near the dartboard in whatever clapped-out boozer you visited on the way to the ground. This was the nasty prelapsarian truth, which, along with urinating where you stood, drinking Bovril and abusing black players, disfigured the national game for a generation or two.

In the late seventies and early eighties, accounts abounded of fans being showered with darts falling from the sky, from Roker Park to Stamford Bridge. There is a famous photograph of a Manchester United fan with a dart in his face being led away from the ground by a policeman. The weapon is embedded at an angle in the bridge of his nose at the very edge of his eye socket, and must have missed piercing his eyeball by a matter of millimetres. Curiously, he doesn't appear that bothered. I wonder what he's doing now? Perhaps he's got a framed copy

of that picture hanging behind the bar of his local. It might, conceivably, be his screensaver or his Tinder avatar.

The eye, with its pupil for a bullseye and iris for the twenty-five, is a soft target, whose injury is the stuff of nightmares. I remember getting a job in the summer of 1990 as an operating theatre orderly at King's College Hospital in Camberwell. The first operation I witnessed was an incision to the eyeball, enlarged onto a TV screen so the surgeon could see what he was slicing; a grisly video installation like a late 20th-century echo of Salvador Dalí and Luis Buñuel's 1929 surrealist masterpiece *Un Chien Andalou*. That film assaulted its viewers from the very first scenes, one of which depicts a woman's eyeball being slashed with a razor blade as a thin cloud passes in front of the moon. It's shocking, even now. Appropriately enough, the scene was shot, according to Buñuel, using a real calf's eyeball. In a very real sense, it was a bullseye.

There have also been a number of more recent instances in film where the dart, and its violent misuse, has featured to dramatic if gruesome effect. In the much-celebrated *The Football Factory*, Billy Bright, the most acutely psychopathic character in a broadly dysfunctional cast, gets his two sons to throw darts at the chests of two burglars, whom he has dressed in T-shirts with dartboard patterns. The two boys are remarkably good shots, and both the unfortunates take blows to the bullseye, which sits over the heart. In the end, though, it is not a dart so much as a firm kick in the bollocks from one of Billy's charming offspring that forces them to reveal which of them stole the PlayStation.

In *Shaun of the Dead*, when the sole survivors of the zombie apocalypse head for the Winchester pub, Simon Pegg and Nick Frost have reason to give thanks for the fact that their local still has a dartboard. When the zombies finally smash down the door and enter the pub, a dart is one of the weapons used on them by Liz. Unfortunately, her aim leaves something to be desired, and she strikes the back of Simon Pegg's head, leaving the dart lodged uncomfortably in the base of his skull. But in the grand scheme of things, it's a small comic detail in an otherwise blood-soaked finale. Darts almost always gets a cameo role rather than a romantic lead.

There is also a comic darting interlude in Mel Brooks' *Young Frankenstein*, in which Gene Wilder, playing Dr Frankenstein, visits the oche. He is armed, puzzlingly, with five darts, which just feels wrong. All of his shots miss the target, most of them smashing through a glass door, and one of them impaling a cat. We don't see the cat's injury, but we hear its comedic feline shriek off camera, apparently the result of some Brooksian ad-libbing during the shoot.

And in 2013, the cult US sitcom *It's Always Sunny In Philadelphia* featured a scene in which one of its principal characters gets his hand impaled on the bullseye in some misguided game of bravado in the Irish bar they all hang out in.

It's a gruesome scene, which prompted some viewers to wonder whether David Lynch had been hired in as a guest director. Or perhaps Luis Buñuel.

The 2007 short film *Dartsville* begins with the memorable voice-over: 'Now life's pretty simple here in Dartsville, cos there's only two things a man can do: throw darts.' It's a film that also features maiming by way of darts. In fact, it is not just the unfortunate, bespectacled Dee Jay who gets hideously disfigured (a dart thrown by his best friend Randy pierces his glasses, and removes an eyeball), the actual game of darts gets a pretty impressive mauling to boot.

Dartsville is an overblown comedy turned up to 11, set in an imaginary, and yet unimaginably, backward Hicksville town, where everyone sports a mullet and wears sleeveless T-shirts cut off at the midriff. The film tells the story of a darts-obsessed father and son, and how the son avenges his abusive father's darting loss of face by winning the annual 'tourney'. In a fundamentally reductive portrayal of the game, every dart is pitched baseball-style at the board, with a lift of the leg and a whoosh of the arm, and it is only ever the bullseye that is aimed for, as if nothing else matters. I can imagine darts purists watching the film in unamused horror, and they'd be right as well. There is something sneering about it, because the white poor are the film's bullseye. They're an easy target.

Dartsville almost redeems itself at the end, with the half-decent pay-off, 'You see, there comes a time in every man's life when he realises that everything he's ever known is absolute crap. Except darts.'

And, proving that in the darting constellation fiction is not necessarily stranger than fact, there was a minor, but very real furore back in 2011 when the maverick (and not very good) Italian striker Mario Balotelli was sanctioned for lobbing darts out of the window at members of the Manchester City youth team. There followed, in the online community, a plethora of jokes about none of them hitting the intended target.

Of all the players in the league most likely to throw darts at children, it was probably going to be Mario Balotelli, a man I interviewed on the Wembley pitch after he'd been part of Manchester City's FA Cup-winning team, during the course of which interview, he became the first player in the history of the venerable competition to use the word 'shit' live on national TV.

In some ways, Balotelli was born not for football, but perhaps for darts, where his rough edges and extrovert personality would have been welcomed with open arms, and without the need for broadsheet newspapers to fill their pages with sanctimonious columns and overwrought reflections on the deep divisions within contemporary Italian society. A simple pair of chequered trousers, a pouch with three darts, a couple of pints and a bit of hair dye would have done the trick. The fact of the matter is that darts, like Mario Balotelli, are really rather unlikely to kill anyone, even when they form an unholy alliance.

Darts players, in my experience, find all manner of ways of hurting themselves, without resorting to the extreme measure of misusing the tools of their trade, although at the 2018 Masters, Dave Chisnall, throwing for the match, managed somehow to stab himself in the crotch with his second dart. But there is a spectacular variety of ways in which they can pick up tournament, or even career-ending, physical impairments. A twisted ankle is common. Kirk Shepherd famously twisted his ankle when he stumbled into some of the stage furniture celebrating a win in Wolverhampton at the Grand Slam. But then again, Shepherd often found walking in a straight line something of a challenge after an evening preparing for action.

Peter Wright did the same thing to himself when playing against Adrian Lewis and could barely walk the next day, let alone jig across the stage in his trademark characterful slacks. And Lewis himself played a match at the European Championships with deep lacerations to a finger and his thumb that required stitches. This was a bar-room injury resulting from an act of selfless intervention. 'A glass fell from a table and I tried to catch it on the bounce, but it shattered in my hand.' Lewis is far from alone among darts players in coming to grief in a pub.

But the attrition of the repeated walk to the oche, the twist, throw, pluck and return should not be underestimated, especially when it affects those players with a more dynamic muscular action. Belgian rising star Kim Huybrechts has battled a bad back in the past, as have Gary Anderson and Mervyn King and Vincent van der Voort. Even the great Michael van Gerwen, a man whose physiology, at first glance, appears to have few bones or muscles to strain or fracture, succumbed to an injury that denied him the opportunity of defending his 2016 UK Open title. A few days before flying over to the UK, he found himself flying through the air and landing on his back when negotiating some particularly slippery kitchen tiles in his Netherlands home. This fall was not without its irony, given that van Gerwen had previously worked as a tiler.

And again, in 2017, he had to withdraw from the German Masters after suffering from an inflammation of the ankle known as bursitis, an injury more commonly found, according to the NHS Choices website, in elbows. 'Your risk,' according to the official advice, 'of developing bursitis is increased if you regularly take part in physical activities that involve a lot of repetitive movement, for example running (bursitis in the ankle) or playing darts (bursitis in the elbow).' Van Gerwen, a man who doesn't knowingly run, contracted bursitis of the ankle.

An amateur player called Andy Relf, who also happens to be the President of the Darts Injury Society (an office which must be among the most niche in the world), lists three ailments from which he suffers after years of practice: a torn rotator cuff muscle (from throwing), torn anterior cruciate ligament (the result of a knee joint constantly thrust into a right angle) and a displaced navicular bone in his foot (pushed out of alignment after being repeatedly pushed against the oche). It sounds pretty ghastly.

Bad backs may be one thing; permanent disability is quite another. Remarkably enough, there is a professional player who has completely lost the sight in one eye, as a result of a 'penetrating eye injury' and yet continues to function at an extremely high standard, rising through the rankings to the top 30.

Jamie Caven is one of the most highly regarded men on the circuit, a warm, positive, friendly presence at any tournament he takes part in. He lollops around the players' bar and warm-up area, bald, dozy-looking and grinning. But everywhere he goes he meets friends, for a more affable, generous and cheerful man you'd be hard pushed to meet. At the age of just 15 months, while he was being taken out for a trip with his uncle, he suddenly started to scream. He'd been stung by a wasp, or so the medical practice concluded, when, six operations later, they had to concede that they would never be able to save the sight in his right eye.

That he can throw darts at this world-class level is something of a medical and technical mystery, in a sport that is surely all about hand-eye coordination and 3D visualisation. In fact, it's almost mystic. In his own words, 'I do not really see the target and I do not really see the flight of the darts,' he writes in his wonderfully titled autobiography *The Way Eye See The Game*. Only a darts player would try to pun his way around a life-changing injury.

And if his partial blindness wasn't a big enough disadvantage, he also has to contend with another, equally serious condition. Caven has an extreme form of type 1 diabetes after his cancerous pancreas was removed when he was in his twenties. These days, he injects himself as often as four times a day with insulin, a necessary habit that has earned him one of the best nicknames on the circuit. Darts being a fairly unreconstructed environment, and not a bastion of political correctness or sensitivity, Jamie Caven's medical treatment has been rewarded by the nickname 'Jabba'. His darts persona is therefore based on the sheer mirth of diabetes, and the need for medication.

But not everything is jolly in the world of darts. Pain can be inflicted intentionally, sometimes maliciously. The leading darts player who deliberately stabbed the hand of a pub landlady he found unreasonably irritating during an exhibition evening will go unnamed, as the recipient of the wound might well still harbour a justifiable grudge, even though the incident happened 20 years ago. But it serves as a grisly reminder that the game is a metaphor for airborne combat; and a rather lifelike one at that.

Jocky Wilson, forever prowling the scene like your best mate's untrustworthy older brother, was responsible for quite a serious injury involving a fellow professional during an exhibition. The player in question was the 'Prince of Style' himself, Rod Harrington. I had often heard tell of this particular encounter, but like so many other darting stories I put it down to exuberance, hyperbole and addled memory. I was wrong.

Tracking down the still immaculately groomed Harrington, I asked him if the thing with Jocky Wilson had really happened. 'Oh yes,' he assured me, when I relayed to him the version of events I'd heard, 'but it was worse than that.'

Harrington used to have a great darts trick, an almost unbelievable trick, in fact. His big showpiece number would stun the audiences at exhibitions on the circuit. It went like this: he would stand next to the board, get a player to throw at the treble 20, and catch the dart in mid-air with his hand, as if he were trapping a mayfly. How you get good at this very particular and challenging skill, and how much blood is spilled in the process, was anyone's guess. But Harrington had perfected the art.

'Can you still do it, Rod?' I asked him, astounded at the very thought of it.

'Fuck, no.'

Perhaps he had some of his enthusiasm for the trick taken away from him that evening in a pub in Windsor. Something was winding Jocky up, turning him from a rough-edged and unpredictable Scottish darter into a rough-edged and thoroughly predictable Scottish darter. He was going to do something quite dangerous, quite soon. It was only a matter of what, and to whom. And, as it happened, the dangerous thing was done to Harrington.

'Oi!' the Scotsman yelled at his exhibition partner. 'Catch this, you cunt!'

And with that Jocky Wilson threw a dart, overarm, as hard as he could at the two-time World Matchplay winner.

It landed in his midriff, just above the waistline, pierced the skin, and stuck. It was Harrington's wont to wear well-tailored white shirts, and soon there was a pool of blood spreading out like a duelling wound in a Musketeer film. He looked down at the injury, aghast. 'What did you do that for, Jocky?'

The thing is that no one knew. How could they know? Because in all likelihood Jocky didn't even know why he'd assaulted a fellow professional with a small arrow. It may have had something to do with lager. In fact, thinking about it, it almost certainly did.

Testimony such as that would almost seem to justify a formerly widely held view of darts' immorality. In the sixteenth century, a minister from Devon called John Northbrooke wrote a killjoy tract entitled *A Treatise against Dicing, Dancing, Plays, and Interludes: with Other Idle Pastimes.* This puritanical diatribe takes the form of an imagined conversation between two characters known as *Youth* and *Age*, who debate the evils of, well, things that *Age* doesn't approve of, basically. *Age* doesn't like the theatre at all, for example, and suggests that actors should be punished by being 'burned through the ear with a hot iron of an inch compass'. You get the idea.

And that's before he's even mentioned darts, which he dismisses with not quite the same passion. In perhaps the least interesting passage in the treatise, the game of arrows gets a dishonourable mention when *Age* warns *Youth* of the many 'ydle playes and vaine pastimes' of which 'throwing the darte' is most definitely one.

Much of the more contemporary moralising literature on the subject of the dangers of darts draws heavily on a very specific (and mostly North American) interpretation of Evil and the weapons of Evil. Darts are mostly to be considered a very bad thing, according to the Bible. Indeed, in the King James Version, Ephesians 6:16, St. Paul advises, in no uncertain terms, 'taking the shield of faith, wherewith ye shall be able to quench the fiery darts of the wicked'.

That phrase has been oft-quoted in contemporary evangelical literature, and not always comprehensibly. Joseph Hall's mysteriously titled and disappointingly out of print *Satan's Fiery Darts Quenched* features the following cryptic, almost satanically garbled passage, according to an extract on its Amazon page:

> It is thy malicioufaeflc that would make the affliction oFmy body the bane of my foule: but if the fault be not mine, that which thou intendeft for a poyfon (hall Jam. i. 4. prove a cordial!

And, if that horrifying script wasn't enough to scare you witless, then another book makes the moral threat of the humble dart much more explicit. Janet Warren Lane's *Fiery Darts: Satan's Weapon of Choice* documents the many small wounds that the Prince of Darkness likes to inflict.

'The smallness of a dart,' writes Lane, 'makes it subtle, thus, dangerous.' Mostly, according to the work's author, a retired schoolteacher and minister's wife from Polk County, Iowa, these Satanic darts seem to invoke in their victim an almost irresistible temptation to commit adultery. Each dart is, in isolation, a negligible blow, but their cumulative effect can drag its victim down into the moral swill, whence they will never return.

There is, for Warren Lane, little that is good about the humble dart. 'Be assured that Satan is preparing the *fiery darts* to deter you. He will make sure the *fiery darts* are so well disguised, you will not suspect that you are struggling with *fiery darts*,' she writes, using the phrase *fiery darts* three times in quick succession, as if imagining Lucifer engaged in a game of 501, or perhaps 666; a triptych of deviance, an unholy visit to the Oche of Hell, a devilish maximum.

It's worth noting, before we leave the realm of the spiritual and return to straightforward earthly vice, that the Bible also references the use of darts as a distinctly non-metaphysical, ordinary weapon. The Book of Job, for instance, in its description of the mythical Leviathan, notes that the giant fish/crocodile/ whale/beast is not afraid of the puny dart. 'Darts,' recounts the ancient scripture, 'are counted as stubble, he laugheth at the shaking of a spear.'

Nonetheless, for all their seeming pifflingness, darts contributed considerably to the arsenal of any self-respecting Hebrew monarch, as Hezekiah, son of Ahaz and 13th King of Judah, bore witness when he shored up the fortification of Jerusalem and armed his troops with 'darts and shields in abundance' (2 Chronicles 32:5).

The Holy Bible also contains one startlingly unpleasant reference to a very visceral act of darting violence. It is King David's fiercely loyal nephew Joab who, in Samuel 18:14, tracks down the monarch's treasonous son Absalom, hiding in a tree and takes 'three darts in his hand and thrust them through the heart of Absalom, while he was yet alive in the midst of the oak'. Again, you will note, three darts. Not four, or two.

An unholy trinity. Such things are meant to be.

Free Mason

We penetrated deeper and deeper into the heart of darkness.

JOSEPH CONRAD – *HEART OF DARKNESS*

There are other ways to hurt yourself, and to hurt others, some of which are not detailed in the Book of Job.

I was on a train bound for the Midlands for a meeting that I had delayed for long enough, but one that I knew was important. Perhaps it would address a an uncomfortable thought that had nagged at me about the extent of what the game allowed, what it tolerated, what it fostered and what it hid. There was, within darts, a potential for genuine harm I only dimly perceived. From my long conversations, which led to this trip to Birmingham, I knew something far outside of my own experience lay in wait at the end of the line.

The Virgin train rattled through Milton Keynes, home to the PDC Masters Championship, and then, on its Pendolino suspension, swung gently left, describing a vague north-westerly curve ever further from the World Championships and towards the Grand Slam of Darts. The country was a map scored with dart tips. It was the same route I'd taken to Wolverhampton some years ago, on that November day when I had first discovered darts, and sensed its unstable joyfulness.

I have often sensed a simmering potential for something wild at the darts, though less and less often in recent years. There was a tinder-dry threat of explosion in among all the brilliance, waiting for a spark. During my early years of working in darts, things quite regularly kicked off backstage, though not often with any serious intent. Nevertheless, short fuses abounded, and tempers were often ignited, rather than extinguished, by the volumes of booze being consumed. I think of players who are no longer competing at the highest level: Ronnie 'the Rocket' Baxter and Andy Jenkins, a man mountain from Portsmouth. Colin 'Jaws' Lloyd had a temper when he lost, as did Wayne Mardle, for all his floral, happy-go-lucky persona.

In a landscape littered with rough diamonds, Chris Mason is probably the most uncut: hard as nails, in some ways, and unpolished. Few people have offered me such an insight into the red-hot centre of the darting world than he. But then again, few people have made me more alert than he, and not because of anything I'd ever seen him do. More because of what I knew he could do, and what he had done.

I have known him for many years now, and count him as a friend, because I enjoy his company greatly. He's smart, with that kind of quick wit that means he can adapt to any situation, any conversation, any tone. We bump shoulders on meeting, a ritual that has emerged over the years and is entirely at his instigation. It's a slightly awkward manoeuvre that involves clapping and clasping our right hands, and then, with a Viennese waltz-step to the left, angling our right shoulders towards one another, and, well, bumping. Mason performs the dance with total surety but I have never been able to relax my way into the ritual. It's as alien to my instincts as hugging my dad.

'All right, mate?' he'll ask me, in time-honoured darts fashion.

'Good.' And each and every time, I'll wonder what on earth he thinks of me, really. 'All good, Mace.'

He is a powerfully built man in his late forties, stands tall, broad-shouldered, with kindly bovine eyes and slightly fleshy features. His hair is styled into something approaching a flat top, though he has been known to experiment with a fringe. His dress sense, when off-duty, reflects his periodical obsession with working out in the gym, favouring loose-fitting sweatshirts and jogging pants. But when performing his public role as a darts pundit on TV, his lavishly tailored appearance is itself something of a darting in-joke; one he plays up to with assiduous attention to detail.

Mason's TV attire veers wildly around on a spectrum that ranges from 'natty' to 'circus'. A feature of his taste in shirts is an over-complication of the collar that verges on the baroque, with the addition of unnecessary triplets of tiny buttons, or false layers to the cloth, revealed in staggered stitching. Patterns swirl and assail the senses – chevrons, floral, parrots, anchors, spaceships – hell, why not? His shoes are often tapered to a sharpness of toe that challenges the very form of the human foot.

'Nice shirt, Chris,' you might say.

'A bit of a Bobby Dazzler,' he'd reply, with a shrug of the shoulders aimed at re-hoisting his collar into perfect alignment. 'A bit special, this one.'

But its his sub-woofer voice that stands out: a deep, dark, tar-black bass drum rattle, unfathomably reverberating around a larynx that must surely have been modelled on the Cheddar Gorge to have acquired such depth of tone. It is astounding. It can be heard through solid brick walls. To stand near Mason, even if he is scarcely projecting, is to feel assailed by sound waves coursing through your body at a level only granite can tolerate.

His West Country accent, too, is remarkable. He sounds like he is a character from a costume drama, perhaps a mildly untrustworthy quartermaster in a long-running military saga set in the Napoleonic Wars. Or rather he would do, were his everyday language not peppered with extraordinary and quite unbroadcastable profanity. His Bristolian vowels roll forth with lugubrious coarseness and fearful languor. But the fact is that he speaks like he thinks: passionately, solidly, one idea at a time. He is as brightly enlightening about darts as anyone I have ever met. A game that nurtured him, nearly made him and almost destroyed him.

Mason's debut in the WDC (the forerunner of the PDC) World Championships had come over 20 years ago in 1997. At that time, I had just started out as a production runner at Sky Sports when Sid Waddell, Phil Taylor and Chris Mason came to the West London studios to conduct the draw for the competition live on *Sports Saturday* (the slightly low-rent predecessor of *Soccer Saturday*).

I can remember someone in the office pointing Mason out to me as Waddell prepared him for the draw before we went on air. I was warned, in dark whispers, about Mason's past: 'He's just got out of prison for assault, you know.'

I glanced across the production office at the young man with the deep voice and the sharp shirts, his hair tamed to his forehead with an abundance of spray. He didn't look too dangerous, at least not from where I was observing him, with half a dozen office desks between us.

Meanwhile, Mason was blowing his own trumpet to anyone who'd listen. In his late twenties back then, trim, charismatic, assiduously dressed by Boulevard Menswear of Bristol, all he needed to break through into the public consciousness was a major win, or at least a big-name scalp in a tournament that really mattered. He was, at the time, considered by many to be the brightest young player on the scene, perhaps even the future of the game.

Taylor, Mason and Waddell blinked in the hot white light of the studio, where nothing casts a shadow. They were just about to draw the balls from the hat.

'Who would you like to draw, Chris?' asked the TV host Jeff Stelling, live on air.

'Taylor,' replied Mason without hesitation.

And a few minutes later, Phil Taylor was duly paired against Mason. A convenient result all round, everyone agreed.

Later that week, Sky Sports' promotional department went into overdrive. The film *Mission Impossible* had just been released, and Mason starred in his own darting version for the small screen. Sky's directors went to town. 'They had me jumping out of helicopters, bursting through doors,' Mason later recalled with a chuckle.

But the match was something of an anti-climax. 'I got beat 3–0, 3–0, 3–0. I was up there for about 14 minutes. It was the quickest game ever in the history of the World Championships.' Mission Impossible proved to be just that.

Nonetheless, Mason was more than capable of throwing with the best in the world. Some of his finest moments endure to this day on the Internet, such as his nail-biting 5–4 defeat of Martin Adams in the BDO World Championship quarter-finals; a game that will be remembered for 'Wolfie' Adams' astonishing sequence of missed doubles, as well as the respective agonies and ecstasies of the Adams and the Mason camps, sitting powerlessly in the VIP area. It was a match that was watched by over a million people on the BBC, a huge number for a highlights slot late at night.

But Mason's playing highlights, as well as the blond streaks in his hair, were of limited wattage when set up against the very brightest in the darting starscape, and mostly his career played out in the shadow of greater talents: van Barneveld, Warriner, Priestley, and, of course, Taylor, who, as Mason was stuttering into life, was just about to drop a gear and leave everyone else far, far behind. Then, for a variety of reasons, plenty of which were of his own making, the magic deserted him and he retired from the top end of the game.

He still throws every now and again, even as the fading of the light still enrages him. 'I get absolutely irate now just playing local league games. So bitter. So bitter. I feel like my career was robbed off me, through some fault of my own, through my mental situation and through outside influences.' In common with every dart player I have ever met, he is 'available for exhibitions'. But his last TV appearance came in the 2007 Grand Slam of Darts, at which he played three and lost three against Adrian Lewis, Raymond van Barneveld and Dennis Priestley in the group phase. The end of the road, really. But he was lucky to have got that far, given everything that had detained him en route.

These days, Mason and I are part of the ITV's presenting team on their darts coverage. He commentates on matches and works as a pundit in between. Sometimes he and I stand in front of the camera talking about a match we've just seen, or a match that's about to get under way. He's a brilliant analyst of a sport that often eludes analysis, one of the best I've ever come across: forthright, observant, articulate and funny as hell. In fact, everything he does is framed by the fact that he both loves the game and sees its funny side.

He is also blessed with a warm humour, even when he makes, as we all do, the odd slip. Setting the scene at the UK Open one year in Minehead, he wanted to allude to the tournament's special status, a uniquely democratic event that pitches grassroots underdogs against the mighty of the game.

'It's like the FA Cup of football, Ned,' he said earnestly to me, in front of a national television audience.

'But surely that's the FA Cup,' I said.

'... like the FA Cup of darts,' he corrected, without a flicker of hesitation, and a stony-faced glare that hardened infinitesimally as he looked at me, betraying the fact that he was trying not to laugh.

He's a man who has coachloads of demons howling after him and is trying to outrun them. Sometimes he gets away, and sometimes he doesn't. He's tough. But he doesn't want to have to be tough all the time. It's complex.

The terrible, glorious, silly, elemental darts crucible, with which he battled throughout his playing career, and in which he revelled with equal excess, might well have been the worst possible place for a man of his delicate and explosive constitution. It was like putting a hand grenade in a pressure cooker and hoping it would end well.

I got off at Birmingham New Street station to find him waiting for me there, as we had painstakingly arranged a few days earlier. He was wearing some kind of gentlemen's tweed cap, à la *Peaky Blinders*, and a thick turtleneck sweater. We shoulder bumped, intimately enough for me to draw deeply on the heady cocktail of Hugo Boss, Marlboro Lights and Wrigley's Extra that rose from his aura.

'Where shall we go?' he asked.

I had suggested the lunch, and it was therefore up to me to decide. 'I don't know, Mace.' We almost always have curry when we are working together. Chris Mason, who is a prolific publisher across multiple social media platforms, often posts pictures of curries. I suggested curry.

'Shall we go there?' I pointed at a curry house.

'Nice one, bud.'

Chris Mason comes from a large gypsy family in Bristol. His dad was heavily involved with motoring: racing rally cars, working as a demonstrator for a sports car franchise and at one point owning, and then gambling away over a game of cards a thriving driving school business. The man he lost his business to owned the Bristol School of Motoring, which went on to be known simply as BSM. In other words, he ended up with everything, and the Mason family drew a blank. That debacle left his mum and dad, in Mason's words, 'skint'. After that, his childhood was a tightrope act without much of a safety net, leading him into some extraordinary situations, as his family looked to get by in multiple different ways.

And then there were the darts. From a young age he excelled, just as his father had, who was a stalwart of the Bristol scene, playing on the same team as Alan Evans, Leighton Rees and the 'Limestone Cowboy' Bob Anderson (a former Olympic standard javelin thrower and non-league footballer). Growing up in the shadow of such talent, the young Chris Mason lapped it all up and by the age of ten or 11 was competing, and thriving, in tournaments for under 21s.

When he turned 14, he won a junior tournament sponsored by MFI, which ran in parallel to the senior World Matchplay event that they sponsored. Mason's prize, much to his disappointment and bemusement, was £500 in DIY tokens, which his dad bought off him 'for about 20 quid'. However, not long after that, and roughly coinciding with his first motorbike and girlfriend, he drifted away from the game. Losing, even at a game like darts, upset him unreasonably.

The Birmingham curry house was situated round the scruffy side of New Street station, with its unprepossessing side alleys warmed by blasts of fatty air from extractor fans. We were almost the only customers. Outside, people hurried past the window, scarves wrapped high around their necks, swaddled up to avoid the worst of the cold. Mason sat back, recalling those early years that nearly led to his perdition.

'I used to take defeat devastatingly badly. Darts, even at that age, used to depress me,' he recalled. 'Something wasn't right, mentally. It was already evident back then. I just didn't tick the same as everyone else. I didn't know what it was at the time.' Thirty years later, after a long, and sometimes violent history, he was diagnosed with 'every mental health illness there is', in his words. 'Every one. Every one: mild schizophrenic, manic depressive, personality disorder, everything.'

There was a sense that one day Mason would fall foul of the law. His dad saw it coming. 'He used to tell me I was like a fucking trouble magnet. Everywhere you go. Everything you do. Trouble, trouble, trouble, trouble, trouble.' And that trouble was never going to lead to anything other than more trouble, as much as he might have felt immune from prosecution. 'We come from a gypsy background. The last people you ever call is the police. And even then you don't call them.'

I am not sure in what way he differentiates his ethnicity from those of the settled community, or which term to use, or quite how he relates to the pejorative way with which both 'gypsy' and its nastier variants are routinely used. In the mostly unreconstructed world of the darts community, where everyone is fair game, the traditional targets are still over-abused. The word 'gypsy', when it is used by someone who isn't one, is a loaded word.

In his own recollection, the Masons were 'well known' for being the kind of group you didn't want to cross. Many of his relatives boxed, including Mason in his youth. Despite his clear, raw intelligence, he failed himself, and was failed, at school, 'in everything I did', he recalled. 'If I couldn't get it right, it would trouble me, and of course that affected me at school. So, I was more or less the class idiot.'

His incapacity for emotional self-control started to wreak havoc on his, and other people's lives, on some people who perhaps had it coming, and on other people who simply had the misfortune to come into contact with a young Chris Mason at the wrong moment.

Working by day on building sites, going to the gym, taking a few lines of cocaine, and then going out for a second job as a manically motivated doorman, for 'a horrendous nightclub in Bristol, where people from all the roughest parts were drinking'. This was Mason's norm. People took it upon themselves to try and get a rise from the doormen, who were only too happy to respond in kind. Ritual fights 'down the stairs at the back' were nothing unusual. The beatings became a simple fact of life, one for which he appeared extremely, worryingly, well suited.

'From about 17 to about 21, it was proper psycho stuff. It wouldn't end with someone just getting a slap. You know, there had to be an ending to it. There had to be a conclusion.'

In 1993, a conclusion of sorts was reached when Mason, after a night out in Bath, got involved in a classic British brawl in a kebab shop. In our Birmingham curry house, he told me how it all began to unravel for him. The poppadums arrived. The snap of the spicy crisps broke the tension of his recollections, almost making them seem normal.

'There were six of us and eight of them. They started breaking up "A" boards and they had lengths of two by two. I got my left arm broken, putting my hand up to stop them hitting me in the head. We were getting absolutely battered.' He ran out of the shop, fetched his car, and, seeing the rival gang at the top of the street coming for him, drove the car quite deliberately into the crowd of his assailants, catapulting one of them over the bonnet. Shortly after that, and after eight previous convictions for fighting and other public order offences, he began his first custodial sentence.

On his release, he was enrolled in a mandatory anger management course, which also, rather comically, was attended by eight other men with severe anger management issues, including some well-known Bristol gangsters.

'What do you think happened?' he asked, spooning up some mango chutney. 'Fucking massive fight. Everyone's pulling everyone apart. There were guys with black eyes and bloodied noses, split lips and teeth everywhere.' Then he shoved the loaded poppadum in his mouth and let fly an immense, Bristol laugh.

In the depths of his booming chuckle, I was surprised to hear a small boy version of Chris Mason still making himself heard. The laughing version of Chris Mason is by far the best. He has an infectious humour and is one of those rare individuals who instinctively adapts his own sense of fun to suit the tastes of others. It's one of the reasons why I've grown to like him so much over the years. But here he was delving into the darkest of his dark places.

'Anyway,' he continued, 'after I got out I moved back home. Took my dad's darts out of the board and started playing. Three hundred days later, I qualified for Lakeside.'

Filling his glass with water (we were both being surprisingly abstemious, for which I was certainly grateful, and I think that he was, too), I asked, 'How do you know it was 300 days?'

His answer was simple. 'Because no one's ever done it before.' Mason had risen up the rankings that year like a surfacing dolphin of the darting world, clicking his pleasure as he ticked off the milestones of checkouts and improving averages.

He stayed out of trouble after that, at least for a while, slowly building a career in darts. It was a delicate thing to attempt in the mid-nineties. Politically, he had to navigate the splintering of the two codes, skilfully managing to keep a foot in both camps, playing in both BDO and PDC events, until he finally committed to the PDC in 2001. He was battling other players of a similar standard, including the likes of Ronnie Baxter, who beat him in a thrilling 11–13 semi-final at the Blackpool World Matchplay, and of course an increasingly untouchable Phil Taylor.

But he was also battling himself, and the game itself. Prescribed multiple medication regimes for his various mental health issues, the brutally exposed playing environment of the darts world led him to experiment with alcohol, cocaine and whatever else he could get his hands on. 'I was on this roller coaster. I was doing well. But then I started self-medicating. I was just trying to find the balance of how I could feel normal. That's all I ever wanted to feel: normal in the head. Not psychotic.'

He put down his glass of water, and paused.

'Then there's the thing with the dog. There's this mythical thing with a hammer.'

Instinctively I flinched. I had known Chris Mason for a good few years, and we had often spoken about his early childhood, stories which probably should remain untold. But I had never spoken to him about the night on which Neal Harley and Jane Graham's house was broken into by a group of men, one of whom was Mason, and two of whom were wielding a baseball bat and a hammer. It had started, seemingly, as an argument between two former lovers (Mark Gibson and Jane Graham) about a dog, and it ended with a serious violent assault. Harley was left with a broken nose and other injuries after being beaten by the intruders.

I was surprised that Mason brought up the subject. This was the albatross around his neck, the stain that cannot be removed. The whispers about his past had always been in the background, like a faint, de-tuned radio: so much static hiss.

For the record, Chris Mason was convicted, in 2003, along with Mark and Simon Gibson, of aggravated burglary, an offence that carried a mandatory three-year sentence. It is also worth saying that to this day, Mason maintains his innocence, insisting that he only got involved later, having been standing outside the house when he heard the children screaming, and broke up the fight.

'I ran into the house. The kids were crying in their bedroom. I go in there, fucking shout and scream, put an end to it. We all leave.'

We were the only diners in the Indian restaurant that lunchtime, and I became conscious that the waiter, fiddling with some optics at the bar, had stopped what he was doing and was listening. Mason was talking steadily, without great emotion, but his words were putting us all, the waiter included, right into this extraordinary moment.

'Next thing, police helicopters, everything.'

When he'd driven at those lads in Bath some ten years previously, he had raced away from a police car and a brief chase had ensued. Now, once again, he fled from them. 'I checked into a hotel. Then, at six in the morning, the police are in the hotel room and I'm nicked.'

At the end of his trial, the jury (who Mason alleges were somehow nobbled during their deliberation, dramatically changing their voting intentions overnight) returned a unanimous verdict. Mason also questions the validity of some of the testimony. He believes still that some of the witnesses were going to be paid by newspapers for their stories, but only upon his successful conviction. But his grievances mattered little. He went down for the crime.

His 14-month odyssey at Her Majesty's Pleasure was eventful, to say the least. He began his sentence in an open prison, in Lewes, but managed to get on the wrong side of a prison officer who listened in on a phone call in which Mason was arranging a liaison with his wife 'for a bunk up', in his own words, during an authorised visit outside of the prison walls. They thought he was planning an escape. They waited for him and pounced. Taken straight back into custody, he was reclassified as a flight risk, and sent to the austere surroundings of Camp Hill, one of three Edwardian prisons on the Isle of Wight.

'Twenty-three-hour bang-up. Fucking awful. It was horrific, like horrific.'

At first he was placed in a cell with a black man who objected in no uncertain terms to having to share a cell with a white man; the first time, according to Mason, he'd experienced racial abuse that wasn't solely attributable to his gypsy heritage. Then the prison authorities moved him on to the wing of the prison under the command of a senior prison guard, a simple twist of fate that might well have saved his life.

'Oi, Mason! What're you doing on my block?' The officer was as shocked to see him as was Mason to discover that one of his old mates from the darts world was in charge of locking him up and letting him out every day.

The bond of the board proved strong. Within days, the prison officer had erected a completely illegal dartboard with an oche and spotlight in an empty classroom next door to Mason's cell. Then, after his wife had delivered his trusted darts to the prison, the guard and Mason fell into a routine. 'Every morning he knocked on my door, "Ssshhh," he goes. Then he handed [the darts] over and said, "There you are, off you go." Every day he'd let me out and give me two hours' practice. He proper looked after me.'

As the winter of his long incarceration on the island, behind those rain-soaked, roughly hewn grey walls, dragged on, Mason, a convicted, violent criminal, according to the words of his indictment, paced up and down from dartboard to oche, clutching three sharp weapons. But far from inflicting harm to anyone, the flight of each dart rebuilt a bit of him, reconstructed a broken connection, healed another tear in his fabric he'd managed to shred. The time spent gazing after the throwing arm, and lifting the next arrow into the breach, honing his field of vision into the only thing that mattered: this was the important time, banishing the white noise, silencing the banshees, shrinking his world until once again it became manageable. That prison officer knew exactly what he was doing when he hung up that dartboard and paced out the correct measurement for the oche. He'd thrown Chris Mason a lifeline.

Eventually, Mason was moved from the Category 'C' confines of Camp Hill, back to the privileged status of a Category 'D' establishment, another open prison. He was sent to Standford Hill prison on the Isle of Sheppey, where the coast of the Thames Estuary opens up to the North Sea. From here, while containers headed past for Tilbury, passing Gravesend to the port and Purfleet just inland on the starboard, he set about preparing for life after prison. In these coastal towns of Kent and Essex, London's tidal fringes, the game had grown popular 100 years previously. And here, Chris Mason was hoping to reinvent himself within it all over again.

In this new institution, and full of rediscovered self-confidence, he struck a deal with the prison authorities who were putting out a construction contract to tender for the building of a new officers' mess. Mason, an experienced builder, got together a gang of chippies, brickies and assorted trades, and pitched for the work.

'I can't believe your fucking front, Mason,' the officer had told him.

'Well, let's get one thing straight: My name's Chris,' Mason had replied, with typical chutzpah. 'We'll start from there.'

But Mason won the contract, saving the prison tens of thousands of pounds in labour costs, and, in so doing, negotiated for himself an increased wage, an extra outside visit every week, a dartboard and, for reason's best known to himself, a sandwich toaster.

'A sandwich toaster, Mace? Why?' I asked, amused by the very specific clause the prisoner had inserted in the negotiation.

'Because I could,' he said with a grin. 'A Breville.'

Shortly after that, Mason saved the life of a prison officer, whom he found collapsed, having swallowed his tongue, as the result of a fall. He resuscitated him, put him in the recovery position, and ran for help, later receiving a commendation for his efforts. 'I know plenty of lads who would have stepped over him and gone back to their wing.'

After that intervention, he could, in Mason's words, 'do no wrong'. Dartboards began to flourish all over the prison: one on the building site; one in the recreation wing. He even stuck one to the back of his cell door ('you couldn't use screws, you see'), invisible to the guards, comically enough, who flung the door wide open and never inspected the back of it, as if they were all acting out a scene from *Porridge*. And the net result of all this time spent practising was that by the time of his release he was more than ready to get back on the circuit.

'It was no coincidence: I was straight back into it, and making finals, semis.'

Yet, there was to be no fairy-tale ending to the story, no great triumph at the oche, no epic act of redemption. Mason did not rise to the very top, nor win the World Championships. At best he could hold his own, but never really threatened to break through. He competed admirably, at a very good level, for another few years, but it became more and more of a struggle. On rare occasions, he'd let his frustrations bubble to the surface, as they did at the World Championship in 2007 when he lost to Phil Taylor, prompting a foul-mouthed tirade for which he later apologised.

And, below the surface, his private life continued to boil with trouble. He was arrested once again and then convicted of making a fraudulent claim for housing benefit. On this occasion, the police arrived at the Bolton Arena to take him away about ten minutes before his first-round match at the UK Open, a very public shaming. Then his marriage to his second wife, Lorna, never an entirely comfortable match ('we were like petrol and matches'), fell acrimoniously apart when he was arrested on the basis of her complaint for threatening behaviour, something he doesn't deny. But the transcript of the interview he gave to the police on that occasion suggests a man in deep trouble. Over a 20-minute interview under caution, he simply answered 'fuck off' to every question that he was asked. The judge handed down a restraining order, which Mason breached twice when he sent Lorna text messages on various matters. It was extremely messy and at times Mason was suicidal.

'If there'd been a facility there for me to have either hung myself, shot myself or taken a lethal injection, I'd have done it.'

In the end, the torment and the pressure of holding it all in put an end to his career as a competitive darts player. It was hardly a surprise.

'It's remarkable that you managed to keep a lid on it in that environment,' I tell him.

'It's a vile environment.'

'It's a remarkable trick that you played. I don't know how you managed it.'

'Neither do I. It was so draining.'

'Are you able to look back on anything with any pride?'

'No.'

We had spoken for so long that eventually the waiters, who'd been circling for the past half an hour, allowing Mason to talk in ever more sombre tones, now approached our table with polite caution.

'I'm sorry, but we're closing.'

We stepped out into the city, again. We did the awkward shoulder bump thing one more time.

'Thanks for talking to me, Mace.'

''S'all right, bud.' He smiled. 'There's fucking loads more where that came from.'

As my train pulled out of Birmingham and we started to cut through Warwickshire and Northamptonshire, turning south all the while, I fell to wondering what it could possibly be like to be Chris Mason.

I knew something of his instinct for self-destruction, and I knew a good deal about the difficult upbringing. His wild adolescence had been far removed from mine, in every conceivable respect. Having never been the recipient of his vindictive side, and having always only enjoyed his affectionate company, I was left with no choice but to put my censoriousness to one side.

Here was a man who had pulled himself back from the brink. The point of intersection in our lives was a simple beam of light, behind the cameras, in whose gaze we both stood and talked about darts, the spectacle that had both saved him and offered him another path to ruin, and which had brought us together in such an unlikely collaboration. The game, played out behind us, was bigger than me and bigger than him.

Bigger than both of us.

Ordinary Shoes

Certainly the affair was too stupid–
when I think of it–to be altogether natural.

JOSEPH CONRAD – *HEART OF DARKNESS*

There is an obvious tendency towards a certain body type among darts players. Eric Bristow ate vindaloo almost every night of his adult life, and was in the habit of ordering two, just in case one wasn't enough. The same went for kebabs.

They have been known to smoke (in Michael van Gerwen's case, almost professionally), and they have been known to drink, almost all of them, quite a lot. So, the game of darts is rather an outlier on the sporting spectrum, to say the least. Here's one fact that marks it out as decidedly different from, say, basketball.

There is a specific article in the rule book of the Darts Regulation Authority (DRA) that relates to footwear. Rule 5.17.1 actually prohibits the wearing of training shoes, or indeed any 'tracksuit' attire. Should there be any room for doubt as to what kind of shoe is deemed inappropriate, the rule book specifies that 'the final decision will rest with the Tournament Director'. But the intent of the rule is clear: as long as the darts player is wearing shoes that are clearly not designed for running/football/ gym etc., they will be OK. For that reason, most players favour a pair of boring black shoes, made remarkable only by their sheer ordinariness. Phil Taylor turned up for a tournament a few years ago in trainers, having forgotten to pack his schoolish black shoes. Glancing at the obliging and beleaguered PDC press officer Dave Allen, he enquired what size he wore.

'Seven and a half, Phil,' replied Allen, suspiciously.

'That might do me, bud.' Taylor requisitioned the footwear, leaving the chief media officer to go about the rest of the day in his socks. The following day, Taylor kept Allen's shoes, forcing him to walk barefoot to a shop and buy some new ones.

Most darts players, with the exception of the nattily attired James Wade, who has recently taken to wearing brown shoes with blue trousers (worth, he proudly told me, £200), and of course Peter Wright, whose outfits are simply ridiculous, don't greatly care about their shoes or their trousers. A good case in point would be 'Goldfinger' Andrew Gilding, an extraordinary loping figure, bald of head, short of sight and splay-footed, whose trousers split down the backside during the UK Open a few years ago as he was bending to retrieve a bounce-out from the floor. Unfazed, he calmly requested some assistance from the PDC riggers and spent the rest of the weekend sporting a pair of strides that had been patched up with gaffer tape.

So, given that startling image, one could be forgiven for returning to the most frequently asked question of them all: is darts a sport?

This question gets asked of darts, argued about, contested, laughed over and generally discussed with more prejudice and passion than it does about any other sport/pastime/game/ activity/performance I can think of.

No one agonises too much about Formula One, which is simply noisy marketing. All those swirly/twirly things that crop up once in an Olympic cycle are not scrutinised too closely. Snooker, the closest thing to accountancy in the sporting world with its waistcoated parsimony, never gets its status as a sport questioned. Boxing, undeniably athletic, is also unlike most sports in that, far from being a metaphor for combat, it *is* combat, legitimised violence. But its place in the sporting pantheon is never questioned. Archery's all good, apparently, of course it is. So is shooting, unquestionably, a sport.

But darts gets it every time, for two reasons, and for two reasons only: lots of players are fat; lots of players have drunk beer.

Never mind the fact that weightlifters are routinely flabby, gymnasts barely into their delayed adulthood, jockeys and cyclists neurotically underweight, swimmers fat-necked, narrow-waisted and big-footed, sumo wrestlers morbidly obese, rugby players and NFL linebackers steroid-chiselled freaks. Never mind that all manner of blood-doping, mechanical-cheating, testosterone-recovering, nandrolone fast-twitching, match-throwing, non-trying, spot-fixing illegitimacy permeates almost every sport in the world that sells a ticket or two and pops up from time to time on television. Never mind all that! Some darts players are fat, and they wear black slacks, and shoes that they bought at British Home Stores in the sales! How can you do sport if you've had a pint?

Actually, the terms of the question are meaningless. Darts is darts. Horse racing is horse racing. But are they both sport? Who cares. It's like insisting that tomatoes are a fruit. Or, equally, that they are not a fruit. They're tomatoes, and that's that.

Nonetheless, there is of course a need, or perhaps a desire, to label and classify human experience. We need to know what it is that we are looking at. 'Is it art?' for example, remains one of the most enduring questions, to which Britain's favourite cross-dressing potter Grayson Perry rather brilliantly suggested that (and I paraphrase), 'if it's in an art gallery and there are men with beards and oligarchs' wives looking at it, then it probably is.'

For a while, after the formation of the PDC, and even before Barry Hearn's headlong rush at legitimacy, there was a genuine, almost fervent desire for darts to be considered a sport. The apotheosis of this lobbying campaign came in 2005 when Bob Russell, the sitting MP for Colchester, hosted an 'Exhibition for the Sport of Darts' at the House of Commons, where members of both houses were invited to join the likes of Bob Anderson, Colin Lloyd and Phil Taylor to throw a few darts and have a quick drink. The fact that the beverage in question turned out to be Chablis did nothing to undermine the occasion, not even for committed ale drinker Sid Waddell, who recalled having shrieked, 'I've heard of four lords-a-leaping, but this is the first time I've seen four lords-a-tossing!' Seventy members turned up, including Richard Caborn, the sports minister, who checked out 97 in two darts, according to Westminster folklore.

The following day Sport England announced that it recognised darts as a sport, and Sport UK soon did the same. The blessing that these two august (not to mention well-funded) governing bodies felt fit to bestow on the game filled darts with new-found status and a sense of purpose. All of a sudden, certain things started to change.

One of those changes was surprising. I was working for ITV on the Grand Slam of Darts in 2009 at the Wolverhampton Civic when I walked past a man in a suit looking lost. He was hanging around the stage door round the side of the venue. Thinking he might have been a cab driver waiting to pick up one of the players from their private bar, I asked him if I could help.

'Yes. I'm from UK Anti-Doping.' He smiled meekly and held up a bulging briefcase as if to show his credentials.

In that gesture, my worlds collided. The rest of my professional broadcasting life was centred around the wonderful, dubious sport of cycling. A few months prior to this mysterious and unlikely encounter at the back of the Civic, I had been hounding Lance Armstrong around the Tour de France, waiting to see his race number posted on the Anti-Doping random test board for suspicious riders. Doping, doping controls, anti-doping and dopers were in keeping with the anarchy of professional road racing, a sport whose history and present travails seem riddled through with corrupted science and cheating.

'Sure,' I said, uncertainly. 'I'll just find someone who can help.'

Tommy Cox, the legendary tournament director, later explained to me that, as part of their contract with UK Sport, they had to undergo the same anti-doping tests as any other member sports. But they could voluntarily opt out of certain controls. It will not surprise you to read that one of these is alcohol. Indeed, one of the many other differences between cycling and darts, in these terms, is the relative ease with which darters are able to oblige the urine testers, almost on demand and often too copiously. In the arid world of cycling, with physiologies on the brink of metabolic collapse and drained of hydration, the process could take upwards of an hour. Not so at the darts, where, frankly, it was like opening a tap.

Now that there was a legitimacy to their self-regulation, darts' ambitions grew exponentially. For a long time, and especially in the lead-up to the London Olympics of 2012, there would be the call for darts to be included in the IOC family of sports. Adrian Lewis had a collection of the best turned-out phrases.

'A lot of Olympic competitions are based on judges' scoring,' argued 'Jackpot', 'which is never as foolproof as winning a race, jumping the highest or counting down from 501 and finishing on a double or the bullseye. You get medals for horses doing tap dancing, and bobbing around in a swimming pool with a clothes peg on your nose, so don't tell me darts is less of a sport than those events.'

Needless to say, it didn't happen. But the lobbying for the Rio games picked up again in the run-up to the 2013 World Championships. Phil Taylor, who had watched the London Olympics with envy, joined the ranks of those calling for darts to be allowed a chance. 'I'd love to think I could compete for a gold medal before my time is up.'

That particular fight has not been entirely laid to rest just yet, with talk in 2015, according to Alexander von Egen, the mysteriously obscure President of the International Darts Federation, that the IOC was prepared to send observers to forthcoming major championships with a view to targeting an inclusion in time for the 2024 Summer Games. But no one is really holding their breath, I don't think. Their noses, maybe. But not their breath.

With or without Olympic status, darts will always remain apart, and not just because of the waist size and dietary requirements of its greatest practitioners. There's something about the game that makes it stand out.

It is the simplest game ever devised. At a certain level, it's primeval. Once, when filming a spoof 'History of Darts' insert for ITV, I insisted that a junior producer got dressed up in a Flintstones-style caveman outfit. He obliged, hoping it might further his career, which I very much doubt it did. Then we all traipsed off to Oxleas Wood in South London, where we nailed a dartboard on a tree and filmed the young production hopeful throwing a flinty stone at treble 20. We later subtitled the sequence, so that when he said, 'Ug!', the caption read '180!'

But, away from that (terrible) bit of television, there is a serious point to be made here. The practice of throwing something at something is elemental. Most other sports that involve throwing something accurately in the right direction have introduced complications, like the sheer weight of a shot, the bias on a bowling ball, extraneous equipment such as bows and arrows, or simply done away with the need for accuracy and made it all about distance, in the case of the javelin.

Darts is simply a matter of:

'Can you hit that target?'

'Yeah, I reckon.'

'Bet you can't.'

'Bet you I can.'

'Go on, then.'

'What with?'

'This.'

'What's that?'

'A dart.'

'Damn, missed.'

'Told you it was hard.'

For this reason, the subtleties of the game are so minuscule as barely to register to the untutored eye. That said, any time spent watching the game in the company of a real expert like Wayne Mardle or Chris Mason is a fascinating induction into a world of subtle variations of throw, angle, pitch of attack and speed of follow-through. But these are almost invisible, and to the outsider, they might as well not exist. You cannot have a defensive set-up. You can't change your formation. You can't use a pacesetter. You can't really play on the counter. You either hit, or you don't hit, in which case you miss. Sometimes the darts bounce out, but let's not get too technical.

Martin Amis was fascinated by the reductive nature of darts; its 'dumbfounding starkness'.

'Hand, projectile, target, through a medium of thin air – and that's that. Remove one umpire, both batsmen and all the fielders from a cricket pitch and you get some idea of the dourness of darts.'

But Martin Amis never had the task of interviewing players about the match they had just won, or lost, live on TV. After the initial question about how the game went (to which there is a polarity of possible answers, based around the twin options of either 'very well/delighted' and 'terribly/gutted'), it is difficult to know where to go with the follow-up question given the absence of nuance.

'What was the difference?'

'I missed the doubles. I couldn't check out.'

This would be entirely obvious to anyone watching the game, and the interview, completely surplus to requirements. Likewise, analysis of the game is pretty near impossible, especially when looking at replays of big checkouts. The dart simply goes into the bullseye, or it doesn't.

'How did he do that?' a presenter might ask of a pundit.

'He threw it accurately,' would be the only answer.

One other favourite is the complaint that a player was 'hitting 180s for fun' on the practice boards, but when it came to it, they 'couldn't hit a cow's arse with a banjo' onstage. In fact, almost uniquely among sports, it's generally understood that players' performances are consistently better in the practice room than they are in actual competition, which tells you all you need to know about the mental side of the game. The human frailty is the thing to be explored, because this is a game of the moment, in the moment, leaving little room to admire in hyper-slow motion the delightful cover drive, the muscular poise of the sprinter or the grace of a serve. What we want when we watch darts is to see players sweat and fret and hit or miss. Live.

The problem of texture, or its absence, is even more acute when a match is being previewed. Before a dart has been thrown, there really is not that much to say, since the only way of winning remains the same whoever the opponent, whatever the stage.

'How are you going to beat him?'

'I'll have to bring my "A" game and hope that he has an off day.' In other words, he needs to miss more than you.

The difficulty of the pre-match interview was a subject that Amis astutely picked up on when he described his anti-hero Keith Talent's rather ponderous interview just before his television debut in a darts tournament in *London Fields*.

'Hopefully the best man'll win. When we go out there.' He realised that more was expected of him. 'So let's hope the guy with the, the superior technique will, will run out winner against, against the man with the... least good equipment. Dartwise. At the death.'

In an unsettling coincidence, Amis's fictional TV presenter is called Ned von Newton ('the man with the mike himself. Mr Darts.') Ned has my sympathies. I have often felt the pain of the pre-match interview. Instead of previewing the sporting contest with anything like a technical approach ('we'll adopt a two-stop strategy', 'I'll try and work the baseline', 'we need to keep the ball in motion and effect the full back' etc.), human foibles are the meat and drink of darting rivalries. Therefore we tend to talk of other things than darts when interviewing players before a game.

'I used to room with him and he snores like a bloody tractor.'
'Yeah? Well at least I don't wash my socks in the sink...'
'At least I bloody wash them.'

And the interview concludes, as it always concludes, with a chest bump and a hand clasp and good-natured chuckling. It's a simple game, to coin a phrase from football (also a sport).

As Amis again points out, the game of darts has been almost completely reduced to an endless cycle of 501. A few variations exist (at the World Matchplay, you have to throw a double to get started, as well as to check out, and there are multiple different scoring systems that involve legs and sets), but at its heart, 501 is as stripped down as it gets. Pure.

'Darts,' wrote Martyn McLaughlin in *The Scotsman* in 2008, 'is indubitably a sport.' One of the few broadsheet writers who had managed to avoid getting bogged down in the superficial appearance of the players, McLaughlin grappled with, as he put it, 'the S-word', and he reached an unequivocal conclusion.

'The darts fraternity are too busy, too happy, to care about the debate over whether their game is a sport or not. Healthy profits are being made, record crowds are leaving satisfied and the players seem humbled at their new status. Whatever characteristics make sport great, many could learn a thing or two from those who walk the oche.'

But the greatest compliment ever paid to the sport came from outside. In 2017, the German newspaper *Die Zeit* printed a fascinated outsider's perspective of the World Championships, an ode to a game as curious and foreign as it comes, but one to which the quality German broadsheet paid the highest respect. 'If darts is a game of chance, then so is weightlifting.' The piece goes on to cite darts' 'greatest possible under-complexity' (two words in German) and talks of how:

'darts shines with maximum clarity: a dart, a board, eyes and nerves. It doesn't need anything else. There is hardly a sport that is as simple, yet at the same time as unpredictable, exciting, often even breathtaking. Darts is an eternal penalty shoot-out. Which makes it remarkable that the English are so good at it.'

The article concludes that, far from not being worthy of the title 'sport', on the contrary, darts is 'probably the last true sport'.

That is a bold claim, indeed, on behalf of the game: darts is a last flickering of light in a darkening world, a still-glowing ember in a cooling grate, a hope to which a broken land might turn. Darts might yet save the world from its awful fate, or at least delay it for as long as it takes to count down from 501 and finish on a double.

'Game shot and the match,' as they say.

Heatwave

I am trying to account to myself for – for
– Mr Kurtz – for the shade of Mr Kurtz
JOSEPH CONRAD – *HEART OF DARKNESS*

Another darting winter ran its course, and spring swept in across the country, blowing open the closeted world in which darts normally operates; the semi-dark of the indoors. My attention drifted, just as Marlow's riverboat seems to stall in his journey upstream, its movement barely registering against the slowly unfolding bank.

When I did think about darts it was often through the prism of the one man whose continued presence drew me on, but frustrated me. More and more I understood that Eric Bristow was the reference point for the whole sport, and all the players within its solar system. I read his autobiography again, making notes in the margin this time, notes that consisted mostly of exclamation marks, underlining in red ink his more eye-catching claims.

I always walked the streets with a claw hammer stuffed down the front of my trousers in case of any trouble.

Everywhere I went I took it with me. That claw hammer became my best friend.

And the logical conclusion of such a preference:

If you've got no fear of dying you've no fear of anything. That, I believe, is why I succeeded.

Whether it were Taylor, Mason or Lazarenko talking, before too long every recollection seemed to return to the subject of Bristow, the player whose career spanned the twin golden ages of the eighties and the new millennium. The Londoner who moved north, repositioning the centre of gravity in the darting universe to somewhere near Stoke-on-Trent.

Perhaps Bristow was responsible for the way darts turned out, the place it occupies, the rough diamond it's proud of being. Or perhaps Bristow was simply its natural progeny, the logical conclusion of the game's century-long gestation.

There have been many moments in the history of darts that are understood to have played their part in the development of the game from taproom pastime to the rock 'n' roll stadium tour it has become. Each has contributed, in its way, to the nudging of the sport in one direction or another, for better or for worse: the apocryphal 'Big Foot' court case in Leeds, on whose ruling the game might have disappeared altogether; the decision of the *News of the World* to come on board as the game's premier sponsor, opening a flood of publicity and potential wealth to a humble game. Or, perhaps the commissioning of the iconic *Indoor League* programme. Every one of these events has been rightfully seen as significant. But other little tricks of the timeline, flickers of distant constellations, have played a part in aligning the darting planets into the perfectly shaped and vast tungsten universe we now accept as a natural order.

And in this respect, the name Gravesend surfaces in the story again as another son of Gravesend steps forward.

He was a North Kent kid, a well-turned-out, urbane grammar schoolboy. As he sat at his drum kit, letting the skin of the snare keep the stick in perpetual motion, feeling the hi-hat snap shut with a puff of expelled air, he could not have known that his contribution to the shape of modern darts would be huge. His devotion to a sport about which he knew nothing still lay several years hence. All that Dick Allix cared about at the time was his drums.

It was 1970. Five long-haired men sat gloomily around in their backstage room on Miami's famous strip. The newly erected Marco Polo Hotel was a 13-floor beachside marvel, a music venue built to rival the big stages of Las Vegas. The Persian Room had already hosted Gladys Knight and the Pips and would go

on to welcome the Pointer Sisters. moved was a time of swagger and groove. But that night it had moved to the harmless melody of Vanity Fare, a group of friends from a neglected corner of the Thames Estuary. For an hour or two, they'd been in the spotlight, onstage at the Marco Polo.

Vanity Fare were a folksy pop band from the UK. An early-prototype boy band, they were a nattily hirsute and flared combination of keyboard, vocals, bass and lead guitar, with a drummer holding it all together. They swayed gently onstage as they let flow a ready supply of sugar-spun lyrics and unchallenging harmonies that spoke of nothing much other than being chilled and content and breezy. It was a safer version of what might otherwise have been called 'hippy culture' but while their contemporaries might have been draft-dodging in Canada or manning the barricades in Prague or Paris, the boys from Vanity Fare were singing instead about how simply wonderful it was to be alive.

They harmonised pleasingly on such meta themes as days dawning and fresh air feeling good. Life was sweet, and they knew it. They took a bow, waved to the crowd and filed off backstage.

But all was not as well as it appeared to be in the carefree, nylon-wardrobed world of Vanity Fare. On the evening in question, the mood was far from festive. They had been riding the crest of a wave ever since the band formed in 1966. But now, as they spoke, there was the sudden sense that things were about to fall apart. Now that the show was done, there was a decision to be made that had the capacity to split the band asunder.

After a successful few months on the road through the USA, touring their two Golden Disc million-copy hit singles, 'Early in the Morning' and its hugely successful follow-up 'Hitchin' a Ride', their tour management, keen to capitalise on their growing success over the pond where they'd recently scored a top three and a top five hit, had negotiated a six-month extension to their tour. The band was split. Three of them had had enough while the other two wanted badly to carry on touring: lead guitarist Tony Goulden and drummer Dick Allix were living the dream. After all, for five lads from North Kent, they'd come a long way very fast.

'One day we were playing on Sunday in the Tudor House in Bearsted, and the very next Sunday we were onstage at the Palladium. It was that quick. After that, we were invited to go on the Beach Boys tour. We toured the whole of the UK and Europe.' Allix would later pick his words carefully. 'Sex, drugs and rock 'n' roll? I remember the sex and... and the booze. That's what it was: a few drinks and a bit of rumpy.'

But the 'rumpy' was about to come to a halt. The band couldn't agree on the extended tour and the future of Vanity Fare was decided by a vote. Three hands went in the air in favour of bailing out. In the back room of the Marco Polo, Vanity Fare signed its own death warrant. The band stumbled on, but the best they managed after that debacle was a number 98 in the States. They never entered the UK charts again.

But, in 1970, unbeknown to the 25-year-old Allix as he flew home to an uncertain future, a whole new continent of entertainment awaited his discovery.

There is a pub in Brough called The Buccaneer.

It's marked by a hand-painted sign of an RAF bomber, presumably a Buccaneer, that lends the whitewashed pub a nostalgic aura, augmented by the dark quiet of the interior. You could almost imagine the sudden onrush of a group of wartime USAF bomber crews crashing through the back doors and ordering, and then complaining about, the flat, warm beer. It doesn't appear to have a dartboard. But I bet it did, not so long ago. And I bet those Brylcreemed Yanks had their fun chucking the darts at the board, much to the displeasure of the locals.

Nowadays, instead of the smack of brass on cork, there is only the spirit-sapping sound of a fruit machine. At the bar there is a lunch menu on a blackboard that proudly announces pan-seared tuna. A modest pub in a modest part of the world, the kind of place where you might grab a quick pint before jumping on one of the irregular trains that trundle through the station at the end of the road, en route to Hull or Doncaster. The pub garden, baking in June sunshine, smells of creosote and ciggies. And in the corner wearing a black collarless shirt and a straw cowboy hat sits Dick Allix, 51 years after he sat down at the Vanity Fare drum kit.

Emerging into the bright heat from the dark interior of the pub, I carry a pint of orange juice and soda out to him.

'I don't drink before five,' he apologises, as if in a darts context his abstemiousness seems worthy of explanation. He pushes his shades back up his long, handsome nose, and smiles ruefully. 'If I do, I'm finished for the day.' Not very rock 'n' roll. But, as he points out to me, he's 72. He looks 20 years younger.

I have known Dick, off and on, for almost a decade. But I'd never really spoken to him before. He was, until two or three years before this meeting, an ever-present sight backstage on the televised darts circuit. Still sporting blond hair that nods to 1970s prog rock flamboyance at the back and sides, and with a pair of classy reading specs that hinted at an affinity with John Lennon's autodidactic intellect, he was a man of few words. He sat hunched over a laptop for the most part, observing the comings and goings backstage and tapping away at the keys. Occasionally he would throw about a *bon mot*, or a literary non sequitur, or an opinion of surprising passion on one of a range of subjects; maybe cricket. Maybe politics. Then he would return to whatever it was he was doing on his computer, and the silence would rush back in. In truth, I had not the faintest idea what it was that he contributed to the darts tournament.

But I knew that he mattered. And I knew that he somehow held the key to unlocking the house of darts. I just didn't know to which door.

Then, suddenly, he had retired. Barry Hearn delivered a heartfelt tribute to him at the annual black tie dinner at the Grosvenor House in Park Lane and I lost track of him.

I had travelled up by train that morning, changing at Doncaster, and then took the Hull-bound branch across the flatlands of East Yorkshire, which Hull's most famous resident Philip Larkin had often taken '…swerving through fields Too thin and thistled to be called meadows, And now and then a harsh-named halt…' Brough. To be honest, I didn't even know how to pronounce it.

'How come you ended up here, Dick?'

'Ah, now that's a long story.'

After the showdown at the Marco Polo Hotel, Allix knew that his musical career was over. He recognised his shortcomings as a drummer and would often sit in awe listening to American drummers weaned on jazz and loose in the wrist. He modestly characterises his own style as rather military and regimented, and, well, British, by comparison: jam roly-poly to their ice-cream soda fountain. Rumpy instead of erotic.

The dream may have run its course, but the hunger for the allure of showbiz was still part of his make-up, and as a result he was unwilling to leave behind the music business entirely. His father was a bank manager and his first job had been in a bank, a position he fulfilled, in his own words, 'very badly'. Whatever it was going to be, it had to be a bit groovier than filling in withdrawal chits.

Allix drifted back to London and wound up working on Oxford Street for George Martin, the legendary Beatles producer, in his new Air London Studios. After a spell there he went round the corner to an agency called General Artists, based in Regent

Street, where he worked as a booker, responsible for hiring acts out to venues.

It was here that the word 'Hull' probably first entered his lexicon. An agency called McLeod's used to subcontract work to General Artists, putting artists their way for a fee. McLeod's represented a huge talent pool. Hull was a city bursting with acts, the no-frills fishing capital of the east coast whose low-rise, yellow brick Greatfield Estate had produced the great Mick Ronson. Ronson was one of David Bowie's Spiders From Mars. But rock was not the only show in town, as the hugely charismatic Heatwave would go on to prove. Allix recalls their first booking.

'We put them on supporting the Tavares Brothers (a well-established R&B band from Rhode Island) and they just blew them away. We put the Stylistics on and they had real trouble following Heatwave.'

Heatwave were an eclectic multinational funk/disco band whose lead singer Johnnie Wilder was a recently discharged GI who'd been stationed in Germany. Answering a 'come-get-me' advert from the hirsute young Cleethorpes-based songwriter Rod Temperton, Wilder pitched up in Hull. They hit it off and the band struck up, to almost instant success. Wilder's brother Keith, from Dayton, Ohio, joined up and they hired a drummer from Czechoslovakia called Ernest 'Bilbo' Berger. Then there was no stopping them.

Temperton wrote their smash hit, 'Boogie Nights', en route to a career that won him Grammies and produced such colossal hits as George Benson's 'Give Me The Night' and Michael Jackson's 'Thriller'.

'They were a monster band,' recalls Allix with a mixture of pride and bewilderment. The 'Boogie Nights' single went platinum all around the world, and before long, booking their tours became a full-time occupation for Dick Allix. In the meantime, Allix moved to Hull and began to look after them on a permanent basis.

Brilliant though they were, Heatwave were a handful for any agent. There was always something to attend to, and often enough that meant serious trouble. One of their main session guitarists, Jesse Whitten, was stabbed to death. The creative force behind them, Rod Temperton, left the band to work with other artists. Their Swiss bass player Mario Mantese, after an altercation following an Elton John gig, was also stabbed, allegedly by his girlfriend, leaving him mute and paralysed (Mantese has subsequently gone on to become one of Switzerland's biggest spiritual gurus, drawing thousands of people to his events).

The band, now flushed with international success, moved to America, while Allix remained at home. But the series of misfortunes continued unabated. In 1979, Johnnie Wilder was seriously injured in a car accident while away in the States, during a recording session in Detroit. He would never walk again and could no longer perform. The band, in that guise, never made another album.

Allix needed a fresh start. For a second time, music had left him high and dry. He had to reinvent himself and build a new career. He sat at his desk in McLeod's Agency wondering what would happen next.

Then the phone rang. And he picked up. It was this phone call that would change the face of darts.

Curiously, and somewhat counter-intuitively, Hull was booming as the seventies faded into the eighties. The North Sea was bouncing with mackerel, plaice, herring and all the other somewhat neglected fish of our collective childhoods. And there was serious money to be made.

'The clubs were heaving,' recalls Allix. 'When the trawlers came in, whoa! When they came into the dock from Iceland, they were full to the gunnels. They were tough boys, they'd been at sea for three months, and when the skipper came onshore, and he'd sold his catch, they were all straight into the boozers in Hessle Road. They'd put a mountain of cash on the bar and say, tell us when it's finished!' Somewhere down the food chain, Allix sniffed his opportunity. 'We fed off all that. We sold them the acts.'

Back in Hull, in the late 1970s, the phone rang in Allix's office.

'Hallo. My name is Herman.' The voice at the other end sounded German. That's because it was: Herman the German, they called him. He worked at one of the big clubs in Hull.

'I vont a dart exhibition.' Allix lapses into a German accent straight out of *Fawlty Towers*. 'I vont a dart player.'

This was the time of the first surge of popularity for the game, built on the back of TV exposure. The *Indoor League* was established and the Embassy World Championships were starting to gain massive traction in the country. The word was out, even if it hadn't reached Dick Allix just yet.

'Well, I didn't know anything about darts. Not a thing. All right, maybe I'd thrown a few darts before. But I was crap.'

He took the call and, undeterred by his total ignorance, promised he would deliver something, somebody, somehow. That's when he started thumbing through the copy of the *Sun* that he'd been reading during his lunch hour. He started at the back, with the sport. A few pages in, he struck gold. 'Lo and behold, there was an article called "The World's Top Darts Players" by Dave Lanning. And there, at number one was this chubby fella called Eric Bristow.'

Allix had not the faintest idea how he might get hold of this Bristow character. He did, however, get a number for the BDO, the organisation that ran the World Championships. Within minutes, he was speaking to the whiskered, autocratic Olly Croft, a man against whom, some 15 years later, he would go into battle as darts split asunder and fought for its very survival.

Indeed, during the course of this brief telephone call between two offices, one in Muswell Hill (the BDO) and the other in Hull, it might be said that Croft unwittingly made a gross strategic error. He handed over, for nothing, Eric Bristow's address and telephone number. He might just as well have flung the doors of his office open to the barbarians and written them a blank cheque. Allix booked Bristow. Herman the German was happy. But now there would be no turning back, but Bristow had flown the coop. Darts had just discovered showbiz.

A few hours have passed in the car park of an average pub in a tiny town in the middle of a flat and unvisited corner of England, not far from the Humber estuary. But in that time, Dick Allix's words have set the clocks back to an era almost beyond memory, where phones rang in empty offices and people answered small ads in local papers. Out of such alchemy of coincidence came Eric Bristow, settling his aviator shades on his beaky nose, flinging an overnight bag over one shoulder and jumping onto a train, young and oblivious to all the pints and fags and fights and laughs that awaited him en route to Buckingham Palace and beyond, to honour and disgrace.

Bristow's erstwhile agent puts his hat back on and starts to play with his car keys as the memories wind down to a dwindling residue, as Bristow's story begins and Allix's steps into the shade. One final word, before we go our separate ways.

'I told my wife that if she puts, "He Made Darts What it is Today" on my gravestone, I'll come back and haunt her.' Allix chuckles. But he looks like he means it.

Under the commercial guidance of Dick Allix, Bristow became the brightest star in the darting firmament; the game's first genuine household name. Eric Bristow changed the game for ever. He stood up, chuckled and checked out. He was Eric.

In the late seventies and early eighties, Bristow was unavoidable, a source of outrage and fascination at family dinners across the land. Bristow was discussed with reverence and disdain over pints the length and breadth of Britain. The 'Crafty Cockney' became the divisive and defining symbol of the brash new world of the darter: filthy rich, not bothered what anyone thinks, a loveable rogue. In the shape of Eric Bristow, darts had its anti-hero; a character whose charm and malevolence sat somewhere on a scale that started with Ronnie Barker and ended with Ronnie Biggs.

He became the first celebrity darts player of the television era. It was Bristow that television people wanted to book, to sit alongside actors and musicians in chat show green rooms, to appear on Christmas specials, to fill cheeky slots on variety shows, to play the fool, play the crowd and play the darts.

Always he obliged, with a sneer, and a can of something before he went on. People couldn't get enough of him.

Having left Allix in Brough, I had arrived in York, where I was due to meet some old friends for a game of bar billiards and a curry. The train station was busy with people heading home from work and families en route to a weekend away. The cool space of the old red brick hall afforded some relief from the heat of the early evening. I headed for the pub and sat, reflecting on my next step, over a pint.

I knew what it was that I had to do next, but I was curiously reluctant to do it. I took a long, slow drink from my glass and then I sent Dick Allix a message, thanking him for his time, and asking for one last favour.

'I need to get hold of Eric. Even if it's just over a cup of tea/ pint some time. I don't think he really knows who I am, and I haven't got a number for him. Do you have any idea how I might be able to set up a meeting?'

Allix replied quickly, supplying me with Bristow's mobile number and an offer of help. 'I will drop him a line,' he told me.

'You're a gent.'

I drank up and left. Just in case it all happened very quickly, I switched my phone off, not wanting the evening ahead to be spoilt by a phone call from Eric Bristow.

I needn't have worried.

Lowlands

You understand it was a Continental concern, that Trading
society; but I have a lot of relations living on the Continent,
because it's cheap and not so nasty as it looks, they say.

JOSEPH CONRAD – *HEART OF DARKNESS*

In late February 2016, a boat set sail from Dick Allix's former
adopted home town of Hull. On board were a few hundred
passengers, all of whom had paid to join the two darting stars
on the P&O liner, Keith Deller and Eric Bristow.

As the ship slipped its moorings and its engines roared into life,
the guests made their way to the bar, readying themselves with
a drink to be entertained by the two old rivals from the 1983
World Championship final. Deller had the patter; Bristow had
the presence. Between them, they knew how to work the crowd.

Out into the inhospitable darkness of the North Sea, the
bows of the liner rose and fell gently on the swell. Away across
the skim of salt-blown wind, the lights from the multiple decks
were an incandescent, tiny honeycomb set against the immense
night on the sea. But inside, behind thick steel and toughened
glass, the world was containable, familiar and intact. They were

playing darts and remembering how things were as they pushed on towards their destination.

In the morning, blearily, they would dock in Amsterdam. In darting terms, this is as close to home as it is possible to get while being abroad. Holland is the closest thing to Britain when it comes to flying tungsten. The darting cruisers, disembarking, made their way into town in search of kindred spirits and an afternoon of 501, continental-style.

Hands across the sea.

The Dutch love darts. Of course they do. It's a natural fit. After all, the Dutch like beer, even Heineken. Also they like sport, and their country is cold enough and their winters long enough to drive people indoors. In fact, Holland is a country made for darts, especially when you take into consideration the well-worn fact, which may not be a fact but probably works for a darts book, that the Dutch population is among the tallest on the planet.

Throwing at eye level to the treble 20 *must* be an advantage. Vincent van der Voort, Co Stompe and Raymond van Barneveld are all strapping six footers, while the young, and wonderfully named Benito van de Pas stands at six foot four and gives you the impression that he could lean forward from the oche and simply place the dart in the treble 20. And the Feyenoord-supporting immensity of Vincent Kamphuis, whose flaxen locks and powerful shoulders sit atop an equally majestic girth, must surely top out at an altitude in excess of six foot five. His vast darts shirt bears the proud legend *Facta Non Verba* ('deeds not words') which only Feyenoord fans know about and is probably the only Latin-based darts reference to be immortalised in nylon.

There is something unstoppable about the Dutch darting scene and its growing status in the world. English players still just about hold sway at the major tournaments in terms of representation, but the Dutch are firmly established and enjoy a complete sense of belonging that began in 1998 when van Barneveld became the first Dutchman to be crowned world champion. That opened the floodgates which, in the dyke-constrained landscape of the Netherlands, can have a major knock-on effect.

These days you cannot move for players like Ron Meulen-kamp, Jermaine Wattimena and Christian Kist (almost the only Dutchman I've ever met who, when I first met him, struggled to express himself in English much beyond the necessary repertoire of 'Tops!' and 'Game On!'). And the young guns of Dutch support, whose great hero is of course the incomparable two-time champion of the world and reigning world number one Michael van Gerwen, make sure that their lager-saturated voices are heard and their Day-Glo colours are seen. The famous Dutch orange is ever-present at the World Championships, even though its hue is derived from a nonsense of mistranslation and half-understood history itself: William the Silent was the prince of a town in the Vaucluse region of France that was named after Arausio, a Celtic water god, and not a fruit, or indeed a colour. But who cares? Such nuances may be lost on the Barney Army, unless they are particularly bored at the darts and start wondering why it is that they are sitting there in an orange romper suit with the words 'Hup Holland Hup' emblazoned across their buttocks.

Any cursory visit to Ally Pally for the PDC Worlds will tell you all you need to know about the growth of the game in the low country. Their players are good, getting better, and in some cases, supernaturally gifted. In fact, in Michael van Gerwen, they might just have the best there's ever been. When you consider the records of Phil Taylor, that's some statement.

In 2016, and again the following two years, the Dutch witnessed a grappling of their country's darting past and future when their two greatest ever players met in the latter stages of the tournament. In 2017, van Gerwen got the better of van Barneveld and set a tournament record average of 114.05 in doing so, beating Taylor's previous best of 111.21. He had to be that good in order to get the job done. Barneveld (as commentators routinely refer to him, dropping the 'van' for convenience) averaged 109.34 for the match. That's like losing a Test match after posting 500 in the first innings. And in the 2018 tournament they met once again in the quarter-finals, and van Barneveld once again went down by the narrow margin of 5–4.

But it was the match in 2016, the first of these three outrageously brilliant meetings, which most sticks in my memory. The match that saw the youngster put in his place. It served to remind anyone watching of the fading brilliance of van Barneveld, and of what a player he had once been.

Van Barneveld won the 1998 BDO World Championship at Lakeside, beating Richie Burnett in the process, the man who had stopped him three years previously from becoming the first ever European world champion. It was a significant moment, not just for van Barneveld, but for the game itself, and it had been played out amid blistering tension all the way down to the final and decisive eleventh set. When the winning dart ricocheted from the barrel of its marker and into the double eight bed, the lightly moustachioed, tall Dutchman, wearing a very plain white shirt with a simple 'Holland' embroidered on its back, and bejewelled by the simplest of gold chains, closed his eyes then jumped in the air. This lucky charm had woven its spell. At 4–3 down, and in trouble, Barneveld had taken a moment to kiss the medallion before throwing. An hour later, and the tide had turned decisively in his favour. He was the new Embassy world champion. Then he sank to his knees and buried his face in his hands.

'Look at van Barneveld!' implored the BBC's veteran commentator Tony Green. 'He's crying!' As if this was a thing that dart players weren't normally to be found doing, an odd, continental habit, quaint and faintly comical. 'Look at the tears! Look at the scenes!' The camera picked out the darts player now staring heavenwards, while a boiling sea of fans bounced up and down in the background. 'Oh, this is incredible.' His co-commentator John Part, the man who four years previously had become the first ever overseas world champion, could only sit back in wonder at the significance of the occasion: 'one of the greatest sporting moments we've ever seen!'

Quite a claim.

And when the impeccably reserved and restrained Dougie Donnelly finally got van Barneveld into the studio for an interview alongside a distraught Richie Burnett, he asked whether he was even in a position to talk. 'No, yeah,' van Barneveld gabbled, 'yeah, no, yeah, yeah.'

'I was really emotional. I am the first overseas player to take the title to the Netherlands, and I am very proud of it,' and then he added, 'I don't know if I am going to stay a postman.' Then he started to mumble something about Schiphol airport, and lost the thread of his point. So Donnelly crisply wrapped up the chat and the show went off air.

He didn't remain a postman. Instead he went on to raise the BDO trophy on three more occasions before switching to the PDC, arguably, even at the time, a much tougher crucible, and repeated his success there by beating Taylor in 2007 at the Circus Tavern in Purfleet, claiming the trophy the Englishman had begun to consider his own by rights.

But his success had started the ball rolling for the land of total football. Suddenly they were all about the darts. The year following van Barneveld's fourth and final success at Lakeside, a 21-year-old Dutchman from close to the Belgian border, making his debut at the Lakeside, took his crown in another thriller. This time, not just the language had changed, but the look had too.

Jelle Klaasen's dark skin, slim build, perfect hair and single gold stud through his lower lip were decidedly un-darts. His game was, and still is, frighteningly fast. His nickname, the Cobra, is fully justified. TV directors groan inwardly when faced with the prospect of having to keep up with his furious pace. He takes a little over a second between darts. In fact, during one encounter with Michael van Gerwen, no slouch himself, they threw eight legs of darts in just over ten minutes. For plenty of pub players, a leg every quarter of an hour or so would be considered par for the course.

Klaasen, at his best, is a whirlwind. In 2006, everything about him was different. His skin colour, for a start. Klaasen's family roots are in Indonesia, although he hails from Alphen in the Brabant and is part of a relatively small community of expats from the former Dutch colony who punch above their weight in their adopted homeland. Their number include the former Dutch international footballers Roy Makaay and Giovanni van Bronckhorst.

Though united by native tongue and by passport, the contrast with van Barneveld could hardly have been more pronounced. The reigning champion, 38 years old in 2006, was probably at his portliest, having been on the circuit for the best part of a decade. In the intervening years since his first victory, van Barneveld, now no longer pacing the streets of den Haag with a bag full of post, had filled out proportionately to his reasonably ruinous lifestyle, born of the need to eat and drink enough to sustain the appropriate darting levels. He contracted type 2 diabetes, with which he continues to struggle, although in that complaint, he is far from alone in the darting world. But the longer the match ground on into the fetid Lakeside air, the more he began to succumb to the intense pressure, redden up around the cheeks and perspire.

Klaasen, meanwhile, looked immaculate. Who was this kid with his dark eyes and simple shirt wide open at the collar to reveal a boyish chest? His chin was smooth, though there was a trace of moustache on his upper lip which remained resolutely unquivering throughout. He betrayed not a flicker of emotion. The lights from the stage occasionally caught on the tiny gold stud that pierced his lower lip or teased his sculpted, oily-black hair into life. He was the most un-darts darts player ever to step up and compete. The word was he didn't even drink!

Klaasen snatched the title in 2006 in that all-Dutch final, playing deep into a game that finished 7–5 in sets, with astonishing calm and ruthlessness for a 21-year-old, still the youngest player in the history of the sport to achieve a world title. He closed the game out by thundering home a 101 checkout. It took him 4.77 seconds to throw the three darts that would change his life and for ever wed the Dutch to darts and vice versa. Each time accompanied by a trademark false throw to align the eye with the arm with the dart and the board, and then the unerring result: 25, treble 20, double eight.

'It's there! It's there!' The place erupted. 'Everyone is standing! Applauding!'

Klaasen had risen through the ranks of junior competition in the Netherlands alongside another Dutch wunderkind, Michael van Gerwen. They would often be profiled together: Klaasen, full of youthful poise and elegance, an even gaze and a maturity beyond his years; van Gerwen, with already thinning hair vertically teased into life by significant amounts of spray, a strangely malleable figure, mangling vowels as his fleshy voice chewed through his words. They were an odd couple, but two of the brightest talents on the planet. Van Gerwen, in particular, though he took a while to have the impact of his older compatriot, was talked of in the whispering halls of darting venues up and down the length of the country as a future great.

And yet, it has not been an entirely straightforward story for either player. With seemingly everything within his grasp, Klaasen, the newly anointed BDO world champion, tripped up. Dubbed the 'Cristiano Ronaldo of Darts' on account of his athletic physique and chiselled good looks, as well as his complex and time-consumingly styled hair, he never quite lived up to the enormous expectation that was placed upon him after he had dethroned his trailblazing compatriot Raymond van Barneveld. He switched to the PDC, as had van Barneveld, but the rigours of the circuit cost him, to some extent, his boyish good looks, and as he ploughed headlong into his thirties, to quote Philip Larkin again, 'his beauty had thickened'.

A few years after his World Championship win, and after switching codes, Jelle Klaasen was briefly involved in a potentially ruinous scandal. He was questioned by police and then prosecuted for sending an obscene picture message to a minor. Klaasen apologised profusely, but was sentenced by a Dutch court to community service and to pay damages. The extra complication, beyond the obvious seriousness of the offence, was that the recipient of the message, a teenager with learning difficulties, happened to be a relative of Michael van Gerwen. The two Dutchmen, as far as I have been able to observe, and unsurprisingly, do not waste words any more on one another.

Van Gerwen has risen from oddball maverick talent to the swaggering heavyweight of the darting world. His rise to the top has come about with sudden, almost violent, ruthlessness, mugging the established stars of the darts firmament like a young Mike Tyson entering the ring. Two steps forward, almost at a run, one punch, and it's game over. A sneer, and fist pump,

and the damage is done. The greatest player ever to throw a dart? That's a whole different debate, but his brilliance has been undeniable now for a couple of years.

When he turned up at the Grand Slam of Darts in Wolverhampton for the first time, he came with a colossal reputation, and a girth to match. This was my first encounter with MVG, as he has become known, Mighty Mike. He wore a bright green polo shirt, drank often to the point of flushed slurring, left tournaments early on, had no hair, and hobbled around as if his feet had been run over by a dumper truck. All in all, not quite world class. A tiler by trade, he was enjoying a job that didn't involve grout and adhesive. He lapped up the boisterous, care-worn glamour of the circuit and would rarely spurn a late-night KFC or two, or three. It's a tough lifestyle to keep a lid on, and van Gerwen gave me the distinct impression that his lid had been ripped off and discarded, like a family bucket.

But, still barely 20, and only a year or two on since switching codes from the BDO to the PDC, he was the talk of the sport.

Aged just 17, van Gerwen had already won the Winmau Masters, a venerable tournament dating back to the very early days of the televised sport in 1974. He became the youngest player ever to lift the trophy, two years younger than Eric Bristow had been in 1977, himself a freakishly young talent.

That victory was a good indication of things to come, and the reason why those with a detailed understanding of what constitutes a great talent would insist to me, gazing across the players' bar at this prematurely hairless Dutchman sipping away at a Red Bull or Jack Daniels and Coke, and nod reverentially in his direction. 'He's got it, him. He could be the real deal.' And somewhere across the room, the untouchably brilliant Phil Taylor would be holding court, or noisily winding up an opponent. To compare the two seemed absurd, and though I bowed to their judgement, I found these prophecies somewhat fanciful.

I didn't see it coming, until it suddenly did. In 2014, van Gerwen claimed the PDC World Championship, beating Peter Wright, 20 years his senior, to the title. With that quantum leap, he also took the number one ranking from Phil Taylor in a seismic moment for modern darts. It was the end of one extraordinary era, and the beginning of the next. Over the following two years, he amassed a further 14 major titles with Tayloresque greed. And three years later, he won the Worlds again.

He grew a swagger, too. As the millions started to pile up in his bank accounts, and a new army of fans were recruited from across the nation (not just the Netherlands, his popularity on these shores is colossal), he acquired some of the endearing and not so endearing habits of a serial winner. Now, when he entered a room, there was a sense of ownership. The scene was his, by rights. The strut said it all, and each consecutive win, of which there were so many, only fed into the impression that here was a man who beat his rivals before a dart was thrown.

The mental game, so much a part of Taylor's time at the top, was now taken up by his successor. The king of darts was, if not dead, then being measured up for interment, but the next coronation was in full swing.

The only thing missing in van Gerwen's sudden and continued brilliance had been an instant follow-up to that first world title. It took three more years to achieve, because in 2015 he fell just short of retaining his crown: a brilliant performance by Gary Anderson in the final denied him.

And in 2016, a year later, van Gerwen came face to face with his past, in one of the most extraordinary games I have ever seen. In the Netherlands, a nation watched on in rapt attention.

It was the quarter-final. Mighty Mike, in peak marauding form, faced Raymond van Barneveld as darts stared itself in the mirror, the Old and the New. And while the New was still very new, the Old van Barneveld had long been causing his legion of supporters to sigh and long for the days when he, not van Gerwen, had swept aside the opposition with terrible insouciance.

The truth was that the popular postman, the daddy of all darting Dutchmen, had been sliding ever so slowly into increasing irrelevance. He still looked like the same player, the wonderful fluency of his action would never be affected, but the waning powers of a man nudging towards his fifties had started to betray his talent. Indeed, he had started to approach the oche in the distracted manner that anyone of a similar age could identify, as if he'd walked into a room, patted his pockets and walked out again, without figuring out what he'd intended to achieve.

Everyone had become accustomed to his constant lugubrious presence at tournaments: quiet, unsmiling, shuffling around from practice board to exit with his tall loping stride. He had a string of worries and neuroses to pick away at. Controlling his diabetes meant that he tired easily as his blood sugars see-sawed wildly and his eyesight slipped away during matches. He fiddled endlessly with the weight of his darts, tweaking the flights, restless in his quest to turn back the years. Nothing worked. He cut a fractious figure, and seldom smiled. As a result, he was losing friends on the circuit, despite unaccountably high levels of popular support from the darts crowd, wherever he went.

He tried, in vain, to reinvent himself. He spent hours on the treadmill, Rocky Balboa style. Walking, not running, but on the treadmill nonetheless, even if it might have been hard even for Sky Sports' whizz-kids to cut a snappy training montage to his walk-on music of 'Eye of the Tiger' from shots of van Barneveld in a pair of baggy tracksuit bottoms loping along the rubber belt of a treadmill.

He experimented with a pair of glasses, and then lost them, and then got a Larry Grayson-style glasses chain, and still lost them. Then he forgot about the glasses and relaxed.

Then came this match.

At one point during the hour and a bit it took to complete, Wayne Mardle, commentating for Sky Sports, was left only with the simple, wonderful observation that, 'it's very hard to play this game well' – that from a man who is never stumped for words. But they were also the honest and heartfelt words of a former pro who could only dream of hitting such heights.

Van Barneveld was suddenly back: it was transcendent stuff. On two occasions he followed up his first dart by landing his second in the flights, and impaling itself on the first. The margins were so slight.

Van Gerwen did little wrong; van Barneveld out-calmed him. The game ebbed and flowed. The players traded 140s. They peppered 180s into the board. Van Gerwen took a lead, van Barneveld hauled himself back, broke the throw and went 3–2 ahead in sets. Needing 135 to save the game, van Gerwen produced a stunning checkout. All square in the deciding set, van Barneveld once again had a leg to win, if he could hold his throw.

He paused before his first visit, breaking with the nerveless momentum of his game, and had to steady himself with deep breaths. Then, almost inevitably, he blew it. Van Gerwen returned fire, and after six sets and four legs, it went to a sudden death decider. One leg. One winner.

It wasn't van Gerwen. The odds-on favourite for the tournament, the man who had won every televised major that autumn and appeared unbeatable, left the stage, slumped and shaking his smooth pale head, visibly shocked by his elimination. Van Gerwen had been astonishingly, unreasonably, historically good, averaging 105, at the time the highest-ever losing number at the Worlds. But the Amsterdam postman had just been better.

At the end, van Barneveld, whose calm finally broke, reached out his arms in an ecclesiastical pose, an ecstatic crucifixion in front of a baying mob. The tiger motif on the back of his shirt roared into vibrant colour as he howled a decade of frustration up into the lofty rafters of his ambition, a champion reawakened. Dutch vowels and consonants flew up into the late night air, thick with the sweat and beery breath of the 3,000 gathered there to witness one of the greatest encounters they're ever likely to see.

There is a statue in Canary Wharf, forgettable urban art. The day after van Barneveld's victory, I ran past it. It depicts a stout man, with arms outspread, looking skyward in supplication, or praise or despair, I am not sure. I took a picture of it and sent it to Raymond van Barneveld, who acknowledged the similarity in the gesture. Every time I pass it, I think of that extraordinary game.

Sport thrives on such moments, the last flickerings of greatness. A fading champion drops one heavy blow on the

young pretender and bloodies his nose. Everyone cheers and bays for more, not so much through loyalty, but that endless insatiable thirst for drama that lager itself will not quench.

That makes sense whether you are watching in Amsterdam or Hull or somewhere in between. The beer tastes much the same across the North Sea, and the weather's a bit crap.

Just like home.

Seventy-Six

'Don't you talk with Mr Kurtz?' I said.
'You don't talk with that man – you listen to him,'
he exclaimed with severe exaltation.
JOSEPH CONRAD – *HEART OF DARKNESS*

Russ Bray is known as 'The Voice': a man whose entire *raison d'être* and income stream is associated with one very particular dart. It's the final dart of three treble twenties; the one that finds the impossible gap, muscling into the tiny space left on the board, a fractional jostle of the flights as if the dart is shaking its shoulders, then is still. It's the last dart in 'three in a bed': the final piece of the perfect 180.

In the split-second of ultimate success, Russ Bray starts to emit an exquisite noise, like rainfall in a desert forcing sudden flowers. The blossoming exhortation that follows is the sound, which, more than any other, means darts. It will last no more than a few seconds, but will echo in the imaginations and the memories of all who have been lucky enough to hear it.

It starts with a throaty gurgle, almost a gargle. The staccato drumming of a golf ball-size gob of phlegm that is slapped in hummingbird-wing speed against mucus membranes deep inside a human's throat:

'One huuuuu—'

Then the pitch rises, gently at first then exponentially, surfing a wave of sound ever upwards and, as the windpipe opens, the snot-rattling croak falls away and the battle cry takes over. Here is the climax, the arc of the rumble, heading towards the non-negotiable hard stop of the T. Bray winces, eyes half shut, with the actual effort of making this sound happen.

'...uuuundred...nnn....eeeiiiiGGGHHH–Teeeeeeeeeeeeee...'

Tripping along in the wake of the explosive consonant, the after echo of sound, a long mournful, post-coital exhalation; longer than you might ever have thought possible. Bray moves his mighty lips closer to the microphone, determined to catch every last decibel, every last vowel. He lets nothing spill.

'...eeeeeeee..ee..e.e...e...'

Bray has called it again. He knows that when he calls '180', there is no greater sound in darts. It is his trademark, his 180, and as befits all 180s, it is an unimprovable moment in time. The sport of darts has this sound as its signature tune. For, like the thunder of hooves in the final furlong, the squeak of trainers on the basketball court, or the Doppler effect whine of a Formula One car in full flight, darts is defined by Bray's iconic uber-gravelly voice.

In short, when Bray calls, 'Game on!', then the game is properly fucking on.

I arranged to meet him in London.

I wanted to talk to Bray properly. Previously, our exchanges had taken place over a hotel breakfast in Purfleet, Minehead or Glasgow, when he was sharing ribald chat about this, that and the other. Now, though, I needed Bray's undivided attention.

I was on the scent of Eric Bristow. And Bray had worked with Bristow at exhibitions and knew him. Their history went back the best part of 30 years. When Bray was a competitive darts player, together they had won the Norway and the Finland Pairs, a couple of footnotes in Bristow's career, but the crowning glories of Bray's. If anyone could shed light on the Crafty Cockney, then surely it was him.

An Essex boy in his early sixties, Bray is olive-skinned, close-cropped and slightly bejewelled. He stands well over six feet tall, weighs in at a fairly trim 15 stone, and looks like the Last Cockney.

He speaks the English of the Thames estuary in a manner that makes Phil Mitchell sound slightly effete. This is cockney distilled down to a thick London sludge, edged with threat and croaking the values of an East End animus that I thought only ever existed in the imagination. He is the very essence of that imagined London.

And yet it might have worked out differently. Born to a Canning Town mother and a USAF airman father in 1957, he was very nearly expatriated, along with his brother, to be raised in the United States by his father. Instead, his mother remarried and the family were raised in South Ockendon in Essex; a new town originally built mostly by German POWs and designed using prefab constructions. It originally housed bombed-out East End families.

Bray's stepfather worked at the local Aveley Ford factory where they manufactured the original Ford Escorts, those boxy ones that look like children's drawings of cars. His mother rose through the ranks at the local authority to become a chief accountant, and Bray grew up in a happy, supportive household.

We are sitting outside King's Cross station, our agreed meeting point, at the end of his train line in from Cambridgeshire, where he now lives. It's summer and we're enjoying some warm sunshine, which allows his silver medallion to glint from time to time. As people stream past our pavement cafe table en route to the station, Bray attracts oblique nods and glances. I notice that people are noticing him. He's a name. A face. A voice.

You can hear that famous voice in a bewildering variety of places. It'll bubble up in movie trailers, or advertising crisps, bookies or microwavable food products. Most recently, he's made his musical debut, of which he is justly proud, in the animated film *The Land of Sometimes*. In the shape of a charmingly lazy bespectacled amphibian, he sings (well, talks, really) a song called 'The Ballad of the River Slouch Sling'. The film's illustrious cast includes Ewan McGregor, Helena Bonham Carter, Terry Jones, James Corden and David Walliams, and has, at the time of writing, no projected release date.

In fact, his singing talents were proved to me only recently in a pub near Minehead when he performed a karaoke duet of 'Up Where We Belong' with Richard Ashdown, the diminutive Master of Ceremonies from the rival BDO darts scene, himself blessed with an angelic falsetto. I think it was the last time I cried with laughter.

The ten-year-old Russ Bray must have had a bit of a showbiz glint in his eye, I suggest. Bray puts his latte down. 'I was a bit

mischievous,' he tells me, with a look of faux shame. He then laughs, like Sid James warming up, a geezer's wheeze that could just as easily segue from mirth into a chesty cough. 'I started smoking when I was ten.'

'That's pretty... committed,' I observe, searching for the appropriate accolade.

'And I stopped at 43. No, 53.' The word 'fifty-free' is as rich and dark as a swimming pool of molasses on the Costa del Sol.

For a man who makes counting such an integral part of his professional life, the omission of a full decade is an unusual slip of the tongue. Bray's maths skills are prodigious. But then again, there's nothing unusual about that in the darts world, where things that pass for ordinary are far from it. The ability of players (and referees, of course) to calculate on the hoof without the slightest hesitation is remarkable. Knowing every combination of 'out shots' and what remains on the board is a vital skill, which must be learned until it is glitch-free, instant and unthinking. Anything less than instantaneous calculation breaks the flow of the visit for the player.

I tried to chalk a game in a pub once and was left trying to catch up almost straight away. Subtracting numbers like 57 from 306 may come naturally to some, but not to me. Bray does it without thinking: 249. He also knows which routes the players favour on their way to a checkout. Each player has his own preferences, which referees like Bray grow to know just as well. Besides, Bray has been calling darts scores for the PDC ever since 1996 when he deputised for another caller who had taken ill. In that moment, darts had found its voice, one forged by the bewildering amount of fags that had been inhaled and passed over its vocal cords.

'I was fifty-free when I gave up. Forty-free years of smoking,' he chuckles, having now done the maths.

How can you not like Russ Bray? Listening to him talk is like mainlining a very specific culture. His is the Essex of the seventies and eighties and, just about, the early nineties. Forgotten Britain, in a single, distended larynx and a mash-up of dropped consonants.

One day, during a long-ago tournament, we filmed him trying to teach me how to call a 180 (I couldn't, and the attempt to do so nearly left me mute). The next day, we filmed him as we took him shopping for a new suit to wear onstage (Bray favours some pretty outlandish gear) and ended up forcing him into the most appalling threads we could find, a kind of shiny blue abomination, collarless, as far as I recall, in the style of a kind of bling Jawaharlal Nehru. He hated it, but wore it with good grace onstage the following day, prompting Matt Porter, the much-feared chief executive of the PDC, and effectively Bray's employer, to tell him to 'never wear that fucking disgrace of a suit again'.

'But ITV made me put it on,' Bray pleaded in his defence.

'Then ITV are a bunch of wankers.' Porter concluded the case for the prosecution, not unreasonably.

I remember hiding behind my laptop during this backstage exchange, afraid of what primal darting furies I might have unleashed by forcing Russ Bray, the number one darts referee in the world, into an inappropriate suit for the sake of a laugh as cheap as the garment itself (I seem to recall it cost the handsome sum of £40). Not for the first, nor last time, I felt that I had strayed worryingly to misapprehending the mood, failing to judge the degree to which darts people seem open to gently mockery. What we had filmed had perhaps come dangerously close to sneering, which was the last thing I had intended. You see, I like Bray a good deal.

Ten years on, Bray has forgiven me. Besides, as he tells me, he's lived a life dedicated to having a laugh, ever since childhood.

'I were... y'know... cheeky 'n' tha'.' He shoots me a smile in which the six-year-old bursts through the craggy veneer of the man ten times his age.

'Just the right side of wrong?' I ask him.

'That's it.' He slaps me hard on the shoulder in jocular, if painful, approval. 'Just the right side of wrong.'

It seems that I have accurately gauged Bray's correct level of rascal.

'Don't forget, I became a copper,' Bray reminds me, as a second latte gets plonked down in front of us both.

I'd forgotten that before he became the voice of darts, Russ Bray's throwing arm was clothed in the dark blue of the Metropolitan Police. This was exactly the same time that a young Eric Bristow, almost identical in age, was breaking into houses and straying decidedly the wrong side of right. It would be years before the two men met in the middle, where darts defined the margins. At the age of just 16, Russ Bray followed his elder brother into the police force. It seemed the natural thing to do.

He was also a high jumper of some distinction, representing the police force athletics team. Pictures of him back then show a toned, tanned specimen, standing on makeshift podiums in trademark 1970s nylon shorts, smiling broadly. He once beat a young Daley Thompson, setting a personal best of a more than respectable six foot ten. It was only when he became aware that the Americans, who had the luxury of proper crash mats to land on, rather than the sand pits of their British counterparts, and had developed the Fosbury Flop that he packed it in and tried out his darting arm instead.

Two and a half years later he had learned to play darts with enough swagger to win his first trophies as he represented his unit. At the same time he graduated from the cadet force to become an officer. His insertion into the front line would prove to be a swift, steep and sometimes violent learning curve.

In 1976, aged just 19, he was stationed at Peckham police station at a time when the largely immigrant West Indian population was beginning to simmer with a pent-up sense of injustice. The almost exclusively white police force of the Met had little or no idea of what a hornets' nest of tensions they might be stirring up when they went about their policing. Random arrests, arbitrary beatings, even unlawful detention: all these were not unknown police behaviours. Sometimes there were fatalities, incidents that have gone unexplained to this day.

Our weirdly nostalgic nation still seems curiously fixated by that hot summer of 1976, as if summers have never been the same since. Even those born too late to remember it believe they were there, so powerfully has 1976 bedded down into the national collective unconscious.

The West Indies cricket team came to play, all summer. England captain Tony Greig, somewhat ill-advisedly, suggested that his team would make them 'grovel'. That's not quite what happened.

In his 16 years on the force, Bray's most treasured memory is still the fifth and final Test of a five-match series (won 3–0 overall by the West Indies). Just a mile or two from the heartland of South London's black community in Stockwell, Camberwell and Brixton, the Oval hosted one of the greatest visiting teams ever to be assembled, who just happened to be at their dazzling best. Russ Bray, bussed to the cricket from Peckham police station, and a massive sports fan, hit the jackpot.

'Kennington Oval, 1976.' More than 40 bewildering years later, Bray's eyes light up at the memory of the unnaturally blue skies, the brittle outfield and the 747s wheeling in over the gas towers. 'Viv Richards, double century.'

It was Richards' second century of that astonishing series, as his monstrous 291 helped the tourists to a blithely assembled first-innings total of 687 for 8. Bray watched every heavy hoist over mid-on, every dismissive slog over square leg.

'You know what my job was? Walk round the perimeter and open the gate for them when they come in for lunch and tea. For five days.' To make it even better, Bray was also on police overtime pay. 'The hottest summer we've ever experienced. That was...' The Voice is temporarily lost for words, '...that was the best job I ever had.'

It must be one of the earliest memories I have, not just of sport, but of anything. I cannot remember life in a pram, nor my earliest nurturing on the maternal arm. What I remember best is watching telly; the smell of our calor gas fire in the winter, brought ever closer to the sofa, and the sound of the TV and its wonderful dramas played out to the tune of the best: Coleman, Vine, Walker. And of that summer, I remember Benaud.

Even 100 miles away, I understood, without really understanding, that something different and beautiful and a little dangerous was happening. Listening to Richie Benaud (who Bray would much, much later meet and chauffeur to a wedding during a brief period of time in which he drove a white Rolls-Royce for a living) as I watched the action on a badly tuned black-and-white rental TV set, I can recall the atmosphere that the West Indies brought to bear.

It was not only about the brilliance of their batsmen and bowlers. It was equally something to do with the unstuffy exuberance of their play and their celebrations, matched only by the unbridled joy of the vast crowds drawn to the game from the local streets. The boiling, bouncing mass of pleasure inside that cricket ground. The cans of Red Stripe held aloft. And Russ Bray, in the thick of it all, not yet 20, unhitching the catch on the little wrought-iron gate that led to the pavilion, easing the path of the Caribbean's greatest sportsmen to their egg sandwiches and orange squash. Bray was the gate-keeper to a culture clash.

Then, just 13 days later, a very different story was told. It was 30 August, the other side of London, and no one was thinking about the cricket any longer. Russ Bray was thrown into the front line when that summer's Notting Hill Carnival exploded into violence.

A series of pickpocketing crimes, and rumours of more, led to a violent, and, many would have it, unjustifiable overreaction from both sides. Certainly some of Bray's stories of the policing culture back then are horrifying by today's standards, whereas other stories are simply horrifying by any measure. This was a raw world.

There were 1,600 police that night in Notting Hill, many of them like Russ Bray, new to this world of urban unrest, armed with truncheons and protecting themselves with dustbin lids, drinks crates and traffic cones, whatever they could get hold of. They clashed with a large number of predominantly young black men, furious at their targeted treatment. It was one of a series of lows in race relations in the late seventies and early eighties, in which heavy-handed police tactics undoubtedly exacerbated the violent lawlessness it met with. While some of what he remembers of his colleagues' behaviour from the time is scandalous, other memories are more human. Footage of the time suggests simply that chaos held sway; the police, on the front foot, spilling out, Keystone-like, from old-fashioned minibuses, clutching their helmets with one hand, and their weapons with another, to be met with anger, fire and stone.

'Bear in mind we didn't have shields. We didn't expect it to go off. There were guys standing no more than three foot away, trying to throw house bricks at your head.' It's still a real memory for Bray, as he lines up an imaginary rock.

'There's someone standing right in front of you that wants to hurt you... that don't care if you've got a uniform on.' He shakes his head. But the fear was there on both sides.

The summer of 1976 had been a burning, turning point, and as Bray circled the Oval, and drew lines with the boys in blue, a newer, brasher Britain was licking its lips. Post-war restraint was a bust flush, the old order was no longer fit for purpose and whether or not there were better times ahead, patience had finally run out with black-and-white Britain.

That summer finally cooled off and the nights closed in. November arrived and London went back indoors. And with the darkness came the darts. At the West Centre Hotel in Fulham, John Lowe beat Welshman Phil Obbard to lift his first World Masters title. When the winning dart went in, Lowe turned to shake the hand of the markers onstage, who had been scoring as the game progressed.

One of them congratulated him and said, 'You don't know me, do you? Well, you will soon. Eric Bristow's the name.'

Darts was anti-establishment. The established order of *Top of the Pops* was overthrown, turned upside down by punk; charts that still dripped with the honeyed craft of ABBA and Elton John now had a riot on their hands. It was a revolution. Meanwhile, Bristow, strutting into a pub in California called the Crafty Cockney, stole the title, assumed his new nickname, and returned to London full of cheeky ambition and unassailable swagger, about to shake up the darts world. 'Get stuffed,' was one of Eric Bristow's favourite phrases. That's what the old world was being told to do. Get stuffed.

That was a mission he would never quite decline, even some 40 years later, when the darts world decided that Bristow's ancient prejudices were representative of a time that had burnt itself out and crashed into the Sun. But all that was still to come.

This was 1976, and he'd not even met Russ Bray, who still had years of policing left ahead of him, before eventually turning to the game of second chances; the last-but-one resort. Before Bray started to call darts, darts called him.

Fourteen years later, in 1990, Eric Bristow would save Bray's life. It was one of those trivial close escapes that proliferate in most people's daily lives, but could pass to within a whisker of tragedy.

The first time that the pair got to know one another was on one of Bray's first trips abroad, in Canada. After an afternoon spent necking lagers in their shared accommodation, the two men went out to find a pool hall (Bristow, perhaps unsurprisingly, was a brilliant pool player). Striding out into the road, Bray had failed to look the right way, being unfamiliar with the decidedly non-British habit of driving on the right. He took one step into the road, and straight into the path of an oncoming juggernaut, screaming its presence from the giant chrome horns on the roof of its towering cab.

Bristow had seen it coming. He reached out his elongated darting arm and grabbed Bray by the neck, yanking him back towards the pavement and out of harm's way by the width of a wire as the truck hammered past, narrowly avoiding the recently retired policeman and emerging darts referee.

From there the pair proceeded, as if it were the most natural thing in the world, to the pool hall, where Bristow briefed Bray on his plans to hustle the joint. He intended, much to the impecunious Bray's horror, that they'd open up by playing for $25 a frame. Bray agreed, because he had no other choice. After all, he was playing with Eric Bristow, and you tended to agree.

After their orchestrated slow start, Bristow took control and they left the joint with $200 in their back pockets. 'We have been mates ever since.'

Twenty-eight years later, they still watch each other's backs. That is to say, Bray still keeps an eye out for Bristow, just about.

'He's a good lad. A little outspoken at times, maybe,' Bray explains. 'But that's Eric Bristow and everyone knows it. He's always got away with it. But that one he hasn't.' Bray acknowledges the seriousness of Bristow's extraordinary public attack on male victims of sexual abuse, an attack that earned him instant dismissal from his employment by Sky Sports on their darts coverage. 'He just got smashed down in flames.' Then he paints a picture that is, by now, familiar: Bristow has been cast adrift.

'Now he's just doing odd jobs. Cos no one'll fucking touch him. No one wants to be associated with that. And you can't blame them.'

'Not even in the darts world?' I venture. 'Because, let's face it, it's not exactly politically correct.'

'No it's not,' Bray agrees. It's a habit of his, almost as if it were an inbuilt reflex, to agree with what you say. The corrective comes later, when you've forgotten that perhaps he doesn't actually agree. As it happens, on this occasion, we are as one: darts is not a particularly politically correct arena. Bray moves the debate about Bristow on. More pressingly, in his mind, he delivers a withering attack on the Crafty Cockney's diminished darting skill set.

'But also he's shit,' he points out. And then he amplifies his assessment. 'He's crap, he's absolutely fucking hopeless. I mean, I would smash him to fucking pieces. I don't throw a dart at all any more, but I would smash Eric to pieces.' He thinks about it for a second more. 'I really, really would.'

Bray suggests, quite rightly, that I should talk to Bristow myself. He's right. But I know that it won't be easy. This is what I think of as I watch Bray leave me behind and head for his train in King's Cross, passing through the crowd anonymously and disappearing from view.

But I know that he is right. So, stopping by the side of the road, on my ride home, I send Bristow a text message.

'Hi Eric. It's Ned Boulting here...'

Minehead

The memory of that time itself lingers around me, impalpable, like a dying vibration of one immense jabber, silly, atrocious, sordid, savage, or simply mean, without any kind of sense. Voices, voices…

JOSEPH CONRAD – *HEART OF DARKNESS*

My text message remained unanswered. Eric Bristow was lying low. Dick Allix had contacted him on my behalf and put in a good word. But Dick had come away empty-handed.

'Hi Ned, I'm afraid Eric will not speak with you. It's not personal, it's universal where any media is concerned. To quote: "I'm done with the lot of them." For a reasonably intelligent man, he, at times, shows remarkable stupidity. Your book will survive quite well without his input, I think.'

It was both a relief and a frustration to be snubbed by Bristow, I thought, as I drove along the M5 to my next waypoint. It seemed, on the one hand, that there was no escaping his presence and that all roads led back to him. But, at the same time, he appeared to exist nowhere.

Minehead was somewhere I associated intimately with Bristow. I had often seen him there, the day before the UK Open or the Players Championship got under way, when I'd been working for ITV. Bristow had, on occasions, been paid to put in an appearance by some sponsors while a tournament was going on. His job was simply to turn up, not actually throw any darts, and be Eric Bristow, pint in hand, fag on the go, quip at the ready. No one fitted the job description better, and no backdrop suited the occasion more aptly than the famous Butlin's holiday camp, out of season, and readying itself for the incoming darts.

Like my destination beyond a perfect sun that was setting over the M5, Bristow had simply become a potent symbol, a shorthand for a way of life born from the British at play. It was a bit unreal.

A mile up the road from Minehead, where I work twice a year for three days, lies the heritage gem of Dunster; a pretty, cobbled, gabled, and markedly non-darts village. Dunster has a high street that has appropriated the term quaint. It boasts a clutch of B&Bs and small hotels. Once in November, and again in March, the ITV darts crew descends on this scene, opening up otherwise dormant accommodation, neglected during the winter months. After 12 hours of live broadcasting, time spent dredging nearby Butlin's in Minehead for its swill and grime, sweat and spit, it is with a sometimes guilty sense of relief that we pile into our cold vehicles, switch on the heating and roar away from the venue to find Dunster sleepily welcoming us with log fires and real ale. Here, calm returns, and order is restored, while back down the road, the crazies are battling their way into town in search of more beer or a late feed.

I wake early on most of my Dunster days, soft at the edges from another noisy sojourn in the realm of the darts. With a considerable effort of resolve, and only after a fractious internal tug-of-war, do I summon up the willpower to run out of Dunster in the direction of higher ground.

I grind through leaf mulch up the steep slopes of the splendidly named Grabbist Hill till I reach the top. Here, by the bench on which no one ever sits, I pause, catching my breath. I look from this grand shoulder of land above Minehead down on to the coast, the flat sweep of land buffeted by a steady wind, its barnacle holiday complex on the coastline, dwarfing everything else around. This is the still sleeping encampment of Butlin's, slowly summoning itself into sobriety and limbering up for another day of semi-ironic, mostly inebriated hero worship of the big men of the oche. The contrast between the ochre- and khaki-wooded expanses that fringe Exmoor and the cloistered, artificially colourful world contained within Butlin's fenced-off perimeter far below is as clear a difference as day is from night, or darts from grouse shooting.

Minehead is unique. With part-frozen drizzle whipping in across the Bristol Channel, there is no bleaker place on earth to stroll off an outrageous tungsten hangover than here. A stumble along the seafront outside Butlin's is a ritual of suffering and rebirth. Sand blows across the road. Flagpoles rattle their ropes in the wind. Nothing else moves, except the slow drift of the second hand, inching the minute hand towards the afternoon session and the reawakening of appetite.

Set like a giant franchised jewel into this obdurately north-facing stretch of Somerset coast, Butlin's dominates the understated Edwardian gentility of the old resort. Built originally in 1962, but tinkered with down the decades, its outstanding feature is an outsized tent pole and canvas construction, not entirely unlike a kind of low budget, undersized, variegated Millennium Dome. This giant awning houses the main atrium; a 21st-century pleasure dome, fully equipped with hot food retail outlets that fill the air with an ultra-fine mist of vegetable oil and minced beef.

Around that centrepiece lies a series of two-storey chalet blocks in which, if you have drunk more than your body

weight of watery lager, it is just about possible to sleep before the sound of the steam railway, which anachronistically runs along the back of the chalets, hoots the morning into noisy life. Its whistling passing is a quaint reminder of family holidays back before the darts arrived, administering their financial life support to a facility at death's door.

Though this tired accommodation has seen better days, when the darts is in, every day is one of the best days ever. Twice a year, in the gloomiest of months either side of Christmas, the PDC circus moves to the south-west. Butlin's Minehead welcomes darts to its bosom with a warm embrace and beery breath.

At nine o'clock in the morning there is normally not much to be seen out and about, save for the occasional Peter Storm-clad cagoule-wearing dog walker. Locals know that there is little danger of encountering a marauding posse of darts tourists so early in the day, so it is considered safe. But by ten, the first explorers emerge, blinking into the daylight. Then, at the mid-morning witching hour, the locals melt away.

But by 11 o'clock, the scene has changed again. Now, huddled packs of pale men, and a few women, stream from the holiday camp into town in search of fried food, bent against the grey-soaked sky. This is the recovery hour, where bits and pieces of the previous night are reconstituted in half-remembered scraps and broken flashbacks. The walkways and alleyways, doorways and access roads of the holiday camp are rich with regret: a discarded can of cider, half-filled with rain water and fag butts; a multicoloured Mohican wig, flattened into a puddle; a cold, dew-sodden pizza crust with a mournful mouthful missing, beached outside the door to the chalet. If only it could speak. What tales it might tell.

At the back of the main arena are shrouded echoes of a funfair, de-commissioned for the winter months; a go-kart circuit, some sort of scaled-down roller coaster and a chair-o-plane, whose seats stir limply by its side, awaiting warmer days when they will once again soar joyfully above the tarmac and the hot dog and onion waft.

The go-kart circuit is also closed for the winter, though once we arranged for it to be sparked back into life so that I could squeeze into a tiny kart alongside Andy 'The Hammer' Hamilton to film an interview. Quite why we were chatting in a miniature racing car never seemed worth explaining to the viewer, even if we could have explained it.

There is a mini-golf, too, for the less adventurous. One afternoon, following on from his victory, Terry 'The Bull' Jenkins and I wandered around the mini-golf course, accompanied by a television camera crew, and discussed his career as we stepped carefully over miniature windmills and bridges. It was a very darts interview, made up on the spur of the moment, and shot guerrilla-style without a second's preparation. In order to film, we'd had to break into the mini-golf compound by climbing over the perimeter fence, as none of us could be bothered to wait in the biting drizzle any longer for the lad from Butlin's who'd gone off to look for the keys.

Then, on our way back to the warmth of the players' lounge, Jenkins had pointed at two tiny spring-mounted rocking horses, the kind you find in playgrounds for the under-fives.

'We could sit on them and have another chat,' the world number 14 dart player suggested.

'We could.' Since I could see no reason why not, though I also could see no reason why, I agreed.

And so it came to pass that Terry Jenkins was sitting on one, and I on another wobbly plastic horse, our knees ridiculously high, and both gently bobbing on our saddles, engaged in a high-level analysis of the difficulties of his game.

It only occurred to me later that evening how strangely accepting everyone was of this peculiar setting. My producer, on viewing the tape, had taken our playground setting in his stride, offering only a matter-of-fact appraisal that made no reference to the rocking horse aspect of the shoot. 'Nice interview with Terry.' That was all he had said.

And then I understood the mind-altering otherness of the context. This extraordinary, possibly unique, minute or so of television could really only be realised in the surreal fug of Butlin's Minehead in November when the darts is on. It is a time and a place that warps convention, and challenges norms, mostly because of the absence of anything approaching reality. Here is delusion and delight. Here is the very centre of the darting jungle, and instead of being 1,000 miles up the Congo, it's actually about 45 minutes from junction 24 of the M5.

If darts can be considered a religion, then Minehead, with its forlorn back passages stacked high with aluminium beer kegs, its security cameras and its wet tarmac twinkling with the reflected light from chalets, has become a location for an annual pilgrimage, as if it were some kind of Lourdes in reverse, where the pilgrims leave less healthy than they arrived. Other darts venues are visited by day only; a ticket to an event, an evening out and then a taxi home. But in Minehead you live, eat, drink and sleep the dream.

The flagship of its two-event darting calendar is without doubt the UK Open, an event that used to be held in Bolton and which was created in the tradition of the old *News of the World* championship. It has a grass-roots, down-to-earth appeal, as players can get to the televised finals through any number of open qualifiers up and down the country: simply turn up, win four or five matches, and you'll be on the telly, maybe even drawn against one of the greats. This is precisely the path that was taken in 2016 by Rob Cross, who, less than two years later, was the world champion.

During the UK Open, on whose leviathan opening day there are ten boards in play at any given moment, parts of the Butlin's complex that do not normally open up for the use of the darting fraternity come into play. This includes two of the on-site nightclubs. The most atmospheric of these is called 'Reds', and is red. It is not easy to forget the smell of this place, once experienced. The olfactory senses rebel at a cellular level as they are assaulted by a very particular sweetish, almost faecal stench, with overtones of an elderly dog panting in your face. It is generated and distributed via the acres of rotting carpet in the cavernous, low-ceilinged bunker. What once was red, and might have been plush, is now trodden to a deep bruised black and compacted to form a centimetre of floor covering. Spilt beer and leisure shoes have threshed the fabric into submission. It has subsided into degeneracy. So specific is this mix of carpet mould – Red Bull and vodka and perspiration – that I was astonished when I recently boarded a Virgin Pendolino train in Crewe only to be assailed by the Butlin's odour. I was transported, as only smell can transport, straight to Minehead, and to the sweet, if sometimes sickly, soul of the game.

At the front of the compound stands a modestly sized block of luxury penthouse apartments. They are quite recently built and rendered in a timelessly glamorous art deco style. Facing north, with their backs to the rest, they are the jewel in the Butlin's crown. From the second floor, their tall windows, should the curtains be parted, would gaze out into the cloudy gloom that seems to hang over the wintry water.

These islands of opulence are also, while the darts are in town, the exclusive reserve of the big stars of the darting firmament. This is where the pre-eminent players like James Wade, Michael van Gerwen and Raymond van Barneveld take up residence for as long as they remain in the competition. Their commute to work is about 100 yards, though sometimes I have seen them get a lift in a car, often a Range Rover with a bespoke number plate that plays artfully with the number 180.

When the players are knocked out, as all but the two finalists will be before the tournament wraps up on Sunday night, they check out within minutes (often having packed in anticipation of an exit) and they vanish into the night, roaring through the gates, onto the seafront and then out into the darkness of Somerset. There is simply nothing to hang around for. With each fresh departure, the backstage area of the practice boards and the players' bar becomes more and more deserted.

That's one of the curiosities of a knockout tournament. The longer it goes on, the less intensity it generates. The early rounds, when the place is buzzing with players, all of whom think they've got a chance, are when Butlin's hums with life; figures in brightly coloured darts shirts flit around the place like tropical fish in a vast holiday camp aquarium.

But the crowds do not witness this gradual thinning out of the darting panoply. Their part in the action remains strictly

front-of-house and as boisterous as ever. The signal that the
weekend can officially get under way is the moment when, just
before the first match of the tournament, the ebullient MC John
McDonald takes to the stage on Friday lunchtime. The arena
is only half full, but people are wandering in and taking a seat
on the rows of benches; isolated clusters of lager-drinking fans
become bigger, less identifiable clumps, and before you know
it, there is a crowd starting to feel a lively tingle of beer in the
blood. This is the audience that faces the immaculately turned
out MC when he strides onto the stage, microphone in hand, to
get proceedings under way.

After welcoming the fans and asking them to refrain from
penning obscenities on their message cards, he advises them,
for their own welfare, to 'please, drink responsibly'. He follows
this up with a knowing smile, instantly undermining his advice.
Besides, they're not really listening.

'Thud!'

And so it begins.

This is where the hardcore come and stay, the lifers, those
willing and joyous members of the wider British public
who have elected to lose three days to darts, punctuated by
occasional moments of exuberant, irrational cheering and
uncontrolled staggering down the aisles between the tables on
the hunt for chips, dad-dancing as their favourite players walk
onto the stage, and, crucially, living for those frequent moments
of intense drama as a game narrows into pinpoint tension.

Without those precious, unique, transcendental seconds,
darts is simply a formless piss-up. The close calls, the pressure
throws, the off-the-wire agony of the miss: these crackle with
meaning, and they evince an unconscious and uncontrollable
reaction in the spectator. This is what darts thrives on; the
method in the madness when the concentrated congregation
becomes absorbed in the teetering, unknown outcome of the

struggle. Sometimes, in the midst of total mayhem, you can hear a pin drop, or a dart land.

Thud.

And then the place explodes. The rhythm of a darts match can be mesmerising, to the extent that even the fuzziest head in the crowd will find their attention drawn to the spots of light on the stage where the action suddenly sparks into incandescent life. Players, at some unknowable pheromone signal, will routinely accelerate into blistering form, dropping astonishing 140s and 180s with fluent abandon, matching shot for shot and stride for stride, the pace of the game barrelling vertiginously upwards. Or as one player suddenly hits a groove, their opponent's game will crumble. And then, a leg or two later, the whole impulse of the game swings back through 180 degrees, and the momentum changes.

Great swings of fortune are what makes the game work as a spectacle. The scoring system of 501 allows for the unlikely possibility of a player coming back from the dead, just as James Wade did to beat Mervyn King in the final of the Masters in 2014. He'd been 9–2 down and ended up winning the title 11–10. That's an extreme example, but similar reverses are not uncommon, and they bring the crowd to boiling point.

That's what these fans have come to see, after all. For all the Super Mario hats and aching livers, this is what the point of it is, and it's every bit as intoxicating as the alcohol on sale in the Skyline Arena. These are the moments when the game takes over and the union of stage and board and crowd is complete. This is darts and, at Minehead, it comes for the all-in-one price of £130, including accommodation for three nights and entry to all six four-hour sessions of live darting action.

Over the course of a long weekend, finishing late into Sunday night, tales will emerge from the serried ranks of darts fans that will shock and amuse. There will be talk of raw sewage backing up into toilet pans in the chalets and of young men dressed as Jesus Christ being escorted from the premises. On that occasion the venerable hall soon echoed with chants of 'We want our Jesus back!' 'Don't worry,' McDonald told the crowd. 'He'll be back at Easter.'

But on another dark Minehead night of the darting soul, worrying tales emerged of a finger being bitten off. Not that you should be put off by that. Statistically, you are no more likely to lose a finger at the darts than you are at any other sporting event.

Working for television keeps us at arm's length from the tungsten coalface of the arrows. The cameramen, often wearing waterproof clothing to protect against lager spills, and closely marked by the immense might of the PDC security detail, make occasional forays into the crowd, training their lenses on clusters of bishops, Tellytubbies or men in baby costumes complete with nappies and a dummy.

When the red light on the top of the camera flicks on, so too does Pavlov, and instantly the assorted fandom parades a riotous array of gurns and grins and bounces, all to the certain and unchanging accompaniment of an involuntary 'Yaaaaaaayyyy!' Then the camera detail withdraws again, to await its next mission behind the lines.

The fans in the hall, burping and singing their way through the night, are transmitted into millions of houses. The viewers are given a precisely measured dose of the mayhem, enough for a mild hit, but not so much as to render the viewing experience incoherent. It's a delicate mission. No crowd, no television, no game. But keeping a lid on the whole boiling stockpot is just as important.

And yet, in the midst of the bedlam, swoop into the detail and pick out the individual faces. The Minehead mass is amorphous, wild, ridiculous, but the single face, etched with the lines of pleasure and release, betrays its own reasons for being there, and being happy. Behind each howl of delight that the TV pictures dilute and disperse into a wash of colour and noise is an entirely separate world of primary concerns put on ice: anniversaries celebrated in style, children left at home and missed, painful situations temporarily forgotten and old friendships renewed by three days of robust amusement. This is intended; it is the whole point.

When the everyday heroes of the dartboard make their way to the stage, some bashful, others ebullient, and all of them feted in ways they would never have imagined possible; and, for the minute or two while the music lifts the hall to its feet, there is nothing better than to reach a hand across the barrier and scream a name, and get a smile in return, in acknowledgement of the spirit in which it's intended.

Minehead's amphitheatre magnifies the ordinary until it bursts at the seams. Here there is no national pride at stake, no tribalism to be afraid of, just plastic beer glasses, star-spangled spectacles and folk in Wonder Woman outfits clutching signs in the air saying, 'I'm supposed to be at work!' This is a good catharsis.

Here, only the determined impulse to entertain is to be entertained. And if, towards the end of the night, when it's hard to keep track of who is playing whom, let alone what the score might be, and the occasion loses some of its sharpness, there is always the option to stand on a bench, arms outstretched in an approximation of ecstasy, and holler for all it's worth: 'Stand up, if you love the darts!'

And outside, where the wind has changed to whip in from the north, throwing sea spray over the parapet and onto the road outside the entrance, the song from inside the big tent will catch on the breeze and skitter over the fields and villages that lead to the woodland that fringes Exmoor.

There, crows and owls, their necks drawn into their plumage against the cold, sit in the treetops of those ancient oaks, looking down on the shoreline. And the lights of the darts wink back over the distance, and into the darkness, shoring up their store of happy oblivion against the inky night and all its worries. Until the next day.

That's Minehead, when the darts are flying.

The Phantom

'Why! He's mad,' I said. He protested indignantly.

Mr Kurtz couldn't be mad.

JOSEPH CONRAD – *HEART OF DARKNESS*

When Conrad's Marlow finally gets to Kurtz, he discovers a tribe of native Congolese and a posse of expat courtiers who have fallen under his spell. They will fight to defend him and they celebrate him for a deity. Kurtz treats them, at best, with extreme indifference. It seems to sadden him as much as it delights him to be held up with such adoration.

It had been a long time since I had texted Eric Bristow. And still there came no reply.

There are those, worshipping at his rough and ready church, who claim that Bristow was the greatest ever, even if the statistics might suggest otherwise. Phil Taylor unquestionably wins that contest on numbers alone. But for a game that is ostensibly about numbers, darts is about much more than that; it's also about style.

For many, especially those still equipped with a functioning memory of darts' heyday, the answer to the question of all-time greatness is always going to be Bristow, and Bristow's style. Bristow was the King of Darts. From his first Embassy World title in 1980 through to 1990, he failed to reach the final just once in those 11 years; winning five and finishing runner-up in a further five. But it was the manner of his victories – the way he got inside the heads of his opponents, derailing their game, eating chunks out of their self-confidence, making them lesser players than they were – that marked him out as different from the rest. He threw with a contagiously self-assured style that was matched only by his peerless arrogance. He really was as good as he thought he was; a confluence of aspiration and actuality that eludes almost everyone else on earth and defines what it means to have a special talent.

His career was curtailed by the onset of dartitis, the sport's genuinely mystifying, if daft-sounding, equivalent of the yips. Put simply, he battled with every throw to release the dart. No one has adequately been able to explain the balance of physics and psychology that leads to this bio-mechanical cul-de-sac. Towards the back end of the eighties it started to blight his game, and he attributes its onset to the beginning of a passing of the crown from one great to another, from Bristow to the emergent Phil Taylor, whose talent and promise Bristow had helped nurture in the pubs and clubs of his adopted home town of Stoke-on-Trent. Unwittingly, perhaps, he trained Taylor to succeed him, though he could have had no idea what a force he had unleashed.

The pair met in the 1990 World Championship final, which Taylor won by a commanding, if not humiliating six sets to one. 'We played and Phil won,' recalls Bristow in *The Crafty Cockney*. 'He was the vampire who had sucked all the knowledge out of me.'

Though dartitis spelled the end of his reign at the top of the sport after a decade of dominance, he clung rigidly to the belief that his demise was premature. In Taylor, he had found a worthy successor. 'I didn't mind him winning everything,' mused Bristow later, 'as long as it wasn't against me. I was never going to be as good as I was during the early to mid-eighties so he became a kind of Mini-Me, winning the titles I would have won if I hadn't been affected by the yips.'

But the legend remained intact.

Like in 1989, on the day he had been honoured with an MBE by the Queen:

'You're a darts player,' she'd enquired of Bristow, while pinning on his medal.

'Yes, ma'am.'

And so the one-time burglar and former small-time crook knelt in front of Britain's longest serving monarch. She saw fit to honour him for the accuracy with which he threw darts. Fittingly, his account of the Buckingham Palace reception that followed is mostly a tale of him trying to work out where he could nip out to light up a fag, an act he describes onomatopoeically as 'dink'.

There's always been plenty of 'dink' in Bristow's life. Much as T S Eliot's Prufrock 'measured out his life in coffee spoons', so Bristow has punctuated every waking hour of his adult life with the 'dink' of another fag being sparked up, and, more often than not, another beer being tapped.

These days, Bristow drifts with liquid ease, never rushed, from room to room, bar to bar, always attracting glances of curiosity, admiration and fascination. He smokes prodigiously well, with elegance and rigour. The fag he holds must feel honoured, I've often thought, for the few exterminating minutes of its combustion, to be pinched between the self-same fingers that dispatched some of the greatest darts ever thrown.

He holds a pint with equal poise. He works the room, owns the situation, plays to his strengths, takes control. When Eric Bristow talks, you don't interrupt, you listen. A word of caustic advice here, a rascal observation there, a pithy aside for the stalls or a filthy innuendo directed at the dress circle. He's centre stage. I have seen Phil Taylor breeze past in the background on his way to a walk-on, but your eye would not deviate for a second from watching Bristow.

He has the strangest, hardest face to describe: pasty and pale in his youth, then burnt brownish-red in late middle age from years of Spanish sun. His features walk a disarming line between full-faced and birdish, warm and threatening. But, in that confusion of impressions, he is quite unmistakable.

Think of him and there he is: a man in a scarlet shirt, ready to throw, a half smile playing across his features. Eric Bristow, head back, right arm crooked towards the board, that trademark little finger lifted from the stem of the dart and poking elegantly out as if he were a courtesan with a sherry on the go. That ludicrous little pinky. It hangs in the air, cocked ridiculously, poised, posed, like the index finger on Donald Trump's right hand. It is the grip for which Bristow was derided in his youth: the grip of a 'poof', as his dad George had it. In fact, it's the first line of his autobiography, *The Crafty Cockney*: 'You play like a poof!'

That nasty little word would come back into his life, many, many years later, to devastating effect.

Born in 1957, Bristow came from the streets, growing up fast in an old Stoke Newington townhouse stranded in the midst of rapidly developed and brutal post-war housing estates. He tore through adolescence, a member of the Oxton Boys gang, the product of a tough home, rifling through the bedrooms and living rooms of north-east London for his loot. Burglary was his shtick, and when that got boring, he'd be out on the piss, lager-angry, looking for trouble and getting it. He ducked and dived his way through the minefield of London gangs, swerving the real nasties and mixing it with the others, largely unafraid of consequences, a respecter of nothing and no one unless that someone were tooled up and prepared to scalp you. That might have stopped him, temporarily.

No, this life was not a joke, not even a particularly dark Bristow type of joke (and believe me, there is 'dark humour', 'black humour', 'gallows humour' and 'Bristow humour', in that order of descension). He rampaged through a chaotic childhood, bereft, it seems, of that boring old conventional impulse that makes people question the legitimacy of their actions: conscience. Thus did Eric Bristow walk around from car theft to street brawl to burglary, with a claw hammer down his trousers for protection. He walked a tightrope between a life inside, or a not entirely unlikely death on the outside, until finally his ridiculously brilliant darts, a game that his father introduced him to, allowed him to walk clear of big trouble and straight into the more minor snakepit of fame.

When Bristow first became known in the 1970s, he launched a smash-and-grab raid on the nation's attention, stealing the limelight as he had stolen so many other things in his past. He basked in the tungsten filament gaze of the flashbulb and the studio lantern as if it were the most natural thing in the world to be adored, as if he were lying on the bed of a suntan parlour being bronzed by admiring eyes. Of course, the country would love Bristow. Loving Bristow was as easy as pushing someone off a chair, as easy as necking a pint, as easy as flicking a V-sign, as easy as a casual fucking swear word. He was a man of his age.

In 1979, the Glaswegian documentary film-maker John Samson focused his attention on darts. The result was an intriguing portrait of Bristow in a work called *Arrows*. Samson was known for a series of short films about other unorthodox or marginalised groups and individuals, so it's interesting that he chose a young Eric Bristow as the subject for his attentions. Samson's style was to observe, allowing the simplest of things to sing the loudest: Bristow lighting a fag, leaning out of the first-floor window of his tiny bedroom in his parents' house in London, packing an overnight bag, getting into a car, taking a phone call, lighting another fag. Samson followed Bristow for a day or two, from radio station to practice board, on trains and in cars, to exhibitions and hotels, a pint on the go, or a can of Tennent's flipped open in the corridor of an InterCity. This was the age of Bristow, and didn't he just know it. And always the big aviator shades. Always the faint smile.

Aged just 22, he had already won the prestigious World Masters twice, and was about to win the first of his five World Championships. He was thin, almost gaunt, quietly spoken and inscrutable. And he was starting to earn the kind of money that darts players of previous generations could only have dreamed of. He was announced to the world as the 'first darts player who will earn a million pounds!'

A million pounds was an unimaginable sum in those post-Callaghan years, when the three-day week and power cuts were the memories of recent winters. A million pounds was James Bond money, *The Spy Who Loved Me* era, the kind of money that would buy you Raquel Welch in an age of scrimp and save with Green Shield Stamps. It was an obscenity, and, in his own crafty way, so too was Eric, all beaky nose and mouth, if not an obscenity then at least an affront to good taste.

The opening minutes of the film are indulgently celebratory of the sport, in a kitchen-sink style very much of its time. This is grainy 16mm footage from a 'floor' tournament, set lovingly to a soft rock ballad called 'Arrows' by a little known group called The Crafty Cockney Band. In this introductory montage, there are close-ups of left hands clutching darts and smoking fags. The lead singer croons something apposite about arrows flying true and hitting targets while handbags hang on elbows and smiling faces flicker glances across the room. Bristow navigates his way through the crowd in a red darts shirt, drawing admiring gazes wherever he goes.

Then the action switches to the board, as the tune builds to a crescendo. Darts fly towards their targets. They hit their targets. The smoky crowd rises in applause, caught in the seasick tilt of a hand-held camera, feinting slightly to the right, and then drifting back again.

Then the film cuts to Bristow, now relaxed, having won the game, we are given to conclude, and subsequently lording it at the bar. He pats his shirt pocket as he casually searches for a match to 'dink' the cigarette that sits lazily between his lower lip and his teeth. Then he spots someone in the crowd, out of shot, and breaks into an involuntary smile, the likes of which I had never seen from him. It's a sweet look – young, relaxed, happy – into an off-camera middle distance and is accompanied by the trace of an almost imperceptible wink. These are the gestures of a man for whom life cannot get much better. It probably didn't. Later in his life, the smiles would come pre-plastered with a warning label.

After that beguiling opening, the documentary allows us to join Bristow in the dimly lit studio of a local radio station in Nottingham. He has dropped by at the behest of the long-haired, amber-shaded, flowery-patterned Dick Allix to promote an exhibition he'll be taking part in. Bristow is introduced on air by a certain Chris Ashley, the 'motor-mouthed' sports shock jock of the region, who hosts a programme called the *Trent Show*.

'I'm talking about Mickey Mouse sports,' Ashley announces, in the style of a prototype Alan Partridge, to get the interview under way. 'I'm talking about bowls, I'm talking about squash, badminton, tiddlywinks, croquet...' he pauses for effect '... and darts,' he concludes with a loaded, downward intonation.

Then the shot widens and we see Bristow, inscrutable behind his massive pair of sunglasses. The young darter strokes his chin and the smoke rises into a pool of light from yet another cigarette.

Ashley is on the offensive. 'I tell you what, my missus watches you on the box, right?'

'Yeah?' Bristow curls a disdainful lip.

'She thinks you're conceited. She thinks you're a big-head.'

'Yeah?' He levels his gaze at the DJ.

'She thinks you're conceited,' Ashley repeats, just in case there was any room for doubt. 'She thinks you're a cocky young man.'

Bristow looks down at the table, at his hands on the table. There is a palpable tension in that moment before he decides to take it all in good heart. He looks up, and grins. Then he asks, very softly, 'You finished?'

They both laugh, and the ice breaks. 'I'm just a great darts player,' laughs Bristow.

Ashley's wife was not alone in thinking of Bristow in this manner. For all its withering exaggeration, her summation of his character was one that many people shared, people who I had spoken to along the way. Peter Purves, the former host of the BBC's World Championship coverage had noted that, of all the players he knew in the early eighties, Bristow was the one who stood out. For a start, he didn't share the hotel in which the BBC and the players were billeted during the Embassy, preferring to go home, keeping himself wilfully apart. But he also unsettled Purves, especially when the BBC presenter had the temerity to take him on at darts. 'Eric Bristow used to tolerate me. I played him a couple of times and he always used to psyche me out. He was a terrible man to play against was Eric. You'd be hitting some good arrows, and something would just happen, and you'd stop hitting the good shots. It was weird.' He ascribes almost mystical powers to Bristow's unsettling presence. And he's not the only one to do so.

But Purves, like many others, is also quick to recognise the extraordinary talent. 'Eric was exceptional, at the time. I'm not saying that he was the best player all the time, but he was exceptional and he did psyche people out. He had a certain style about him.' And again, this testimony is echoed 100 times over by everyone and anyone who ever shared an oche with him.

Over the course of his long retirement, Bristow had continued unabated with his onslaught of mind games, shooting from the lip, with scant regard for reputations. Phil Taylor, reacting in 2016 to some stinging criticism of his game from Bristow, could scarcely contain his anger during a live television interview.

'Bristow... you know, hate him, love him, whatever you want to do....' And then his anger got the better of him, as his train of thought petered out. 'I could say a lot about him, but I wouldn't. I know a lot about Eric, but I'd never say a bad word about him.'

'He respects you though, that's for sure,' suggested Dave Clark, Sky Sports' unflappable host, trying to calm a reddening Taylor down.

'Well, does he?' questioned Taylor, with a rhetorical flourish. Clark didn't reply. 'Does he?' Taylor enquired again.

Stories of Bristow's belligerence, perfidious tactlessness and wanton indulgence jostle for primacy alongside the certain acknowledgement, not far beneath the surface of every Bristow story, that all this miscreant devilishness must be set in the context of his genius, his unorthodoxy, his anti-establishment fearlessness. For he was good, not just as a darter (maybe the best? We'll have to deal with that), but also as a superstar.

He embarked early on a path that would lead eventually to the jungle on *I'm A Celebrity Get Me Out of Here!* During his weeks on the nation's TV screens, he surprised those who know him well by keeping a check on his baser instincts. In fact, the nation rather warmed to him as he chirruped and groused his way through his time eating bugs. He finished in the final four, which worked out rather well for him as he'd backed himself to make the last six to the tune of £20,000. During his time in the jungle, he only caused minor offence to his fellow contestants, including when he ridiculed *Coronation Street* actor Helen Flanagan, who was suffering from a skin condition. 'I'd just squeeze her head and get all the pus out in one go,' opined Bristow, chivalrously.

When asked to sum up Bristow, the late Sid Waddell concluded that 'Eric showed that darts could be theatre and poetry', and then rather tellingly, added, 'and how far the anger of losing could be taken…'

Perhaps it was only a matter of time before he necked a hand grenade along with his umpteenth pint of Guinness and exploded his own career.

Twitter was his chosen weapon of reputational suicide. Letting Bristow own and curate his own Twitter account was akin to winding up a clock, blindly setting the alarm, and waiting to see what would happen.

Before the self-immolation, Bristow had been steadily grinding away with twig and flint, running the casual risk of igniting something potentially explosive for most of his online career. By the day of his virtual self-destruction, he'd already publicly posted comments on 16,730 occasions over a four-year period. A reasonable assumption would be that many of these were composed under the influence of beer, thumbing missives on the smartphone as a fuzzy by-product of that night's or indeed the previous night's prolonged spell as a bar-supporting flying buttress to the cathedral of Pub.

Normally, his fellow darts players reaped his praise and his scorn. The current crop of players have been routinely subjected to his witheringly acerbic assessments and scarcely notice the machine gun hammering from the Twitter account of the Crafty Cockney, so used are they to being labelled a 'choker' or a 'clown'. Likewise, his slavish loyalty to his employers at Sky Sports often sat in stark contrast to his less than charitable reviews of the merits of rival darts broadcasters. ITV, for whom Bristow briefly worked before sauntering off into the satellite distance, were often the object of his derision. And no mention of the rival BDO, according to Bristow a backwater of darting mediocrity, could end without him rubbishing them.

And then Bristow took it upon himself, late on the evening of Monday 28 November 2016, to pass comment on the growing number of ex-footballers who had summoned up the courage to report their sexual abuse at the hands of youth coaches.

This had been his opening gambit, as it appeared on the screen: 'Might be a looney but if some football coach was touching me when i was a kid as i got older i would have went back and sorted that poof out.'

That was swiftly followed by this clarification: 'Sorry meant paedo not poof.'

And then this: 'Dart players tough guys footballers wimps. U got to sought him out when u get older or dont look in the mirror glad i am a dart player proper men'.

And so on.

If he had stopped and thought for a handful of seconds about the wisdom of describing victims of sexual abuse as 'not proper men', and then getting himself horribly tangled up with an absurdly offensive misapprehension of the two offensive terms 'paedo' and 'poof', he might have judged that such matters were best left alone. But Bristow doesn't do reflection. He does bravado, and will take anything and anyone down with him, including his own name.

Sky Sports sacked him, almost instantly.

When Marlow finally reaches the end of his journey up the Congo to track down the mythical Kurtz, he has to carry him back, fatally wounded. But he discovers in his own reactions to Kurtz a bewildering mixture of emotions: fear, awe, admiration, envy, horror. Kurtz, an erstwhile servant of 'the company', has gone rogue in that distant outpost, creating a kingdom all of his own, inspiring fearful loyalty in his native subjects and acting with extreme brutality, as if quite oblivious to the consequences, operating outside the law in a horror of his own imagining.

Marlow's whole journey has been leading to the point at which he first glimpses Kurtz being carried aloft by his subjects, and close to death. But the notion of Kurtz, the 'atrocious phantom' had figured in the lives and fears, the hopes and dreads of all the characters to that point. Along the way, his story had guided Marlow's quest round each successive bend in the great river.

Meeting Bristow face to face had been a growing, dark obsession ever since I had launched the first of my distanced attempts to broker an interview with him.

Having, at the time, neither a telephone number nor email address for him, I had at first sent him a direct message on Twitter. My approach was simple: 'Hi Eric. I hope all is well.'

This was, of course, a ridiculous first line. Things are always just great if you're Eric Bristow MBE, even when they are dreadful. I continued.

'I'm writing a book about darts, and I'd love to have a chat with you some time. No book is complete without a few of your thoughts on the subject!'

While I waited for his answer that never came, I trawled his Twitter feed, harvesting a few of those 'thoughts on the subject'. It read, at times, like a hazy stagger through a shopping precinct at three o'clock in the afternoon.

Oct 04. *'This time last week was drinking in new york with 4 lads from corby northants'*

Sep 18. *'Had 2 more fags now back in bar what a athlete i am ha ha'*

Aug 17. *'Well suns come out so walking down the pub to see the lads cos i can'*

This seemingly endless drift through life was not surprising. Bristow, without a job, now had time on his hands, as well as an endless supply of fans more than happy to dip their hands in their pockets and buy him a drink. As he said in his own words, 'I'll continue plodding on, drinking, smoking, eating curries and probably getting into trouble with the law once or twice.'

He still lay hidden from sight, but Bristow's attitude and his talent permeated the very notion of what the game is and where it belonged. Think about him and you have forged an instant connection, hard-wired a circuit to the heart of darts, a bullseye.

So that was it, I now understood. Bristow: the totemic darter.

Big in Japan

It was the farthest point of navigation
and the culminating point of my experience.

JOSEPH CONRAD – *HEART OF DARKNESS*

In a room, far, far away from Stoke-on-Trent, a transparent bowl had been placed on a table in the corner, and it was wriggling with life. The brown liquid filling it was livid with flipping, panicked, not-yet-dead seafood. A becalmed waiter was liberally sousing whatever it was that was dying, in warm, ochre-tinted sake.

We were in the port of Yokohama, just south of Tokyo, the night before the Japan Darts Masters got under way. Barry Hearn, in his sharp-suited munificence, had invited the local tournament sponsors to meet the eight visiting players over a traditional dinner.

Bit by bit, the exotic dish started to attract attention. One by one, the diners turned to look at the spectacle, as still the poor creatures wriggled. The waiter, happy that he had administered enough of the lethal medicine to his bottom-feeding charges, stood back and waited for them all to stop dying so that he could dole them out onto plates. By now he and his giant prawns had drawn the gaze of all the occupants in the room. And, by doing that, the waiter had unwittingly commanded the attention of the greatest array of darting talent ever assembled in a Japanese dining room, or possibly any room, at any time, in the history of the world.

There was, in that soundproofed dark-cherry-wood-panelled dining room, with its ornate Empire-line chandeliers and thick, soft carpet, a bewildering line-up of familiar faces, none of whom were wearing their darts shirts and so looked curiously 'other'. In fact some of them were almost unrecognisable.

Raymond van Barneveld, the five-time champion of the world and pioneering Dutch master, was stony-faced. He sat close to his younger countryman, the buccaneering Michael van Gerwen, almost half his age. They talked to one another only occasionally, as if their native Dutch had been bullied out of them both by years on the circuit, leaving them too shy to converse in their mother tongue.

To their left sat the dark-haired, very tattooed Scot Gary Anderson, in 2015, the reigning world and Premier League champion, with a trademark smile playing across his worried features. The bags under his eyes, as ever, were tremendous.

Anderson had been swapping the occasional joke with Peter 'Snakebite' Wright, a man who normally took to the stage in pantomime trousers with a luminous Mohican and intricate face painting. But tonight, out of costume and off duty he looked curiously wan. He had no sparkly serpent writhing across his temples and his hair was neatly shampooed and lying flat across his scalp in the same way that dolphins' fins droop from years of depressing captivity in Florida sea parks.

Then there was Stephen Bunting, a tall, round, gentle giant, a bespectacled and shy Scouser. 'The Bullet' was the reigning BDO world champion and new kid on the block.

Bunting was sitting to the right of the dark-shirted James Wade, one of the game's great thinkers, a tricky, clever, sensitive and belligerent soul, who had his fiancée, former walk-on girl Sammi Marsh, at his side. Wade and Marsh were soon to be wed. They would not leave Japan without investing thousands of pounds in some pedigree puppies.

Phil Taylor, 16-time world champion and daddy of them all, sat apart from the rest, flanked by his girlfriend Paula and his mate Bob. Paula, who'd known nothing of Phil's professional life when they met, looked warily at the assembled cast. She knew some of them, but this darts crowd was a close-knit family, and as a new arrival, she was viewed with a little suspicion. Taylor looked tired tonight, and every bit a man in his mid-fifties.

He too was staring at the bug-eyed prawns hurling themselves in ever-increasing fury at the sides of the Perspex bowl, bringing the boozy soup from which they were incapable of escape to a state of froth.

But what an assembled cast! In the wake of Taylor's two-decade long unfathomable brilliance, all these men had raised the bar to take the game of darts to previously unimaginable heights. The generation that had gone before them, great though it had been, could only applaud from the sidelines. These were the men who had hyper-inflated the game's extraordinary rise. Year on year, the accepted understanding of what standards it was reasonable to expect from players at the top end of the game had been torn up and reconfigured as these eight, and the others just beneath them in the world order, continued to push on towards ever more excellence, bearing down ultimately on perfection.

Three-dart averages of over 100 were now the minimum entry standard for the latter stages of any tournament. These days 'ton plus' checkouts, those rare and beautiful moments of genius, rain down on scorers' marking sheets like digital confetti. The unicorn-like 'nine-darter', so rare in previous years, was, if not commonplace, then becoming at least semi-regular.

Indeed, as the players took their seats for dinner that night, they were informed by their snow-haired guru Barry Hearn that the tournament sponsor for the inaugural Japan Darts Masters (a smoothly tailored bookie from Hong Kong, who later that evening would darkly hint that he knew of a top Premier League football manager who was 'into me for millions') had just stumped up an extra $50,000 for any player who hit a perfect nine-dart leg.

Van Gerwen promptly passed him a message, asking whether he wanted his bank details for the money transfer. He was only half joking. At the time of writing, Michael van Gerwen has hit five televised nine-darters, including one in 2007 when he was just 17 years old, as well as numberless perfect legs in practice or during exhibitions. But right now, that was the last thing on his mind. The world number one was looking in increasing horror at what they were about to be served. It fell, not to the elder statesman, Phil Taylor, but to 'Jackpot' Adrian Lewis to break the tension. He rose to his feet and the room fell silent.

Lewis, a big friendly bear of a player, whose acres of black darts shirt bears the logo of principal sponsor, Twyford, the plumbers, is everything a darts player should be. He is a delightful man, sloping around the nether regions of each darting venue with a cigarette readied for ignition, or huddled outside the fire escapes with one on the go. You cannot walk past him without being greeted with a winning chuckle and a genuine smile. 'You all right, chuck?' He came to prominence under the watchful tutelage of Taylor, a fellow Stokie. The glorious, slack-jawed ease of his throw! The lack of visible effort, the unflappability: everything spoke to the darting public of the emergence of a divine natural talent. He was once considered to be the heir

apparent to the Taylor throne. Watching him play brought out the best in the commentators:

'It's like clotted cream...' (Stuart Pyke).

'...Off a hot spoon.' (Chris Mason, with a fat dollop of West Country drawl).

It was as if a shooting star from the darting heavens had been orbiting the planet, seeking a host body to pack with all the ability required to raise the game to its highest level. It paused momentarily, shot out of the night sky, and descended towards Stoke-on-Trent. Darts had picked out its man, dressed him in nylon, blessed his arm and called him Jackpot: the ultimate ordinary beauty.

But that night in Yokohama, the big man from Stoke was exercised by the prawns. He pushed his chair back, then, with both meaty fists planted on the table for support, Lewis raised his massive frame upright. He frowned, his brow beaded with roughly equal measures of sweat and perplexity, took one step towards the seething bowl and stopped in his tracks.

He peered forward as if trying to discern something in the gloom. Then he abruptly stood up straight again, stretched out his vast, tattooed throwing arm, and pointed a finger in accusation at the waiter. Now everyone in the dining room looked at Jackpot, rather than the bowl of prawns, and waited on his judgement.

'What the *fucking* hell is *that*?!'

With a certain embarrassment, I looked across at the waiter, standing rigidly to attention behind the food trolley from which he was about to serve, and tried to gauge his reaction to Jackpot's outrage. Meanwhile the diners fell about hysterically, as the restaurant's equally exotic clientele burst into laughter.

From the Japanese waiter, I did not detect a flicker. This was going to be an interesting few days, culturally speaking.

The Japan Darts Masters must be seen in the context of a sport intent on striding, with sensible, non-athletic footwear across the globe. It is tempting, but only partially correct, to think

of darts as a completely British construct. In fact, it has been trying to break free from its national shackles for longer than you might imagine.

There was loose talk as early as the 1930s that an exhibition match might be arranged between Britain and America to be held at Madison Square Gardens featuring the great Jim Pike, but it never came to anything. Pike, though, did maintain that there were 'experts in abundance in Belgium, France, Holland, Poland, Czechoslovakia, South Africa, even Australia and New Zealand'.

It took another 60 years until those experts from overseas started seriously to threaten the hegemony, and it was the Dutch that spearheaded the invasion. And while Belgium have their talents (in particular the brothers Ronny and Kim Huybrechts), and Australia has certainly produced the occasional talent (like Simon Whitlock, for example, the Wizard of... oh, you know the rest), we are still waiting for Polish or French players to shine. And Czechoslovakia no longer exists.

Throwing a dart is clearly something the British do well, and though there has been the occasional interloper to spoil the fun, there had always been an innate understanding that should the sport ever go Olympic, you could surely chalk in a gold, silver and bronze in the credit column before the tournament even got under way. That was before the advent of the great Michael van Gerwen, of course. But, other than the swelling ranks of the Dutch, the foreign stars representing the darting hinterland have come and gone, played their part, but by and large moved on. North America has perhaps, and unsurprisingly had, the biggest impact, especially in the slightly more inclement, therefore indoorsy Canada.

This is the country, and Toronto is the city, that gave rise to the legendary darter, raconteur, bon viveur and all-round smart dude John Part, or Darth Maple, another huge man with a soft-focus, if filled-out good looks, like a darting Cary Grant, a bit blurred at the edges after a few years on the circuit. He won the BDO World Championship in 1994 and then a brace of PDC world titles followed. On the second of those two occasions, he flew straight back home, where, according to American darts humorist Paul Seigel, he 'enthusiastically announced plans to buy Canada a navy'. If he'd won a third, Seigel added, he'd have 'bought Greenland'.

Then there was the odd Swede, particularly Stefan Lord, the restaurateur turned dartist, and a man whose own website accurately boasts (with the help of Google Translate) that 'It is possible for several reasons not to overlook his contributions and their importance for Swedish darts and dart in Sweden. For as yet there is no one had greater significance for the Swedish dart than Stefan.'

And there should also be an honourable mention to Singapore-born Paul Lim, who hit the first ever nine-darter at the Embassy in 1990, netting him a staggering £52,000, which was £28,000 more than Phil Taylor earned for actually winning the tournament. Lim first contested the Embassy in 1982, and 35 years later, at the age of 63, stunned the darts world by ousting former BDO world champion Mark Webster at the 2018 Worlds, and then coming within a narrowly missed double 12 of repeating his nine-darter from 1990 in his second-round defeat to Gary Anderson.

In 2018, according to the PDC, the World Championships were watched on TV in 130 countries. The biggest audience of all was in Germany, a country whose darts fans accounted for 25 per cent of all ticket sales at Alexandra Palace, a percentage made all the more remarkable by the fact that the Germans don't yet have a notable top player to cheer on.

The men at the top of the PDC have only just begun to realise its global potential and are alive to the real possibility of the world, and particularly Asia, discovering a new sporting passion to rival football and cricket, or at least give table tennis and kabaddi a good run for their money.

As much as this global ambition might seem an absurdly ambitious 21st-century notion, players have actually been criss-crossing oceans in search of golden oches for as long as anyone alive can remember.

In the early 1970s the glamour of transatlantic flight, with all its insanely exciting Pan Am cachet, was so remote a proposition for Britons that you might as well have been talking Japanese. Intercontinental flight remained a pipe dream to most.

But, even back then, a flight across the pond was rapidly becoming the norm for an elite group of the top-ranking British darters. In the 1980s and beyond, the likes of Jocky Wilson, Bobby George and Cliff Lazarenko built a month's travel every year around annual visits to tournaments in the USA where they would face the extreme risk of being knocked out incredibly early in short forms of the game (Chris Mason once flew to Las Vegas, played three legs of darts, about six minutes' worth, and then flew back). But equally there were considerable rewards for reaching the latter stages of gargantuan knockout tournaments in the burgeoning, but largely separate, North American game. As a result, players used to room together and pool both their victories and losses to hedge against disaster. John Lowe and Eric Bristow, for example, were a financial duopoly for years, travelling together on American 'beanos', as Bristow remembers them, colossal darting venues hosting 2,500 players, or heading for the Gulf states where they had to use their ingenuity (smuggling, basically) in order to drink, and Scandinavia, where a good time was always guaranteed. They drank, played, socialised, won and lost together, all over the world. Bristow split from his prize-sharing understanding with Lowe just before Lowe netted £148,000 for the first televised nine-darter, leaving Bristow to reflect that it hadn't been 'a good moment for me'.

Darts, despite its spit-and-sawdust origins, has always cast its spores far and wide. Pins appeared in the map and proliferated, pockets of hardy darting interest. They've all played their part in marking the territory: Old England nostalgists in North America, or well-heeled expats in Delhi, as well as a highly irregular army of soldiers, sailors and other tradesmen, who, through the decades, fate has thrown into close proximity with British manhood in the form of occupying or liberating armies, expanding multinational corporations, or other sundry entrepreneurs embracing the maxim 'Have dartboard, will travel'. Or if no regulation cork disc sprang readily to hand, it's not hard to imagine hours of stagnant time during the Suez Crisis or the Korean War being sweetened by the improvised ringing of metal projectile against upturned oil barrel. Darts pubs can always be found, if you look hard enough, from the Shakespeare Club in Almaty, Kazakhstan to the Bojangles Restaurant and Grill in Ulaanbaatar, Mongolia.

Yet Japan, with its huge potential, had remained largely untapped, despite the country having hosted a few notable tournaments in the 1980s. Soft-tip electronic darts was popular, but the real game, steel tip, was still very much emerging. Hearn was keen on some exploratory work. So in late June 2015, the PDC expanded its global portfolio with the addition of a new stopover, in Japan, for its nascent World Series.

The World Series, it is worth noting, is quite distinct from either the World Matchplay, the World Grand Prix, the World Cup or the World Championships (of which, of course, there are two), even though by and large, all these events are structured around increasingly long games of 501 and generally feature exactly the same pool of players competing against each other with endlessly repetitive regularity on an interchangeable variety of different brightly lit stages in different parts of the UK, Europe and the World.

But while most of the other events with 'World' in their title take place either in North London, Essex, Blackpool, Dublin and occasionally Frankfurt or Amsterdam, the World Series can genuinely lay claim to being rather global; if by 'global', we mean one or two first-world countries readily serviced by direct long-haul flights.

So far, the series has featured an opening round in Dubai. Tickets were snapped up by the anglophone expat and tourist community and bought up by the many corporations with a stake in Dubai who like to fly their clients out to the desert state and show them a good time. What Dubai's ruling family made of it all was irrelevant by the time the stage was up, the hall was packed and the arrows were flying. You might as well have been in a heavily air-conditioned Milton Keynes.

The World Series has also, in its short life (it was only called into existence in 2013) visited the USA and Australia, with rounds in both Perth and Sydney, at which the darting press back in the UK who couldn't afford to make the expensive trip to the other side of the world are instead emailed by the organisation a welter of photo opportunities of the leading darters posing with a thumbs up in front of the famous Opera House or cuddling a baby koala, along with some copy likely to include the phrase 'Darting Men At Work Looking To Check Out In The Outback With Double Tops Down Under'.

Naturally, selling the event to the sporting public of Australia has not been hard. The correct combination of drama, beer and boisterousness with a heady mix of showbiz and glitz appeals quite naturally to the rump of Antipodean manhood out for a good time. If you build the bar and the pie shop and the acres of trestle tables and the stage and the oche, they will come.

Also, Australians have a few brightly shining stars of the tungsten firmament of their own, men like the extraordinary Simon Whitlock, whose watery eyes, extravagantly knotted dreadlocks, violent throwing technique and curiously front-on stance have led him most recently to the runner-up spot at the World Grand Prix in 2017. Then there's the brash new kid, the up-and-coming Wayne Rooney of the sport, Corey Cadby, a snarling, gobby wunderkind from Melbourne with an explosive haircut and a personal history that includes a warrant for his arrest in relation to non-appearance at court and theft. All that by 22.

But in 2015, three more venues were added. Auckland threw its hand in, bolting an extra Kiwi leg on to the Series' visit to Australia. New Zealand was a bit like its bigger, brasher neighbour in the way it embraced the sport, but perhaps a bit less so, as they have other stuff to preoccupy them, like vast mountain ranges and the *Lord of the Rings*. Besides, unlike Australians, the New Zealand darts scene's hottest property is a certain Cody Harris, whose father once beat Eric Bristow, but who otherwise passes through the world game with relative anonymity.

But the addition of Auckland to the World Series did not, it must be admitted, greatly widen the cultural horizon of the darting world, which still had a distinctly 'flat earth' feel, limited to a narrow interpretation of the darting world, or indeed the geographical world. No foray had been undertaken thus far into Burkina Faso. Bangladesh had yet to be plundered for potential, nor had the game yet taken Peru, Nicaragua or Chad by storm. And then it was announced that the grand final round would be held in, not Amsterdam, whose big venues were fully booked, but Glasgow.

So the addition of the new venue in Yokohama was of great significance. A stopover in Japan was exactly what the World

Series needed: kimonos, sushi, Mount Fuji, hell yes! Taking darts to a deeply foreign country on the edge of the Pacific, troubled by earthquakes, and resolutely, unflinchingly 'other', was inspired. By touching down in the 'Land of the Rising Ton' (a pun that was to feature in the live TV coverage, and to which I, shamefully must lay claim), the World Series could genuinely start to live up to its rather grandiose title.

Mount Fuji's cartoonish peak had poked unreally out of the mist on our approach to Tokyo airport, and, during my first, jet-lagged day there, the sense of being in a dream only intensified. It was true, I noted, that most Japanese men (excluding those who embraced punk and would make a special 6,000-mile pilgrimage to the British Boot Company in Camden) dressed with impressive and reassuringly bland familiarity. This, with staggering uniformity, seemed restricted to white or off-white nylon short-sleeve shirts and black slacks, not a million miles away from PDC regulation trousers.

But in every other sense, Japanese life contained all sorts of traits that unsettled the accidental tourist like myself, visiting for work. Never before had I ever felt such a hopeless 'Brit abroad'. The toilets needed an instruction manual. The breakfasts were a Russian roulette of pickles and oddities. The language was quite unguessable. The Japanese I met were good at things like manners, dignity and stoicism. What, I wondered, would Japan make of the 50-strong darting entourage about to bring its own unique brand of boisterous mayhem to its peaceful, orderly shores? Was Japan ready?

On the eve of the tournament, the organisers were tense. Barry Hearn himself had flown out to be on-site, although, being Barry Hearn, he was billeted in the ever so slightly grander hotel than the rest of the PDC entourage, a block down the road on Yokohama's expansive (and expensive) waterfront. The reason for this degree of separation, I was told, was that he needed a hotel suite, rather than simply a room.

I could well imagine that this was true. Men like Barry Hearn (there aren't actually any others like Barry Hearn) need hotel suites, especially when abroad, on quasi-state visits. It was easy to picture Hearn, dressed head to toe in semi-tropical, expensive white linen, receiving visits from suitors and contacts during his four-day sojourn in Japan.

'Mr Hearn will see you now.'

'Ah,' Hearn would proclaim, rising elegantly from his reproduction *fin de siècle* settee. 'Mr Morohito! How good to see you again.' A handshake, a smile and a long, culturally appropriate and perfectly executed bow, just a fraction shorter than his guest's, to make a Desmond Morris sort of point. 'And how is the delightful Mrs Morohito? Is she still playing golf?'

'She is indeed, Mr Hearn. And thank you so much for the set of clubs you sent her. They have improved her game greatly.'

'My pleasure, Mr Morohito.' Hearn would have sat down at this point and with a deft flick of his trouser crease folded one leg elegantly over the other. 'Now, then. Have you thought any more about our proposition....?'

Of course, none of this might have happened. Perhaps Hearn simply wanted to stay in a different hotel to get away from everyone else, and as a gentle reminder to the whole entourage of his tangible difference.

Hearn had taken a not inconsiderable risk with this latest jaunt, hiring Yokohama's newest venue and flying not only darts' eight finest players business class across the world but also all the support crew needed to assemble and light the set, keep order in the hall, staff and present the worldwide television coverage and generally make the whole thing tick like the finely tuned Rolex he (probably) unclips from his wrist every night and places gently on the marble surface of the bathroom in his hotel suite before moisturising his eyelids and turning in for the night.

But he would have slept easily after the first night of darting action in Yokohama. He had done his research.

There is a burgeoning darts scene in Japan, albeit one that is based on the 'soft-tip' version of the game. Vast tournaments are already part of the furniture of the darting landscape, where literally hundreds of electric soft-tip boards are lined up next to each other, and thousands upon thousands of entrants take part. A local darts correspondent showed me pictures from a recent event, whose scale was simply extraordinary. Then he thrust into my hand a glossy magazine dedicated to an affluent darts-playing set, which he edited.

The clientele for the magazine, as was obvious from the moodily shot artful black-and-white photography, were sophisticated, millennial, open-minded hipsters. There was a fascinating-looking (I, of course, couldn't read it) profile of one of Japan's darting pioneers, the former champion windsurfer and restauranteuse Yoko Koyama, who rose to the top of the game in the late 1980s, taking on and beating some of the biggest names in the women's game. The publication reminded me of the welter of classily produced cycling magazines that exist to service a bookish, aspirational and moneyed community of readers. Perhaps darts in Japan played to a different market, I concluded.

After the prawn incident on the eve of the tournament, the players enjoyed a night out on the town. Many of the game's young devotees had filled out the city's scattering of darts pubs to catch a close-up glimpse of their darting heroes from across the globe.

The following day, an excited Stephen Bunting related to me over breakfast how he'd popped into one such establishment for a quick glass or two of Ashiro lager, only to find himself mobbed by an enthusiastic crowd, astonished to find themselves

rubbing shoulders with The Bullet himself. Bunting, whose sheer innocent pleasure in everything he undertook was infectious, was on the crest of a wave. Darts had plucked him from the pubs and clubs of his Merseyside youth and carried him aloft on a white crest of titles and accolades all the way to Yokohama and beyond. His diary had filled up with glamorous overseas shindigs, lucrative exhibition matches and even, to his own utter delight and amazement, personal appearances alongside Liverpool footballers at his beloved Anfield. And this trip to Japan was simply mind-blowing.

Facebook and Instagram testified to the world number eight's night out on the town in Yokohama as selfie after selfie was snapped, Bunting's charmingly myopic grin unchanging from one pose to the next as he smilingly worked his way through the crowd of faces in the pub.

'I only went there for a pint,' he confided to me. 'I couldn't get out of the place until four in the morning. It was mega.'

Later that evening, darts took a bold step into a brave new world. The Japanese crowd arrived early for the event. Many of them were diligently, rigorously decked out in Peter 'Snakebite' Wright multicoloured wigs, carrying foam fingers and sporting Jackpot shirts, and were already at a point of delirium by the time the local MC (John McDonald's Japanese equivalent) strode onto the stage and started to whip them up into an even greater frenzy of excitement. It didn't appear hard.

Day one of three saw the eight best players in Japan take on the eight overseas stars. The gulf in ability was cavernous. Every single local player fell to their foreign opponent without so much as forcing them to break sweat. Just once, as I recall, did a Japanese player hit a 180. The roof nearly came off the Yokohama arena. Fans, juddering with emotion, dropped suddenly to their knees in near religious fervour. The well-ordered, but ear-splitting 'mosh pit' towards the front of the stage, seethed with hysteria. At one point, at the moment a home-based hero failed valiantly in his attempt to check out 32, I looked down into the crowd and I saw a party of four women, all wearing dartboard crowns, burst spontaneously into tears.

The songs were impeccably rehearsed by the crowd, in a language they otherwise had no understanding of. 'Stand up if you love the darts!' was followed swiftly by a Yokohama-accented version of 'Peter Wright, Wright, Wright'. And yet, one by one their heroes fell. And one by one their European conquerors walked from the stage delighted and bemused by the experience of lighting up the Japanese crowd with their talents.

'That was fucking nuts,' was the common consensus.

And at the end of play, with all the matches settled in favour of the elite, the crowds made their way, wrung dry from the emotion of the evening, towards the exit doors at the back of the hall. I stopped what I was doing to see something truly astonishing: to a man and woman, they patiently picked up their empty water bottles and hot dog holders and queued at the recycling bins at the rear of the arena on their way out. When the final darts fan had left the hall, there was not the merest sign that they had ever been there. The place was spotless. One or two cleaners appeared to pick up the plastic sacks that contained all the night's detritus. This was, culturally, a long way from Minehead.

Later that night, as the sky darkened once again over the bay, and the lights from the decks of container ships caught on the warm, choppy waters of the bay, we dodged the rain showers and left the arena for the lighted cliff of our waterside hotel, reflecting on a glorious encounter.

A funny little game had crossed an ocean, and harmlessly, joyously spoken to a new crowd with its old voice. Big, and booming, in Japan.

In 1988, 30 years ago, Eric Bristow had come to Japan.

He was starting to despair about his waning powers, but, poking around in the still orange embers of his once white-hot career, he carried away the first prize in the Tokyo World Darts Masters, winning 1 million yen.

He didn't win much more after that, save for a few minor trophies the following year, as he started to succumb to the dartitis that would prove terminal to his career. But, just a short bullet train ride from Yokohama, Bristow had managed to raise his game exactly when it mattered, and had sneaked another victory against the odds. As the well-admired commentator, the late Dave Lanning, put it, 'Taylor is a mugger...'

'... Bristow is a burglar.'

River's End

When actually confronting him I seemed to come
to my senses, I saw the danger in its right
proportion. It was by no means over yet.

JOSEPH CONRAD – *HEART OF DARKNESS*

In the middle of the winter in 2018, preparing for another long flight overseas, I picked a book from my shelves. I could only imagine that it had been brought into our house by a guest and left in the spare room. As soon as I saw the title on the spine, I knew that I needed to read it.

In 2000, the journalist Michela Wrong published *In the Footsteps of Mr Kurtz*, an account of the reign and demise of President Mobutu Sese Seko, the dictator who, for thirty-two years, ran the nation of Zaire into the ground. Zaire, as he renamed it, was the same Congo that Conrad had written about in *Heart of Darkness*, and Wrong draws strong parallels between Mobutu's charismatic malfeasance and the fictional Mr Kurtz. In her book, she details how Mobutu set about accruing enemies and colossal wealth, eventually retreating into the jungle to an obscene palace he had built with his multi-billion-dollar fortune, amassed by the most sustained kleptocracy in post-colonial African history.

I read her book in a sitting. She paints her extraordinary subject first as a monster, and then, over the course of her narrative, guides the reader to the conclusion that Mobutu, for all his ghastly excesses, was at core a perfectly functional human being whose whims had been indulged without restraint, to horrifying effect. By revealing him in this way, she makes the horrors of his reign still more terrifying by the sheer plausibility of his character. It is a startling conclusion.

I wondered about my own exploration. I had been thrashing around wildly, it seemed to me, from the Thames to the Clyde, the Bristol Channel to the North Sea, in increasing uncertainty. And I still had not come face to face with my Mr Kurtz. The sense of a completed journey seemed to swell, as if the tide had come in, and simply refused to go out. The river, that had borne me from Gravesend, could do no more. There only remained the one outstanding issue to be settled.

Having been handed Eric Bristow's direct number by Dick Allix, I had tried again to message him. Still nothing. My next text, followed up by another, sent some time afterwards, had also remained unanswered. A one-sided message page on my phone had started to fill up with green speech bubbles on the right and nothing but blank white space on the left, where the responses should have been.

'The thing is, Ned, he's super, super-intelligent.'

I looked at John McDonald to see if he was joking. McDonald almost always jokes. He is a man not given to making bald statements of fact that are not jokes. But it seemed he was deadly serious. I could gauge the degree of earnestness because his immaculate teeth were not on display.

'Really?' I asked. 'Eric?'

We were waiting backstage for the action to start at the 2018 Masters. I had been telling him, over a Styrofoam cup of tea, about my interest in Eric Bristow that was bordering on an obsession, about how I'd begun to mythologise the man, to build up the impression of a brooding, divine figure, hidden from view. Dick Allix had spoken to me about Bristow's intelligence, too. I knew that there were different ways of seeing him, which made it harder to get a bearing on him. He seemed to exert a presence, without ever being present.

'Academically brilliant,' Mcdonald continued. 'His maths is exceptional. He went to a top grammar school.' This was true. But it was not the whole truth. It was a school at which, in order to bunk off a German exam for which he hadn't prepared, he rang up Scotland Yard and pretended that he'd planted a bomb. The subsequent evacuation did the trick. School didn't suit Bristow.

'He could do *The Times* crossword in no time at all,' Mcdonald scribbled onto a page of thin air with a flourish of his imaginary pen. 'And he writes beautifully.'

It had never occurred to me that Eric Bristow might be considered a wonderful writer. All I knew of his literary skill was that he avoided punctuation and that he hadn't written back to me. Not one reply had been forthcoming to my attempts to contact him. Text messages went unanswered. There was no word from him, nor had he been sighted in months, a man who appeared to be being steadily erased from the darts world. His TV work had been cancelled. His presence at tournaments had stopped, his appearances at exhibitions had slowed to a trickle and he was no longer courted by the media. Stories multiplied about his increasingly uncontained bitterness, the way he spoke to the public, the recklessness with which he joked about anything and everything (from Oscar Pistorius in front of an audience that contained wounded South African soldiers, to innocent cab drivers in New York). No one, it seemed, was safe from the Bristow scorn. After a long time in the limelight, there was a growing sense that Eric Bristow was disappearing from the world.

Before he had entered his period of purdah, my personal history with Bristow had been restricted to a handful of encounters, and I had not seen him at all for a number of years. I had only ever spoken to him just once or twice, and never so that he noticed me. You have to make some impact for Bristow to register your presence, and on my first visits to darts tournaments I shied away from making any kind of impression. When ITV started to get back into darts, covering the Grand Slam from Wolverhampton, he used to do alternate shifts in the TV truck working as a 'spotter'.

This is a highly specialised job, unique to the sport of darts and normally reserved to ex-pros, whose job it is to anticipate the next dart a player is going to throw so that the cameramen can frame up a close-up of the relevant part of the board. Spotters do this partly by knowing the 'preferred route' a player favours when checking out a high or irregular finish, and partly by reading the minute eye movement and realignment of the throwing arm a player makes in the fraction of a second before throwing. This sounds easy, but it isn't. There are only three or four darts 'spotters' in the entire world. This makes them rarer than astronauts, or living Presidents of the United States of America.

When Keith Deller, Bristow's 1983 Embassy nemesis, wasn't performing this function for ITV, Bristow would often fill in for him. The same pair, at the time, used to perform the same function for Sky Sports on their coverage of the sport.

From the depths of the ITV truck I'd routinely overhear Bristow's gruff tones coming over the radio earpiece, barking instructions to the cameramen.

'He's staying up!'

'Double eight!'

'Bullseye!'

If a player had the temerity to use an unusual route towards the double, or to choose a number Bristow had not anticipated, leaving the close-up stranded on some irrelevant double, as a dart thudded in elsewhere, Bristow's reaction would always run along similar lines. He was affronted, as if it were a personal slight.

'Fuck me. Fucking idiot.' That would be followed, seconds later, by a neat summation of the offender's character. Something like: 'Fucking plonker.'

I had little to do with him back then, though he was working ostensibly on the same production team and staying in the same hotel. I was fairly sure he didn't know my name, and more certain that he didn't care who I was or what I did. There was nothing remarkable about that as it was the same disdain with which he seemed inclined to treat pretty much everyone. But from time to time I ended up doling out undercooked bacon at the same breakfast buffet as him, or would see him in the players' bar, or push cautiously past him in the company of a cluster of smokers by the fire exit at the back of the venue.

'Afternoon, Eric.'

'Awright.'

And when I did exchange a word with him, which I did from time to time, I felt a peculiar, unreal sense of something approaching awe. This man, after all, had been a stellar fixture in the circus of the famous when I was a kid. I found it hard to accept that I was now on any kind of terms with him, however meagre the exchange.

But there was never any eye contact with Bristow, just perhaps the merest inclination of that regal head in my general direction. A puff on a fag, but then a haughty turning away of his imposing frame was as much as I was ever proffered by way of recognition. I would shuffle past him, anonymously, and into the light of the venue.

The mere mention of his name, frequent and unavoidable in the closeted world of darts, elicited a nod, a smile, a wink, a cackle, a shaking of the head or drawing of breath. To bring up the subject of Bristow, especially in the company of his contemporaries, was to invite a flurry of memories, not many of them fond.

As Peter Purves noted, 'He was a big fella, too. He was about six foot two or three.' Bristow had presence. As he entered his sixties, he bore himself well, his shoulders back, if sloping, and covered in shapeless and almost-shabby black. That jacket was mostly for smoking, and he'd shed it when he re-entered the bar. But the most noticeable identifying feature of Bristow was the constant presence of the trace of something of a smile about his angular face. The pinched lips carried the shadow of a permanent grin or, perhaps more accurately, a smirk. Perhaps a sneer.

Or is it unkind to describe that look as a sneer? It could just be a natural consequence of living with the loftiness that comes with being Eric Bristow. He just exudes a certain, if it isn't too much of an unnecessarily highfalutin word, hauteur.

It probably is.

Yet Bristow has been, and still is, revered. Trawling through publications, and searching for traces of Bristow across the nation's cultural landscape, led me to another tale of discovery, another journey undertaken, another dart-related Bildungsroman. It came in the shape of the almost completely unknown film *Heartlands*, which, much like the ill-fated *London Fields*, has never enjoyed a cinematic release. What is it about darts films and success?

Produced on a relative shoestring budget by the now disgraced Harvey Weinstein and shot in 2002, the film stars a number of established British comedy actors from Paul Shane, Celia Imrie and Ruth Jones to a very young James Corden, as well as darts referee Russ Bray, playing himself with devilish charm. But the film features a brilliant performance from Michael Sheen in the

lead role of Colin, a gently impassive darts dreamer whose hero is Eric Bristow. Eric Bristow is played by Eric Bristow MBE.

Colin has only one thing on his mind, and that's darts. In one exchange with a couple he has met in a pub, he embarks on telling a story about a match between Bristow and Cliff Lazarenko. 'Eric needed 134 to beat Lazarenko...' relates Colin excitedly. He gets close to the denouement, before he is interrupted by the girlfriend.

'And he got it,' she predicts, wearily.

'Let him tell the story,' complains her boyfriend.

'But it's another darts anecdote though,' she points out.

Colin, crestfallen, nods his head. 'No more darts stories,' he promises. Then he looks to the ground. 'God knows what I'll talk about now.'

Over the course of his character's metamorphosis, and throughout his journey of self-discovery (on a moped to Blackpool to surprise his errant wife who has eloped with the captain of the local darts team), Bristow's name hovers spectrally over the narrative, held up as the example of everything that the diffident Colin isn't.

Bristow is unafraid, decisive, adventurous; all the qualities that Colin lacks. Bristow would act without hesitation, primally. Bristow, the timid Colin imagines, would simply have gone to Blackpool and returned the same day with his wife.

In the end, after his slow, revelatory transformation, and turning his back on his unfaithful wife and his failed past, Colin strides off from the Blackpool seafront towards a bold new future.

As he passes a cafe window, he catches sight of someone, and it stops him in his tracks. He turns slowly, and at the same time, Eric Bristow, seated inside, turns to look through the window at Colin. Their gaze meets. Then Bristow, smiling generously, nods him on his way, and our hero breaks into a broad smile as

the credits roll. It's a genuinely moving moment, in which the thought, the *idea* of Bristow plays a credible, powerful role in the hero's self-transformation.

So, Bristow could be an idea, as well as a real man.

This golden halo effect is also part of him: Just like the bronzed darting God that he was, there is more to his meaning than meets the eye. Representative of an age and an attitude, his natural status and authority bore down on his detractors, as much as his own wilful self-destructiveness scratched at that very image. But this was all a collage of impressions I'd received at a distance. What I still could not glimpse through all the fug of outrage about his behaviour was the man himself. There was no way through to him, to take the pulse of what he thought was right and what he thought was wrong.

The last words I exchanged with Bristow, face to face, had come about a short while after his fall from grace and had ended with him curling his lip and looking away. That awkward encounter, his frosty rebuttal to some innocuous remark about the form of a particular darts player, had come about in a pub, close to midnight. Bristow had had a pint in front of him, and Bobby George sitting to his right. The situation wasn't ideal for a heart to heart.

In January 2018, I met Allix again. It was at the Dorchester Hotel on Park Lane after another of the PDC's annual black-tie dinners. The speeches had finally drawn to a close (Barry Hearn had once again been on excoriating form), Peter 'One Dart' Manley had turned the air blue with some more than robust end-of-pier humour and the awards had been handed out, mostly to Rob Cross.

Allix was making his first visit to the annual dinner for a number of years. After the evening's formalities were concluded, he made his way through the sea of tables to where I stood talking with a colleague, arriving at our side to shake hands just as the band were striking up a surprisingly tight version of Chic's 'Le Freak', a track that reminded me instantly of the trademark funk of Heatwave.

'I bet this song takes you back.'

Allix couldn't hear me, though. The music was deafening.

'How's the book coming along?' he bellowed into my ear.

'It's OK, thanks,' I answered, swapping sides so that I now was shouting at his right ear. 'Still no word from Eric, though.'

He smiled ruefully at me and shrugged his shoulders.

'What's the title of the book?' he hollered.

'*Heart of Dart-ness.*'

He raised his eyebrows. Then I chanced my arm, thinking that Allix would understand the reference. 'Have you read *Heart of Darkness*, by Joseph Conrad?'

'I've seen *Apocalypse Now*,' he told me.

'My book's a bit like that, without the helicopters,' I added. 'Looking for someone at the end of the journey.'

'Colonel Kurtz?'

'I think I'll give Eric one more try,' I said.

Allix looked faintly amused and sympathetic. 'Well…'

'I know. On my own head be it.' I completed his sentence for him.

He nodded and then made the gesture of something passing at very low level right over the top of his head.

I had one more ace left to play.

One Saturday night in February, Jesus Christ was at Infernos nightclub in Clapham. He had the best seat in the house, naturally, just alongside the two Santas in the front row. As I arrived at the venue, Russ Bray, prowling across the stage dressed devilishly in a black shirt, black jacket and gold chain, was just warming the crowd up.

'Nice to see Jesus Christ here,' Bray growled at the lank-haired Messiah, who raised his pint in recognition. 'Though you're a bit fucking late for Christmas.'

Jesus yelled something back about being a bit early for Easter.

'Not long before you die, then,' Bray came back at him. The place erupted with laughter.

I picked up a beer at the bar and found my seat, alongside a party of friends, whom I introduced myself to. Steve, sitting to my right, was wearing a Hawaiian shirt. He was a bespectacled man from Bromley in his late thirties and worked in IT. He was there because he'd treated his girlfriend, Louise, to a night at the darts. She, I later discovered, worked for a trade union, which, we agreed, seemed like a retro occupation in an era ill-suited to regular employment. And sitting just along from Louise, supping a pint of bitter at the end of our table, sat Kath, celebrating her 98th birthday by spending a night at the Legends of Darts. We were a happy crowd, thrust together on either side of a trestle table, covered with a paper tablecloth.

HEART OF DART-NESS

The occasion was a darts exhibition night – The Legends of Darts – one of the most prestigious on the circuit. It had attracted some of the biggest names and most popular performers. Wayne Mardle was part of a star-studded line-up that included Keith Deller, Bobby George and Eric Bristow, all hosted by the inimitable Russ Bray. The location was perfect as well. Almost akin to the Circus Tavern in Purfleet, Infernos was a low-ceilinged, intimate and slightly down-at-heel nightclub in south London. When I had walked in, I had been struck almost instantly by the smell. It was the same as Butlin's, that distinctive smell of darts: sweet booze and Toilet Duck.

Meanwhile, onstage Bray had by now introduced Keith Deller to the oche, who, after a lively little walk-on to 'Things Can Only Get Better', and a slightly arthritic lunge, which had set me wincing in sympathy, had started to take on a succession of plucky hopefuls drawn from the midst of the raucous crowd. First up to challenge him was a chap called Engelbert (or so he said), a tall, well-spoken young man in a bowler hat and a T-shirt that said 'Real Men Love Cats'. Deller was thrashing him, but was probably only averaging about 45 in the process. This, I observed, was an altogether different experience of darts from the one I was used to. I recalibrated my expectations and settled in to enjoy the night.

It was around about then that two things happened. Firstly, Louise tipped an entire glass of Pinot Grigio across the table so that a wave of white wine sloshed over my lap. Secondly, and only after a prolonged fuss of apologies and paper napkins, there was a sudden, intangible shift in the intensity of the atmosphere in the room, as if its walls had just contracted a few inches and the ceiling minutely lowered. Something, or someone, had just appeared. Steve nudged me and pointed at the side of the stage.

'There he is,' he said. And turning to Louise, still flustered after her wine mishap, he pointed him out with sudden urgency. 'Bristow, Louise. Over there.'

She turned to look, and so did I. Sure enough, tucked away in the shadows, just to the right of the stage on which his old mate Keith Deller was now battling Patrick from Wapping, there was a flash of scarlet, like the oily dab of red paint from the brush of Goya hinting at something awful. Peering deeper into the gloom revealed the detail. Eric Bristow had emerged, drink in hand, red-shirted, and inching slowly through the crowd to the back of Infernos to begin his walk-on.

'You talk about darts to anyone of my age, or older, and there's only one name they'll mention,' whispered Steve, almost reverentially in my ear. 'Bristow was like a god.' I turned to look, first at Bristow, and then back to Steve, who seemed to have been transported to some far-off place. He gazed at where Bristow had now stopped to pose for his umpteenth selfie. The Crafty Cockney's progress was slow, as by now the crowd had begun to cotton on to his presence, and he was drawing ever more admirers. He moved through them with almost regal languor.

Louise, her sparkly bowler hat sitting at a rakish angle, was gazing on with delight. 'I can't believe it's him. He was such a big name when I was a kid.' She played with a foam hand that lay in front of her on the table as she spoke. It had been used, in part, to soak up some of the wine. Steve was still shaking his head in awe, not just at Bristow but at the whole scene: the tables of revellers, the colours, the music, the sheer bubbling joy of the place. 'Not bad for 20 quid, this, is it?'

But I was suddenly overcome with anxiety. It had been months since I'd booked my ticket to Infernos for this exhibition. I had done so at the height of my paranoia about Bristow, when I had been lost in an endlessly repeating cycle of unanswered messages and ever more damning verdicts from his peers about Bristow's reportedly withdrawn state of mind and general ill-disposition to all and sundry.

I don't know what I had wanted to extract from the visit, but I knew that I would at least get to see him again at Infernos, face to face. Beyond that dimly understood ambition, I had not considered what I might do. There was no plan after the initial ploy of getting myself within his physical orbit. But here he now was, approaching steadily, one photo at a time, through a sea of star-struck well-wishers.

What, I wondered, were these well-wishers looking for in those precious few seconds with Bristow when he placed an arm across their shoulder, or a hand on the waist, as he fist-bumped, hair-ruffled, or kissed his way through the masses? In his eyes, what did they see? Was this some sort of a rascal comedy, a playful tragedy? Was he dispensing blessings from a bygone age? Or was it just that Bristow stood tall beside them, alive, flesh and blood, that he was the living link to a nation's adolescence that mirrored their own youth, a connection to a sunlit past that nagged away at an unsatisfactory present?

He was very close to where I sat now, surrounded by a dozen people, variously slapping him on the back or kissing him, pouting for the camera at his side or grinning in his presence. I stood up, almost physically alarmed by his sudden reality, after so many months, if not years, of his invisibility. I moved towards Bristow, torn in two by my own anxieties, but caught up in his aura. That was the bit I hadn't expected, to be swept up in it all.

Then, at our table, he stopped at Kath's seat. She looked up from her pint, a tiny, frail, elderly lady. He loomed over her, a vast man, with a fearsome beak of a nose. Dropping down to his haunches, he lowered his big frame to her height where she sat, and, placing one meaty arm across her back, he drew her close and whispered something in her ear. A huge smile broke across her features. She looked him in the eye, and, with the thumb and index finger of her right hand, tenderly pinched his cheek. He grinned back, stood up, and walked on, casting one glance back at Kath, who was still smiling broadly.

I walked across to intercept him, suddenly emboldened by the feeling that nothing harmful could happen here, that tonight was a place of warmth and gentle humour, of sharing the capacity for fun that Britain, fuelled by beer and games, can produce when it's at its best. I decided that I would reintroduce myself, tell him how I had been reaching out to him for months. I would let him know only that I had wanted to connect, that I only wished to hear him talk to me in his own words; to find out what it had been like, over all these years, to be Eric Bristow. I was suddenly sure, as I strode the few steps towards him, that the time was right for such directness.

'Eric!' I yelled at him. He turned my way, unhurriedly. His birdlike black eyes met mine, and I stopped advancing.

Was there a flicker of recognition? I couldn't be sure. All that I could be certain of was that in that instant all my resolve collapsed. I found myself unable to form a thought, still less a sentence. Only one word sprang to mind.

'Eric,' I said again. And I shot out a hand.

He stretched out his right hand, took mine, and nodded. It was a tiny gesture: just a dip of the head, but laden with a sudden, fleeting seriousness. Then he let my hand drop and walked away. My smile stayed with me, until he had disappeared from view, submerged once again into a crush of people.

'Did you get a picture?' Steve asked as I sat back down again at our table.

'No, I just...' but my reply petered out. What, exactly, had I done?

I stayed for another half an hour before finally saying goodbye to Steve and Louise and wishing Kath a happy birthday. After that I ate a burger and caught the train home.

I sat in Greenwich Park, a few yards from 0 degrees longitude, that notional line that splits the planet like a knife through an apple. Below me lay the Naval College, stuffed with tales of sea battles, polar exploration and exotic trade. Behind that, a mile away, rose the colossal artifice of Canary Wharf, encrusted with cranes winking red and swinging their payloads through the late afternoon air, high above the streets. And, splitting the view in two, I could pick out the archetype of this landscape. Here the curling ribbon of the Thames sweeps inland all the way around the Isle of Dogs, bending back on itself in a perfect horseshoe. This is the river's defining loop, the three-dimensional articulation of the *EastEnders* title sequence.

It was growing dark, and very cold. I was about to head home when suddenly my phone buzzed. Clumsily, and pulling off a glove, I fished it out of my pocket. The name above the message looked almost fictional, a made-up scene played out for the small screen.

Bristow.

'Good luck ned not for me are you earning out of book or doing it for charity?'

I sat bolt upright on my park bench, put my coffee down and read the message again. And a third time.

The deliberate lack of punctuation, I had noted after years of following him online, was something of a Crafty Cockney hallmark. I stared at the screen. There was a lot to absorb in such a short message: an introduction, a pat on the back, an enticement and something that felt like an accusation. It was hard to know what it all meant.

But the question at the end was a reasonable one, even if the only answer I could give him undermined my case: I was not writing the book for charity. Nevertheless, his accusation of self-interest on my part unsettled me. *Should* I be writing the book for a charity? There was a distinct spike to his enquiry, though, recognisable from Bristow's story. I knew very well what he was getting at.

The secondary fallout from Bristow's sacking over the offensive tweets had been almost as damaging to his reputation as the initial offence. The following day after his fall from grace, his representatives had appeared to be selling interview opportunities with Bristow to the media for £5,000 each. Certain outlets, such as ITV's *Good Morning Britain*, had seemingly agreed to his terms, and Bristow had duly appeared on their show, offering a confused defence and an unconvincing apology for his words. The BBC, though, had not only refused to pay the fee, they had gone further and publicised Bristow's agent's request for money.

This apparent exploitation of his situation for personal gain further enraged his critics and he was forced to climb down again. Thereafter Bristow quickly issued a statement designed to limit the damage in which he assured the public that 'any monies received' would be 'donated in full to a relevant charity'.

So, in Bristow logic, that was the line he had drawn. No interviews. No profiteering. It was a surprisingly moral position, and one that I had to think about. Then I hit upon a compromise. Worth a try, I thought.

I replied by text to Bristow, telling him that I wasn't writing the book for charity, but would happily make a donation to a cause of his choosing in exchange for a bit of his time. No more than a minute or two later, he declined my offer.

'Well good luck sir dart boys or tv not my life at the moment'

Something suggested to me that he might be sitting alone, at home or in the pub, and was in search of company. And it just happened to be me that he'd ended up talking to, simply to pass the time of day. This was an unexpected turn of events and I tried one more time to get him to open up. I thanked him for getting back, told him that I understood his position and then I sent him one more question, on the understanding that I'd subsequently leave him alone.

'Do you still like the darts?'

He went silent again. I feared that I might have asked the wrong question, of the wrong man. I plodded home, considering what it was that he had meant by finally answering my call. Then I put it to one side and understood that it had not amounted to much, and that I shouldn't expect to hear from him again.

But later that evening, as I was settling down for the evening, my phone pinged with another text message. It was Bristow.

I tried to imagine the sequence: Bristow, perhaps picking up his phone, looking at my simple question, 'Do you still like the darts?' Maybe he'd put the phone down, gone away for a bit to get something to eat maybe, refill his glass, have a 'dink'. Then, hours later, picking up the phone again and seeing the message still there, unanswered, he had, for whatever reason, decided to reply.

I love darts even watched every dart at the bdo have programme here with every mens and womens average that I have filled in 3 programmes

Again, there was that wilful, obdurate lack of punctuation.

I texted him back. I told him how I was pleased to hear that he was still so interested in the game, as his previous message had given me to understand that he'd fallen out of love with it. Perhaps, I thought, Bristow was not the cold heart that I had taken him for. Had I got him wrong? And, if I had, exactly how wrong?

He replied again.

Also fill in 6 pdc programmes worlds blackpool Ireland premier league and minehead

Suddenly, after so much silence, this exchange felt like a torrent.

Maybe he wasn't out at the pub. Maybe he was at home in his living room, leafing through all these darts programmes, all filled out, like World Cup wallcharts. It was a disarming image, not without pathos. The former champion, in his prime the darling of the small screen and darting halls, the standard bearer for a sport and an epoch, now sitting at home, watching on as the world he left behind ploughed on without him, dutifully tracking, with a pen on paper, its inexorable movement beyond his possible influence. The act of filling in the scores and noting the averages seemed to suggest a deep-set attachment to the game, as well as a human need to feel connected. I thought of him, perching his reading glasses on his famous aquiline nose, biro in hand, linking the loneliness of an older man with the quiet concentration of the boy he once was. Perhaps next to the programme, beside a half-smoked pack of fags, there was a *Times* crossword, completed.

'You're obsessed!' I told him, risking a jocular, teasing tone. But nothing more came back my way. Gradually, I began to believe that he had lost interest in the discussion, that he had said all that he wanted, and would henceforth withdraw back to the shadows. The lead had gone cold again.

Then this thought overrode them all: Bristow is a human being. That simple fact almost shocked me. This briefest of encounters, conducted at fingertip's length across a mobile phone network, had presented me with a different image to the one I'd be carrying with me all this while from Gravesend to Minehead, Yokohama to Glasgow.

Perhaps, after all, the man at the end of the river was just a man with a life behind him full of happiness and regrets. Perhaps there was no real horror here, just a jumble of frailties and strengths, all losing their potency. Maybe Bristow reflected from time to time with pain at his actions or pride in his achievements or maybe not. This is what we all do, we who live imperfectly. Quite an ordinary life, Bristow's, after all, but an ordinary life lived to the full in an extraordinary setting.

And in that regard, Bristow was not alone. I remembered an impression I had taken away from the recent retirement of Bristow's protégé-turned-nemesis, Phil Taylor. I had ridden up to Alexandra Palace on New Year's Day 2018 to watch him throw his final dart in his comprehensive defeat at the hands of Rob Cross. Taylor's last visit to the board was a typically hefty 140, chasing an impossible deficit in the final leg of his career. Those darts slipped almost unnoticed from his grasp, and Cross checked out. It was suddenly over.

Then, save for a few minutes of elaborate farewells, he passed from view. But before disappearing altogether, he held one last audience with the press pack he'd generally bickered with for 30 years. I had watched on from a discreet remove, scarcely able to believe that Taylor would no longer be around. Then, suddenly, amid the platitudes, and interrupting one innocuous question, he looked his interviewer fixedly in the eye, and said something rather startling.

'I'm 58.' Taylor paused. 'My dad was dead at 57. I've outlived my dad.'

And in that clear thought I quite abruptly realised the reduced truth of it all: here was a boy who had become a man to whom this game had given a life. The greatest player ever to throw a dart was a human being from Stoke. It was really rather simple. And for Taylor, read Bristow. For Bristow, read Taylor.

Darts, with its everyday soul never far from the lived experience of normal lives, does that to people who might not otherwise have tasted such adventure, lifting them up and then returning them, either with a bump or gently setting them down in an armchair, to a place not far removed from where it had all begun: a place that looks a lot like home. Here was no jungle, and no Mr Kurtz. There was no 'smell of napalm in the morning', just the stale scent of cigarette smoke clinging to a black leather jacket. The heart of dartness might have turned out to be closer than I ever imagined.

It was there all along. It was here all along.

Then, just when I thought that it was all over, another message landed. Bristow had the final word, as I suspect he often does.

'You're obsessed!', I'd told him.

'No love it and its been great to me'

Acknowledgements

Many people have helped me piece together the fragments of my darting education. First among my guides are the two principal pundits at ITV Sport: Chris Mason and Alan Warriner-Little, who have been patient, honest and amusing company. Along with ITV's spotter, Keith Deller, I would have been lost without them. The commentary teams of Stuart Pyke, Peter Drury, John Rawling and Dan Dawson, as well as ITV's production team spearheaded by Phil Heslop, Stuart Smith, Dave Francis, Matt Smith, Richard Ashdown, Nick Moody, Jacqui Oatley, Paul McNamara, Karen Jones, Mary Hutchinson (and her astonishing home-made pickles!), Bev Coates and Lewis Hurt have all added to my understanding and enjoyment of the game. Special mention must go to Paul Roberts, Adam Maynard and Chris James, in particular, who have been at my side throughout a decade of covering the sport.

At the PDC, Matt Porter, Rod Harrington, John McDonald, Lawrence Lustig, Mark Leak and Dave Allen have been a great support, as well as Katie and Barry Hearn and Tommy Cox. The players have been a joy to get to know, and though there are many whom I have got to know down the years, I would like to thank Raymond van Barneveld, Michael van Gerwen, Terry Jenkins, Jamie Caven, Justin Pipe, Alex Roy, Kevin Painter, Paul Nicholson, Gary Anderson, Alan Norris, Mervyn King, Mark Webster, Colin Lloyd, Paul Hogan, Rob Cross, James Wade, Adrian Lewis, John Part, Wayne Mardle, Peter Wright, Bobby George and many others too numerous to mention.

My great and particular thanks go to the people who gave up the time to tell me their stories: Justin Irwin, Chris Mason (again!), Mensur Suljović, Olive Byamukama, George Jewiss, Peter Purves, Russ Bray, Dick Allix, Cliff Lazarenko, Phil Taylor, Andy Fordham, Stephen Fry and the late Jim Bowen. Special acknowledgement should go to the late Eric Bristow, who, right at the end, made contact with me and led me to think again.

Thanks to the literary estate of Joseph Conrad, who would have been appalled by the misuse of his greatest work, no doubt. The same is almost certainly true of Dr Patrick Chaplin, on whom I have leant heavily. His thorough research into the history of the sport is unimprovable, so I didn't try. And thanks too, to Martin Amis, who took darts seriously, and to the editorial team at Blink Publishing, including Justine Taylor whose copy edit was a work of genius. Matt Phillips, this book's editor, deserves my particular thanks once more for his clarity of thought, vision, humour and encouragement.

But mostly I would like to thank all those who play and watch this 'beautifully ordinary' game, to quote Barry Hearn. They are the true custodians of a remarkable slice of human activity that has only one purpose at its heart.

Fun.